FIVE YEARS OF THE ALLIANCE FOR PROGRESS

An Appraisal

FIVE YEARS

OF

THE ALLIANCE FOR PROGRESS

An Appraisal

SIMON G. HANSON

Editor, Inter-American Economic Affairs

Washington • The Inter-American Affairs Press • *1967*

Printed in the United States of America

Preface

In 1959 the chairman of the Senate Foreign Relations Committee explained that "the deterioration of our Latin-American relations is not so much a material matter. It is an attitude, a matter of good manners. Regarding them as important people and being courteous to them is very essential. Our international manners are often atrocious."[1] By 1960 he was protesting that the Eisenhower Administration's program for $500 million in aid to Latin America, surely a "material matter," had come too late and speculated that it stemmed from the fact that "the President on his recent trip sensed behind the courteous welcome that all was not well," and from "the situation in Cuba . . . All over Latin America there are areas containing the same kind of dissatisfaction and readiness for revolution."[2] By the time the Alliance for Progress had run five years, his prescription had departed from the need for better manners to *very* material considerations: increased contributions to the Alliance for Progress, acceptance of gradual expropriation of U.S.- owned enterprises, a drawing away from military and economic oligarchies.[3]

During the same years another "expert" on our Latin American policy, the chairman of the subcommittee on American Republics affairs of the Senate Foreign Relations Committee was revising *his* prescription, but in the opposite direction. In 1960 Senator Morse had returned from a trip to South America to report that there is nothing wrong with U.S. policies in Latin America that

---

[1] *Christian Science Monitor,* April 29, 1959. "I don't know anything positive that we have done that has alienated them. We just haven't done anything affirmative to conciliate them and make them feel that we are interested in them. In this case I think it is not so much a material matter . . ."

[2] *Congressional Record,* August 19, 1960, p. 15611.

[3] *The Two Americas* (The Ninth Brien McMahon Lecture, Storrs, Conn. 1966). "It will require a renewed commitment and increased contributions to the Alliance for Progress. It will also require a drawing away from military and economic oligarchies. It may require the acceptance of gradual expropriation of United States-owned enterprises."

could not be cured by more money.[4] Five years of the Alliance found a disillusioned Morse lamenting that "the result of our extensive aid has been to produce more pleas for money from the countries that have received the most. What has gone to them before has apparently produced little or no economic stability or improvement in these countries."[5] His "discovery" followed quickly: "Money alone is not the key to the Alliance for Progress."[6]

The confusion of these experts is in part explained by a report on Senator Robert Kennedy's oratorical safari to Latin America: "As the plane banked and rolled through a high pass in the Andes, the Senator scanned a large loose-leaf briefing book entitled EASY ANSWERS TO HARD QUESTIONS."[7] For five years, starting with the assumption that they had answers for all questions, indeed as startled newsmen put it, "solutions even for problems that did not exist," the "fresh minds" which had been assembled for the messianic mission to export democracy to Latin America, revise its social and economic structure from Washington, and accelerate its economic growth, had offered up a succession of "easy answers."

There were no easy answers. But victimized by their own propaganda and fearful of the loss of political capital domestically if the truth were admitted, their situation was very awkward. When Senator Kennedy took off for Latin America "to see" as he put it "if the Alliance for Progress is doing as well (sic) as it was in President Kennedy's time,"[8] a Republican senator (Case of New Jersey) with perhaps even more impressive creden-

---

[4] *Report of Senator Wayne Morse to the Senate Foreign Relations Committee,* "South America: Argentina, Bolivia, Brazil, Chile, Colombia and Venezuela," (Washington, 1960). "There is nothing wrong with U.S. policies in Latin America that could not be cured by more loan money, some additional technical assistance and human welfare grant money, and a great deal more sympathetic understanding of Latin American problems."

[5] *Congressional Record,* June 8, 1965, p. 12316.

[6] "Individual Views of Senator Morse on H.R. 11380," Senate Foreign Relations Committee, p. 12.

[7] Andrew J. Glass, "The Compulsive Candidate," *The Saturday Evening Post,* April 23, 1966, p. 42.

[8] William V. Shannon, "The Making of President Robert Kennedy," *Harper's Magazine,* October 1966, p. 68.

tials as a liberal than those of Kennedy, pointed out that there was really no reason to think that the Johnson administration had lost ground in the appeal to the great mass of Latin Americans from what the Kennedy administration had achieved in that respect: "I don't think the Kennedy Administration achieved very much. I think its heart was in the right place but I don't think we got very far frankly. It was more a public relations matter." [9] The basic lines had already been established when the Johnson administration took over: the *reduction* in the rate of economic growth, the sharp *curtailment* in private investment capital flow, the *intensification* of political instability, the *widening* of the gap between the rich and the poor.

Confronted with the ineffectiveness of the great expenditures which daily became difficult to deny, a new crop of explanations appeared. Walt W. Rostow, an adviser to both Kennedy and Johnson, recalled that he had in 1961 informed President Kennedy that "the first five years of the Alliance would be regarded as a disappointment." [10] At least his credentials as a forecaster remained unimpaired. The chairman of the House Foreign Affairs Committee, confronted with demands for correction of the ineffectiveness of the program, protested that "we must regard this aid as providing a kit of tools to assist in the conduct of foreign policy, a different type of program than if we make adjustments to make the aid more efficient. . . . A large percentage of the independent nations in the world do not have capable governments or a reasonable number of people qualified to deal with political and economic problems. . . . Many such countries are important because of the number of people or geographical location or nature of their resources. It is not to our advantage to force them into the communist camp." [11] The job of the Congress, in Congressman Morgan's view, was to keep the pork barrel full and access to it easy.

When in 1966 the subcommittee on foreign aid expenditures of the Senate Committee on Government Operations, shocked by the pervasiveness of the discontent with the Alliance for Progress here and abroad, sought to ascertain the causes of the malaise, it

---

[9] Transcript, TV appearance, September 19, 1965.
[10] Transcript, NBC, The Today Show, September 23, 1966.
[11] *Congressional Record,* July 12, 1966, pp. 14646-7.

found "the growing literature on the foreign assistance program to be largely unenlightening; publications by international organizations virtually useless; witnesses from the Agency for International Development and the Department of State, as participants in and advocates of the program, more intent on defending their actions than in exploring any weaknesses; legislative oversight made more difficult than in the case of domestic programs by the sheer dimensions of the aid and the fact that it is conducted in distant lands; and the embattled history of foreign aid seems to make witnesses on its behalf exceptionally wary and defensive toward any questioning of their activities, however constructive the intent of the interrogators." [12]

In the specific case of the Alliance for Progress, after five years incredibly large vested bureaucratic interests—national and international—had developed which in pure self-interest comprised barriers to impartial analysis. And there was the further difficulty in a highly political environment that to stop doing what is wrong might be a confession of past error.

The independent analyst can hardly, then, expect to achieve the breakthough in appraisal which is so sorely needed and which even the best-intentioned legislative committees have been unable to achieve. But this book attempts to provide some measurement of the achievement of five years of the Alliance and a better understanding of its real potential.

The editors of the quarterly journal, *Inter-American Economic Affairs,* which publishes an annual review of the Alliance for Progress, have permitted the author to use material freely from these reviews. To that journal and the many others which have permitted quotation and reference, acknowledgement of the assistance is gratefully made.

---

[12] *United States Foreign Aid in Action: A Case Study,* submitted by Senator Ernest Gruening to the subcommittee on foreign aid expenditures of the Senate Committee on Government Operations (Washington, 1966), p. viii.

Contents

Chapter I

The Record

In five years the United States disbursed $4 billion in a program designed, in the words of President Kennedy, "to assist free men and free governments in casting off the chains of poverty." [1] During that period the rate of economic growth dropped sharply from the average for 1950-55 and 1955-60 and the change in the growth rate per capita was even more adverse. During that period the distribution of income became even more unsatisfactory as the gap between the rich and poor widened appreciably. During most of the period a very heavy proportion of the disbursements went to military regimes which had overthrown constitutional governments, and at the end of the period, with almost half of the population of the area under military rule, a significant portion of the aid was going *not* to assist "free men and free governments" but rather to hold in power regimes to which the people had lost their freedom.

Definitions. Before we examine the record, some explanations of the data to be used are in order. (1) There is the obvious distinction between "actual disbursements" and "obligations and loan authorizations (commitments) entered into." (2) Fiscal year data are used because of the relative availability of such data and because it has been found that they do not significantly distort or prejudice the findings. Strictly speaking, August 17 is celebrated annually as the starting point for the flow of the largesse of the Alliance and would be the more proper date for statistical analysis if the data were available in that form.

(3) In this book we distinguish between real loans, grants, and

---

[1] Inaugural address January 20, 1961. "To our sister republics south of the border we offer a special pledge—to convert our good words into good deeds—in a new alliance for progress—to assist free men and free governments in casting off the chains of poverty."

Table I

DISBURSEMENTS OF AID TO LATIN AMERICA
(millions of dollars)

	Total	Real Loans	Real Loans Excluding Mexico
Fiscal 1957	$248	$100	$ 86
1958	469	290	235
1959	667	580	500
1960	427	208	186
1961	431	210	163
Alliance for Progress:			
Fiscal 1962	$1,031	$593	$469
1963	771	157	134
1964	621	77	67
1965	768	102	54
1966	817	135	93

concealed grants. A "real loan" is made with reasonable expectation of repayment, the interest-rate structure more than covers the cost of money to the United States, the grace period is consistent with the discipline which should accompany the movement of funds from one country to another, and the term for repayment is consistent with serious intention to repay. A grant is a grant. A "concealed grant" (sometimes labelled "soft loan" to confuse the public and particularly the Congress into believing that it does not involve subsidy or donation by the donor) carries an interest rate that does not cover the cost of the funds to the donor, the grace period is excessive for financial discipline, the term of repayment is such as to place ultimate payment beyond the generation concerned or repayment may be contemplated in local currency, i.e., free of meaningful repayment to the donor or lender. Questioned by the House Appropriations Committee, the administrator of the Agency for International Development conceded rather begrudgingly that the typical "concealed grant" which the Agency preferred to call a "loan" was better described as 40% subsidy and 60% loan.[2] And even this only if the repayment were ultimately forthcoming, which appeared unlikely.

A member of the Board of Governors of the Federal Reserve System has suggested that "the bulk of the credits being extended to the less-developed countries probably will never be repaid, at least on schedule. They will probably be forgiven, repudiated, stretched out or refunded." [3] And it has accordingly been suggested by some analysts that perhaps the distinction between real loans and concealed grants might also be abandoned. This argument gained favor when shortly after the end of the five years of the Alliance the Export-Import Bank, which is by law limited to real loans made on condition that there be reasonable prospect for repayment, announced that it had initiated the practice of waiving (writing off) certain obligations, in this first case some $9 million in arrears of interest on Bolivian debt. It is true that during the first five years of the Alliance large portions of the grants and concealed grants were being used indirectly to service European credits. And an increasing volume of the "real loans" made by the United States were suffering a rollover of service. Indeed, much of the servicing of "real loans" was being made possible by the donations and concealed donations, so that it was generally believed that as time went on, the real loans would largely depend on expansion of donations for servicing. Nevertheless, some merit attaches to the distinction between real loans and concealed grants which is adopted in this book, as will perhaps be apparent from subsequent analysis.

To what extent was aid expanded? The unceasing flood of propaganda regarding the Alliance for Progress during the first five years tended to distort the scope of the expansion of aid. The mood of the public under the barrage of daily announcements of new grants and loans was caught well by the cartoonist who depicted one character commenting: "I see where we put another $357 million dollars into Upper Tzedakah." And his friend asking anxiously: "Does that give us controlling interest or did we buy it outright?"

Actually in the five years the United States disbursed $4 billion, compared with $2.2 billion in the previous five years. The expansion was significant, but especially if account be taken of the 17% increase in population over which the aid had to be

---

[2] *House Appropriations Subcommittee,* "Hearings on Foreign Assistance and Related Agencies Appropriations for 1967," Part 2, p. 46.

[3] J. L. Robertson. Paper prepared for the Conference on Trade and Aid, University of Nebraska, October 3, 1963.

Table II

DISBURSEMENT OF AID
(millions of dollars)

	Fiscal 1962	Fiscal 1963	Fiscal 1964	Fiscal 1965	Fiscal 1966
Argentina	$66.7	$61.7	$13.9	$22.8	22.1
Bolivia	27.2	34.1	42.8	31.8	26.1
Brazil	354.8	173.5	104.3	233.7	190.2
Chile	136.4	135.8	108.0	103.6	122.6
Colombia	107.7	65.6	80.9	76.0	63.8
Costa Rica	6.0	10.3	6.9	10.7	10.9
Dominican	12.4	32.0	39.9	36.4	81.4
Ecuador	16.6	15.6	21.0	17.0	23.8
El Salvador	9.4	9.3	14.0	10.4	20.4
Guatemala	8.4	7.9	13.5	10.2	8.3
Haiti	9.9	3.7	4.0	2.0	2.8
Honduras	7.2	5.4	4.8	7.0	9.5
Mexico	129.5	40.3	29.6	79.5	60.3
Nicaragua	9.7	8.5	9.4	6.5	9.5
Panama	7.9	15.1	14.3	14.7	21.0
Paraguay	9.3	13.6	8.5	7.2	5.0
Peru	25.8	26.5	37.4	36.5	64.9
Rocap	—	1.1	4.0	5.3	11.6
Uruguay	4.7	10.0	3.6	3.9	2.4
Venezuela	76.0	30.1	45.1	34.6	44.1
Regional	5.4	72.3	15.7	18.1	16.9
TOTAL	1031.4	771.8	621.4	767.8	816.8

spread, the degree of increase was much less than is commonly believed to have occurred.

The really significant change was in the character of the aid. In the earlier period at least two-thirds of the assistance had consisted of real loans. In the five years of the Alliance, only one-quarter involved real loans. And by the final year of the five, the proportion had declined to 16%. See Table I.

A further refinement of the data is appropriate. Mexico did not share proportionately in the grants and concealed grants and in fact by the end of the fifth year it was being washed out of eligibility for such assistance because of its willingness to make

Table III

DISBURSEMENT OF AID
(millions of dollars)

| | Fiscal 1962 | | | Fiscal 1963 | | | Fiscal 1964 | | | Fiscal 1965 | | | Fiscal 1966 | | |
	Real Loans	Donations * Food	Other	Real Loans	Donations Food	Other	Real Loans	Donations Food	Other	Real Loans	Donations Food	Other	Real Loans	Donations Food	Other
Argentina	65.7	—	1.0	36.5	—	25.2	7.0	—	6.9	1.6	—	21.2	5.4	—	16.7
Bolivia	—	5.3	21.8	—	11.0	23.1	0.1	12.1	30.6	—	6.1	25.7	—	6.8	19.3
Brazil	194.3	78.6	81.9	45.7	83.2	44.6	2.7	75.6	26.0	0.3	88.3	145.1	1.2	48.3	140.7
Chile	46.3	23.4	66.7	20.4	18.6	96.8	27.2	12.1	68.7	21.0	21.9	60.7	21.1	13.9	87.6
Colombia	55.2	14.6	37.9	3.2	12.6	49.8	2.7	18.7	59.5	6.8	9.4	59.8	6.8	11.7	45.3
Costa Rica	1.6	—	4.4	1.9	0.1	8.3	1.0	1.7	4.2	0.4	1.6	8.7	0.1	0.9	9.9
Dominican	—	0.8	11.6	1.1	11.5	19.4	1.9	13.0	25.0	2.7	6.0	27.7	5.0	10.7	65.7
Ecuador	0.4	3.6	12.6	0.3	2.8	12.5	0.1	6.5	14.4	0.1	3.3	13.6	1.0	4.3	18.5
El Salvador	7.2	0.8	1.4	0.4	2.6	6.3	1.0	3.5	9.5	0.9	1.7	7.8	0.1	3.3	17.0
Guatemala	1.1	0.7	6.6	1.1	1.2	5.6	3.4	3.0	7.1	2.0	1.1	7.1	1.5	1.0	5.8
Haiti	—	0.7	9.2	—	0.9	2.8	—	2.2	1.8	—	0.7	1.3	—	1.1	1.7
Honduras	0.3	0.2	6.7	—	0.3	5.1	—	0.7	4.1	—	0.4	6.6	—	0.6	8.9
Mexico	123.6	5.1	0.8	23.1	14.4	2.8	9.5	18.6	1.5	47.9	5.8	25.8	42.3	1.2	16.8
Nicaragua	6.5	0.7	2.5	0.5	1.4	6.6		1.9	7.5		0.9	5.6		1.4	8.1
Panama	2.0	0.4	5.5	4.0	0.7	10.4	2.4	0.8	11.1	4.2	0.5	10.0	4.3	0.5	16.2
Paraguay	—	6.9	2.4	0.2	8.4	5.0	0.1	3.4	5.0	—	1.9	5.3	—	0.7	4.3
Peru	14.0	6.1	5.7	8.8	6.6	11.1	9.2	9.7	18.5	7.0	6.2	23.3	27.2	7.1	30.6
Rocap	—	—	—	—	—	1.1	—	—	4.0	—	—	5.3	—	—	11.6
Uruguay	0.8	0.3	3.6	1.4	1.6	7.0	1.4	1.0	1.2	0.2	0.7	3.0	—	0.6	1.8
Venezuela	74.4	0.5	1.1	8.5	1.2	20.4	7.7	10.3	27.1	6.9	4.2	23.5	18.8	4.1	21.2
Regional	—	—	5.4	—	—	72.3	—	0.1	15.6	—	0.3	17.3	—	0.7	16.2
TOTAL	593.5	149.7	288.2	157.0	178.8	436.0	77.4	194.7	349.2	102.2	160.8	504.9	134.8	118.2	563.3

* Including concealed donations.

sacrifices of its own and to rely on self-help to achieve the objectives of adequate economic growth with social amelioration. Thus, by the fifth year, real loans to Latin America excluding Mexico came to only 13% of the total. See Tables I, II, II.

Pledge and Performance. The United States had pledged one billion dollars per year in public funds for the Alliance over the projected ten years of the program. In a sense, the disbursements ($0.8 billion per year) fell short of this promise and thus evoked protests from the Latin Americans. But the test of compliance with the pledge is the volume of funds authorized rather than disbursed, because it had been understood from the start by Latin America and the United States alike that certain conditions must be stipulated to assure effective expenditure and that failure to comply with these stipulations might delay conversion of commitments into actual disbursements.

The fact is that the United States more than fulfilled its obligation. In five years the United States authorized $5.6 billion in aid, well over the billion per year pledge. And again even more importantly, for the area outside Mexico there was the qualitative characteristic, that real loans took a decreasing share of the commitments while grants and concealed grants dominated. By the fifth year, grants and concealed grants came to 93% of the aid committed to Latin America excluding Mexico; and the total aid exceeded $1.1 billion for Latin America. In fact, there was $940 million in commitments of grants and concealed grants even with Mexico excluded. See Tables IV, V, VI.

Table IV

CHARACTER OF AID AUTHORIZED
FOR COUNTRIES OTHER THAN MEXICO

	Real Loans	Outright Grants	Concealed Grants
Fiscal 1962	13%	29%	58%
1963	7	29	64
1964	10	27	63
1965	11	27	62
1966	7	24	69

Additional aid under the Alliance banner. This does not exhaust the devices used to aid Latin America, however. One form

Table V

AUTHORIZATIONS OF AID
(millions of dollars)

	Fiscal 1962	Fiscal 1963	Fiscal 1964	Fiscal 1965	Fiscal 1966
Argentina	78.9	153.8	11.2	28.0	35.8
Bolivia	34.2	68.3	78.5	16.8	38.0
Brazil	202.5	155.4	366.8	279.6	390.6
Chile	215.4	89.0	134.6	135.1	116.4
Colombia	71.3	126.7	133.5	37.9	120.6
Costa Rica	10.4	14.8	16.1	15.3	14.7
Dominican	36.6	49.8	18.6	88.9	115.8
Ecuador	36.6	36.4	28.5	31.2	30.7
El Salvador	23.1	22.5	15.5	19.1	10.4
Guatemala	9.6	13.4	14.4	13.0	5.5
Haiti	7.8	5.8	4.4	2.3	3.5
Honduras	3.3	13.4	9.7	4.3	13.6
Mexico	141.6	49.7	109.6	200.0	128.1
Nicaragua	12.9	5.1	7.5	23.0	20.5
Panama	25.3	9.8	18.0	18.7	14.3
Paraguay	8.0	9.4	10.4	9.9	15.2
Peru	75.4	24.3	86.5	34.2	42.1
Rocap	—	11.1	24.3	43.4	3.8
Uruguay	6.7	22.1	7.4	2.1	6.8
Venezuela	68.1	46.4	45.9	41.7	8.8
Regional	122.8	29.6	67.0	21.2	17.6
TOTAL	1192.3	957.0	1207.8	1065.7	1152.9

of assistance was unauthorized by the Congress but reached very significant totals even compared with the authorized aid under the Alliance. This was the assistance provided by U.S. participation in the International Coffee Agreement. The legislative history of the congressional approval for U.S. participation indicates clearly that the Congress did not intend to provide a $400 million or $500 million addition to Alliance financing by this vote. The Congress was urged to allow U.S. participation in a cartel which would prevent further declines in prices below prevailing levels. The State Department by its own decision seized the opportunity, once the legislation had cleared the Congress, to expand tremendously the donations being given Latin

Table VI

AUTHORIZATIONS OF AID
(millions of dollars)

	Fiscal 1962		Fiscal 1963		Fiscal 1964		Fiscal 1965		Fiscal 1966	
	Real Loans	Other Aid	Real Loans	Other Aid	Real Loans	Other Aid	Real Loans	Other Aid	Real Loans	Other Aid
Argentina	51.9	27.0	24.1	129.7	1.4	9.8	22.7	5.3	29.1	6.7
Bolivia	—	34.2	—	68.3	—	78.5	—	16.8	—	38.0
Brazil	—	202.5	—	155.4	—	366.8	6.0	273.6	18.8	371.8
Chile	46.4	169.0	15.5	74.5	16.5	118.1	8.3	126.8	—	116.4
Colombia	—	71.3	3.4	123.3	23.5	110.0	6.5	31.4	3.4	117.2
Costa Rica	4.5	5.9	—	14.8	—	16.1	—	15.3	10.2	4.5
Dominican	9.6	27.0	—	49.8	—	18.6	12.7	76.2	8.9	106.9
Ecuador	—	36.6	1.3	35.1	—	28.5	8.0	23.2	6.3	24.4
El Salvador	6.0	17.1	—	22.5	4.6	15.5	—	19.1	2.5	7.9
Guatemala	—	9.6	—	13.4	—	9.8	—	13.0	—	5.5
Haiti	—	7.8	—	5.8	—	4.4	—	2.3	—	3.5
Honduras	—	3.3	—	13.4	—	9.7	0.4	3.9	—	13.6
Mexico	105.3	36.3	25.8	23.9	54.0	55.6	163.2	36.8	127.9	0.4
Nicaragua	—	12.9	—	5.1	1.2	6.3	—	23.0	2.8	17.7
Panama	2.0	23.3	—	9.8	7.4	10.6	3.5	15.2	—	14.3
Paraguay	—	8.0	—	9.4	—	10.4	—	9.9	—	15.2
Peru	17.1	58.3	10.7	13.6	28.2	58.3	14.2	20.0	3.0	39.1
Rocap	—	—	—	11.1	—	24.3	—	43.4	—	3.8
Uruguay	2.1	4.6	5.0	17.1	—	7.4	—	2.1	—	6.8
Venezuela	—	68.1	0.4	46.0	31.5	14.4	12.5	29.2	—	8.8
Regional	—	122.8	—	29.6	—	67.0	—	21.2	—	17.6
TOTAL	244.9	947.4	86.2	871.0	168.2	1039.6	258.0	807.7	213.0	940.1

America by consenting to price-fixing arrangements designed to raise prices immensely above the levels that had existed at the time of negotiation of the agreement. The deviousness of the Executive performance in this respect may be seen in this sequence: When the level of coffee prices had been advanced 5%, the President of the United States purported to be so aroused that he asked his adviser on consumer affairs to bring this matter before the Advisory Committee on Consumer Interests, with suitable publicity to stem public protests which might be damaging politically. But when prices rose another 16% as a result of the State Department connivance with the cartel to make possible a vast boost in Latin American exchange receipts without having to go through the Congress, the President's adviser on consumer affairs announced that the prices thus achieved by the State Department were *not too high*. It was then thought politically safe to take this position. Sixty cents, the White House had said in its initial fear of public reaction, represented too high a price for coffee resulting from the cartel's action, and correction was in order, indeed imperative. But when the price reached 70.1 cents, the White House had become convinced that the public lacked the capacity to comprehend what was happening to it and the capacity to focus responsibility for the $400 million per year burden thus imposed, and so it insisted that 70.1 cents is not too high.[4]

The International Coffee Organization has estimated that the value of this cartel action, in which the State Department collaborated and against which President Kennedy in a letter to the Congress had promised that the U.S. would use its veto power, was $600 million annually to the producing countries, perhaps two-thirds for Latin America alone.[5] Senator Douglas has put the cost to the U.S. consumer at $400 million per year and has suggested that it actually does not accomplish the objectives of the Alliance for Progress in optimum manner: "What

---

[4] See Simon G. Hanson, "The Experience with the International Coffee Agreement," *Inter-American Economic Affairs*, Winter 1965, pp. 27-65.

[5] A memorandum by the executive director of the International Coffee Organization published in *Diario las Americas*, July 3, 1966, boasts that the value of coffee exports had been boosted from $1.88 billion in calendar year 1962 to $2.5 billion in 1965, as a result of the cartel's action on prices.

a price increase of this kind' does is to compel the poor and those of moderate means in the United States and other consumer countries to subsidize among others the rich planters in the producing countries. There is a real question whether this is the best form of aid." [6] Since, as we shall show later, the misdirection of Alliance assistance was a common failing and the goals were usually missed as a result of improper usage of funds, this criticism does not set up a unique weakness in the flow of U.S. treasure.

What is important is to make clear that the United States met its pledge. It provided more than the billion per year in authorizations, which was the test. And its actual disbursements taken together with U.S. action to encourage the gouging of the consumer of coffee through cartel action came to more than the pledged figure.

Private direct investment. President Kennedy had warned that "it is impossible for us to supply all the funds that are necessary for the development of Latin America. They must come through private sources. If local capital and American capital dry up, then all our hopes of a decade of development in Latin America will be gone." [7] To this end, private direct investment in the amount of $300 million per year from the United States had been established as the target figure. It was not an especially large figure. In fiscal 1960 U.S. direct investments in Latin America had been $258 million, in fiscal 1961 $214 million.

Again, what is important is that this was not a commitment or obligation of the U.S. Government. This government cannot commit private firms to invest certain sums of money. If anything, it represented a goal for the Latin Americans themselves— an obligation to establish such a climate of investment as would assure at least $300 million annually in U.S. investments. The climate was not forthcoming, and the desired level of investment failed to materialize. As Table VII shows, in five years private direct investment fell one billion dollars short of the target. In no single year was the target figure reached, and in no year was the level of fiscal 1960-61 reached. It must be reiterated that

---

[6] Paul Douglas, *America in the Market Place* (New York, 1966), p. 190.

[7] Statement, May 9, 1962. *Congressional Record,* May 25, 1962.

Table VII

DIRECT INVESTMENT IN LATIN AMERICA
(millions of dollars)

Fiscal 1960	$258
1961	214

Alliance for Progress:

Fiscal 1962	—$ 24
1963	11
1964	83
1965	180
1966	190

this failure is not attributable to the United States. It represents one of the factors for which responsibility rested with the Latin Americans.

Thesis tested. The United States had now completed its test of the Morse thesis that "there is nothing wrong with U.S. policies in Latin America that could not be cured by more loan money, some additional technical assistance and human welfare grant money, and a great deal more sympathetic understanding of Latin American problems." [8] The results were dismal in the extreme.

Table VIII

CHANGES IN GROSS NATIONAL PRODUCT

	% Change in Total	% Change Per Capita
1950-55	5.1%	2.4%
1955-60	4.8	1.9
1960-65	4.4	1.5

Source: Agency for International Development

Growth Target. As Table VIII indicates, the goal of a 2.5% per year per capita growth in gross national product had not been achieved. In fact, the pace of growth had slackened. When

---

[8] Morse, Senator Wayne, op. cit.

the State Department tried to gloss over the failure by asserting that at least in the fifth year the rate had been achieved, the UN Economic Commission for Latin America pointed out that this had come principally because of recoveries by Brazil and Argentina from grievously unsatisfactory performances in immediately preceding years, and that without these countries representing more than a third of the area's gross national product, the figure became a sickly 1.9% growth per capita.[9] (See Tables IX and X)

Table IX

ANNUAL CHANGES IN GROSS NATIONAL PRODUCT BY COUNTRIES

	% Change in Total GNP			% Change in GNP Per Capita		
	1950-55	1955-60	1960-65	1950-55	1955-60	1960-65
Costa Rica	7.4	4.8	3.9	3.5	1.1	0.2
El Salvador	4.5	3.9	7.7	1.8	1.2	4.2
Guatemala	2.3	5.3	6.2	—0.9	2.2	3.1
Honduras	4.1	4.4	4.8	1.0	1.3	1.7
Nicaragua	8.3	2.3	8.3	5.5	—0.8	5.2
Central American Econ. Comm.	4.5	4.4	6.3	1.4	1.3	3.0
Argentina	3.1	2.6	3.0	1.4	0.9	1.3
Bolivia	0.8	—0.1	4.3	—1.5	—2.4	2.0
Brazil	5.7	5.8	3.3	2.6	2.7	0.2
Chile	3.0	4.2	3.9	0.7	1.9	1.6
Colombia	5.5	4.0	4.4	2.6	1.1	1.5
Ecuador	5.3	4.4	4.3	2.3	1.4	1.3
Mexico	6.2	6.1	5.9	3.1	3.0	2.8
Panama			8.1			5.1
Paraguay	2.9	2.4	3.8	0.7	0.2	1.6
Peru	6.0	4.3	6.6	3.7	2.0	3.7
Uruguay		—0.1	0.4		—1.4	—0.9
Venezuela	9.0	7.1	5.2	5.1	3.2	1.6
Latin America (17 listed countries	5.1	4.8	4.4	2.4	1.9	1.5

Source: Agency for International Development.

[9] *Comercio Exterior de Mexico*, Banco de Comercio Exterior, July 1966.

Table X

GROSS NATIONAL PRODUCT
CHANGES FROM PRECEDING YEAR

	1961	1962	1963	1964	1965
Costa Rica	—0.4	6.3	5.1	4.0	4.7
El Salvador	7.8	8.9	7.7	7.6	6.5
Guatemala	3.7	2.6	13.0	5.7	6.6
Honduras	4.2	5.8	3.3	4.6	6.4
Nicaragua	6.0	10.3	7.9	6.9	10.2
Central American Econ. Comm.	4.3	5.9	8.6	5.9	6.8
Argentina	5.7	—2.8	—4.2	8.4	8.4
Bolivia	3.2	4.2	4.5	4.6	5.0
Brazil	6.9	5.3	1.4	—2.0	5.0
Chile	3.7	6.1	1.4	2.6	5.9
Colombia	4.4	4.7	3.5	6.1	3.5
Ecuador	2.1	4.8	3.5	6.2	4.8
Mexico	3.5	4.8	6.3	9.9	5.1
Panama	10.5	8.6	8.3	5.3	7.8
Paraguay	5.6	1.8	4.0	2.8	4.8
Peru	8.2	9.3	3.8	7.8	4.3
Uruguay	3.0	—2.2	—1.0	1.1	1.2
Venezuela	1.0	5.8	4.8	8.0	6.4
Latin America (17 listed countries)	4.7	3.7	2.6	5.5	5.7

Source: Agency for International Development.

The Inter-American Development Bank warned pessimistically that "only a few countries have sustained economic growth trends strong enough to assure achievement of the goals of Punta del Este." And it went on to lament that "in most Latin American countries economic growth is irregular, an indication that the basic conditions for sustained economic progress have not been achieved." [10] The disappointment was general. At the Buenos Aires meeting of the Inter-American Economic and Social Council, the Peruvian delegate lashed out at the lack of progress, protesting that the growth rate had been less in the first four or five years

---

[10] *Sixth Annual Report.*

of the Alliance than it had been in the first half of the previous decade.

The clear demonstration that a simple overspill of U.S. affluence through government donations was not the solution to the problem was enough to panic the growing bureaucratic establishment just settling down comfortably to their generation of personal affluence. The U.S. bureaucrats fired off their daily salvos against the vulgarity of those congressmen who remembered "how small of all that human hearts endure that part which laws or kings can cause or cure." In the international establishment, the Panel of Nine Experts resigned in a jurisdictional dispute within the proliferating bureaucratic organization and informed the Secretary-General of the Organization of American States that "the Alliance is going through a critical time. There are symptoms of discouragement, skepticism and despair." [11]

Social Amelioration. Data on the distribution of gross national product are even less satisfactory than the GNP data. But there was general agreement that for the bulk of Latin American workers during this period, real wages actually declined. The *New York Times* was undoubtedly correct when it mourned that "in the whole of Latin America the rich are getting richer and the poor are getting poorer." This, though the reduction of mass poverty was accepted as the crucial test of the realization of economic development. The head of the Confederación de Trabajadores Venezolanas, in the United States as a guest of the State Department, insisted that the memory of John F. Kennedy had been betrayed because "the benefits have not accrued to the masses of Latin America. . . . The administrators of the Alliance turned their backs on the workers and neither the poor nor the middle class benefited." [12] The Vice-President of El Salvador declared the Alliance a failure: "Rich industrialists, the landowners and the military have benefited from the Alliance but there have been no real improvements for the mass of the people. If this money is to benefit generals and politicians and the ruling aristocracy, let the U.S. keep it. We do not want to be a rich country full of poor people." [13] To this, Assistant Secretary of State Gordon

---

[11] OAS, Press Release, May 9, 1966, E 40-66.
[12] *Diario las Americas,* July 13, 1966.
[13] *Diario las Americas,* December 3, 1966.

had a weary answer: "It is easy to get excited about the rhetoric
of social justice and political democracy (but) I don't want them
pursued in merely rhetorical terms. . . . You can't have real social
justice without something to distribute." [14]   His associate in the
gaggle of "fresh minds" to whom our Latin American program
had been turned over seemed not even to mind the delay in improvement of distribution.   When at a press conference he was
challenged on the policy of imposing a $400 million per year
burden on consumers of coffee in the United States and seeing the
gains siphoned off to safe havens in Switzerland without permitting any improvement in real wages for the workers in the
industry, Walt W. Rostow, the President's Special Assistant,
brushed off reporters with the assurance that eventually the benefits would trickle down to the masses.   Gordon, after an educational experience as Ambassador to Brazil, was less confident:
"We must not deceive ourselves by the hope that somehow or
other general economic growth will trickle down into adequate
social investment and agricultural modernization." [15]

   Agricultural Progress and Reform.   Somehow the claims were
beginning to fall apart.   When Congressman Reuss noted that
"as far as the agricultural sector in Latin America is concerned,
the Alliance for Progress has failed to progress," he asked an
expert witness: "How effective has the Alliance been in attempts
at land reform?" The answer was sobering: "The effect has been
very negative so far." "The plain and simple fact," Congressman
Reuss continued, "is that the goals of the Alliance for Progress
are just not being met." [16]   The Agency for International De-

---

[14] *Hearings before the Senate Foreign Relations Committee,* "Nomination of Lincoln Gordon to be Assistant Secretary of State for Inter-
American Affairs," February 7, 1966.
   [15] *New York Times,* February 26, 1966.   At the Rostow briefing of
the press, May 14, 1965, Rostow had indicated that we were no longer
concerned with the need for improvement of the condition of workers
on the plantations, etc.   The new approach was to hope that eventually
some of the loot from operation of the coffee cartel *might* trickle down
to the masses by way of modernization and mechanization and a migra-
tion to the cities.   The earlier thesis of course was that improvement in
the standard of living for the downtrodden could not wait and that violent revolution might occur unless something immediate was forthcoming.
Now, the trickledown theory apparently prevailed at the Inter-American
Committee on the Alliance for Progress.
   [16] *Hearings before the House Banking and Currency Subcommittee,*
August 29, 1966, p. 2.

velopment had already read into the record the concession that
"no great progress has been made except in isolated cases in the
technical improvements in agriculture, in increasing agricultural
productivity or in carrying out programs of agrarian reform." [17]
And the Inter-American Development Bank conceded that "there
has been very little actual land redistribution during the last four
years." Indeed, when the administration itself listed the achievements, it found itself limited to three agricultural reform programs,
two of which dated before the Alliance had gotten under way!
And the third could only remotely be linked to the effectiveness
of Alliance financing.

"For all the new land-reform laws," The Economist (London)
reported, "the crisis of land-hungry men is deepening. Spotty
attempts at paternal social-welfare programmes are not what is
needed. . . . Everybody now sings the litany of land reform. The
singing is so lusty that one might believe the landless wageless
peasant-serf had had his day. Years of rhetoric and controversy
have led at last to new land laws for most of the Republics. . . .
It looks like a breakthrough. Yet, despite their high-sounding
preambles, the new agrarian reform laws have, in fact, been so
cautiously written and so blunderingly executed as to have had
little impact on the iniquitous land-tenure system under which
nearly two-thirds of farming land is in the hands of one percent
of all landowners." [18]

The postwar dogma that modern economic development is dependent wholly on industrialization, so popular in Latin America,
had not been challenged by the "planners" of the Alliance. In
an area still properly labelled agricultural, agriculture was
neglected. "Consider the record of the Government," Professor
Theodore W. Schultz mercilessly testified. "There is still not a
single first-class agricultural research center in Latin America to
show" for the effort. "Why? Latin American governments have
not vetoed such research. The reasons are predominantly our
own making, namely, (1) crash programs, (2) the agricultural
extension bias, and (3) selling agriculture short in economic

---

[17] *Hearings before the House Appropriations Subcommittee on Foreign
Assistance and Related Agencies Appropriations for 1966*, p. 855.
[18] June 10, 1966.

development." [19] It was a matter of priorities. But was not "planning" the core of the effort the Alliance was supposed to develop?

Planning. For five years, every appropriation for the Alliance was based on testimony regarding the progress in comprehensive planning and the piously affirmed claim of focussing disbursements precisely where the comprehensive planning is most effective. Indeed, even the *first* justifications before the House Foreign Affairs Committee emphasized *how well* the planning effort was going. "The attention that Latin American governments are paying to development planning reflects their recognition that we mean business. Chile, Colombia and Brazil have completed comprehensive development plans. . . . It is expected that Venezuela will submit its plan soon." [20] Each year the State Department returned to the hill to emphasize the broadening list of effective national plans. Yet, outside of some "shopping lists" hastily assembled to stimulate the flow of funds, the planning was largely a fraud. In 1965 an advisor to the World Bank testified:

> "The experience of the Alliance for Progress has been that the practical choice is often reduced to partial planning or no planning at all. Every Latin American country was originally expected to prepare a ten-year comprehensive plan in order to qualify for aid under the Program. But it soon became evident that most Latin American countries were unable or unwilling to prepare such plans, and that the few which were willing to formulate plans would need much time before their plans were prepared. The Bolivian comprehensive plan has never been viable and almost nothing has been done to implement the Colombian ten-year comprehensive plan. Instead, a four-year investment plan has become the basis for coordinating public capital disbursements. Only Chile, Ecuador and Venezuela still have comprehensive plans but they have had little influence on private investment." [21]

"If our Alliance is to succeed," President Kennedy had said, "each Latin American nation must formulate long-range plans for its own development, plans which establish targets and priorities, ensure monetary stability, establish the machinery for vital social change, stimulate private activity and initiative, and provide for

---

[19] *Hearings before the House Agriculture Committee,* "World War on Hunger," Serial W, Part 1, p. 160. (February 1966).

[20] House Foreign Affairs Committee, *Hearings on the Foreign Assistance* Act of 1962, Part III, p. 455.

[21] Albert Waterston, *Development Planning, Lessons of Experience* (Baltimore, 1965), p. 100.

a maximum national effort." But he had gone beyond this: he had promised that in the "allocation of outside resources, these plans will be the foundation of outside resources."

Former Secretary of State Acheson had put it a bit more bluntly: "We can't have the Latin American countries screaming for worms like a bunch of young robins in a nest. We must see some progress from them first." [22]

But so deeply entrenched was the feeling that money can solve all problems whatever its use, and so worried was the Executive Branch that the appropriations might be slowed by the Congress if the conditions were shown to be contrary to requirements for effective use, that the central concern of the State Department became the concealment of the failure. Once the State Department had to claim planning where no planning existed, internal reforms where no reforms existed, social gains where they were conspicuously absent, the likelihood of effective negotiation with the Latin Americans for action to complement the great expenditure of U.S. treasure disappeared. The combination of loud shrieks of distress at Latin America's backwardness by the professional do-gooders who had never had it so good, coupled with the "satisfaction" with Latin America's behavior expressed publicly for congressional consumption combined slowly to imprison the United States in a futile exercise. Lip-service is all we ask, the anguished administrators cried. Is it too much to *pretend* to an interest in planning?

Showcases. The five years were marked by successive selections of "showcase" countries which were intended to show what could be done with proper programs and proper cooperation. Each showcase promptly collapsed. In the fourth year the disaster was the worst. Colombia had been selected for its long record of lip-service to planning. It was given disproportionate sums of money, with maximum lack of attention to what was being done by the country itself. It was praised to the sky before congressional committees for the manner in which it was *planning* the mobilization of its resources and the spreading of the gains broadly. In 1965 the Colombian showcase cracked as had previous selections by the State Department. "It is not that the Plan broke down," officials conceded, "but rather that it had just never been put into prac-

---

[22] *Newsweek,* May 14, 1962.

tice." [23]   By mid-1966 it was politically safe in Colombia to say
publicly that nothing actually had been done to implement the
plans. This was not quite correct, however. The United States
had committed $370 million for the showcase, plus $80 million
per year in a windfall from the underwriting of the coffee cartel.
But somehow, U.S. money alone was not enough. Even in the
heavily endowed coffee industry, real wages fell. And falling
in line with the U.S. thesis of "money can do it all," Colombian
officials protested that since some $900 million in Colombian
funds had been drained away by their citizens to safe-havens
abroad, it was the duty of the United States immediately to re-
plenish the supply, and if possible with even less restrictions on
use of the funds. So lacking in comprehension of the purpose of
the Alliance were the Latins that they viewed the flight of capital
not as something which they must find ways to cope with, on
pain of losing aid from the United States, but rather as a condition that was to be remedied by greater infusions of U.S. capital.
"Look at how much money the United States has sunk in other
areas of the world," the much-respected Caliban wrote in *El
Tiempo,* "and they hate the United States now. . . . Latin America
should come ahead of Vietnam and other areas. . . . We need the
money but without ominous (sic) conditions. And here in Colombia, anti-Yanqui sentiment is at a minimum. *Indeed, in spite of
the theft of Panama from us."* [24]   This at a moment when the
refusal to adopt sound self-help measures was again occasioning
external concern with the hopeless task of gaining recognition
for the real meaning of the Alliance for Progress.

Significantly, far from using the breakdown in Colombia to
insist that this "screaming for worms" must stop and a beginning
made on self-help, the American Embassy in Bogotá now began
issuing statements assuring the Colombians that there had been
no suspension of allocations for Colombia in reaction to the obvious collapse. This in response to press coverage that claimed
the failure to have become so notorious that even the State Department felt it would endanger the whole program to continue
the flow of funds.

Education. After five years, Senator Wayne Morse discovered

[23] *El Espectador* (Bogotá), July 13, 1966.
[24] December 4, 1966.

that "figures for the Alliance for Progress show a distressing lack of emphasis on education." [25] Of the technical cooperation funds for fiscal 1966, he claimed, only 10.8% were directed to basic education, and 7.7% to technical training in industry and agriculture. The figures — $8.5 and $6.0 million respectively — seemed unimpressive in a billion dollar Alliance program. And in the budget for Agency for International Development development loans for fiscal 1966 ($493 million), he found only $3.2 million for basic education.

The House Foreign Affairs Committee working on the fiscal 1967 program reported that the Alliance "has not made satisfactory headway toward the 1971 target of providing six years of education for all children or of extending life expectancy by a minimum of five years."

Housing. The Committee discovered too that not enough progress was being made toward providing decent housing or good working conditions. After years of phony claims on the effectiveness of the approach to the housing needs of the masses, the Agency for International Development conceded that it had discovered that the housing effort of the Alliance had reached too high an income level and that it should not have been aimed largely at housing for the relatively well to do." [26]

Priorities. It should not have required five years for the Congress to discover that the priorities adopted for expenditure of the U.S. contribution to the Alliance were highly unsatisfactory. Even in the first year, the United States under the banner of the Alliance had typically (a) used some $200 million to bail out U.S. businessmen who had over-extended themselves in Brazil and were now benefited by the Alliance in the form of retroactive cost-free insurance cover; (b) underwritten the largest single program of military-hardware purchases ever voted in Latin America ($280 million of equipment for the Argentine armed forces) from implementation of which it was saved only by political shifts in the Plate; (c) paid off accumulated budgetary deficits in Ecuador with the effect of encouraging fiscal irresponsibility; (d) made a campaign contribution of $150 million in a vain effort to hold

---

[25] *Congressional Record*, July 18, 1966, p. 15307.

[26] *Hearings before the House Foreign Affairs Committee on Foreign Assistance Act of 1965*, H. R. 7750, pp. 32-33.

President Frondizi in power against the wishes of the Argentine people; (e) bought a decisive vote at Punta del Este without which it would have been so difficult to conceal the failure of the conference that the Kennedy Administration would have suffered politically within the United States; (f) provided dollar-gap coverage for defaulted dollar bonds which had been denounced and repudiated a generation before by the President of the United States; (g) matched dollar for dollar a flight of capital from Mexico; (h) outlined a campaign contribution of $120 million immediate and $350 million bait to the Chilean government as a demonstration that the U.S. Secretary had not been serious at Punta del Este when for internal political consumption he had worried aloud that the U.S. Congress might want to wash its hands of the Alliance if Chile and its associates continued to resist effective action on the communist menace in Cuba; (i) devised a scheme whereby in some nations most of the funds for the Alliance for Progress would be absorbed in an attempt to soothe American business interests which had chosen the utility field instead of some more profitable area of endeavor and now having milked the properties of their earning power and without just claim on the U.S. Treasury sought full indemnification for their error in judgment; (j) heavily financed Costa Rica despite the insistence of the Costa Rican Central Bank itself that top priority attached to fiscal reforms and acceptance of sound fiscal practices rather than external loans, and thereby deepened the instinct for fiscal irresponsibility which the government no longer concealed after such encouragement from the United States; (k) provided funds to offset a great flight of capital from El Salvador and made loan commitments for the same purpose in Argentina at a time when an Argentine government bank (repeat *government* bank) was helping wreck the credit-strapped economy by providing special facilities for the flight of capital from Argentina; (l) financed Colombia while the mounting corruption and the exfoliation of the bureaucracy (in proportions startling even for Latin America where corruption was indigenous and the swollen bureaucracy a perennial curse) defeated hope for responsible economic activity in the future.

By the fifth year the variety of purposes to which Alliance for Progress funds were being directed continued to contrast sharply with the objectives of the Alliance. Typically, there was money for a deal which aimed to stabilize the price of copper in the United States and had the effect of providing a subsidy principally for the fabricating subsidiaries of a leading American copper company. There was money to pay subsidies to labor leaders *after* they had studied in the United States under U.S. financing and now returned to their own countries to serve in the *free* *l*abor movement. There was money to pay the downpayments and periodic installments on European, Canadian and U.S. investments taken over by Latin American governments in an amount exceeding a half billion dollars, in actions encouraged by American Embassy intervention with the assurance that U.S. donations and concealed donations would be available to help, provided the settlements were over-generous enough to the foreign stockholders. There was a continuation of preferential treatment precisely for those countries which had deviated most widely from the principles of self-help. There was for instance the discovery that Costa Rica was not achieving satisfactory economic growth, per-capita growth was only 0.7% per year in a decade and gross domestic capital formation was declining an average of 2% per year, and the parallel revelation that it was receiving disproportionate aid from the United States whatever gauge might be used. In that case indeed there was the astonishing finding by a Costa Rican President that it was simply going to be necessary to raise taxes and launch some self-help measures unless disproportionate aid from the United States could become institutionalized. U.S. aid was promptly expanded to avert so dire a policy change by the Costa Ricans. There was the continuing use of funds to cover budget deficits. There was the happy Secretary of Defense McNamara explaining that "by this military assistance we are able to substitute *our* expenditures for *theirs* for military purposes." And the accompanying fact that the substitution never worked out to a deversion of funds from military waste to urgent social and economic requirements. This was nicely demonstrated when the Brazilians, the larger part of their imports from the U.S. now financed by U.S. donations and concealed donations, their external debt defaulted by rollover of service, and real wages for their people declining scandalously, announced in London four months into the fifth year of the Alliance that they had $18 million to spend immediately on sophisticated military equipment and could well sign contracts for much larger sums spread over a period of years. Of course, there was in the same fortnight a footnote in the *New York Times* out of Sao Paulo, reporting that military doctors were emphasizing the gravity of the public health problem in Brazil by citing figures that only two out of every five men called up for service in the armed forces are medically fit, with malnutrition high on the grounds for rejection.

"We are all grossly derelict," the Administrator of the Agency for International Development asserted piously, "in the limited attention we have given to the evaluation of the experience." [27] But Senator Gruening produced an answer quickly enough: "When the attention of AID officials is called to some colossal error, some act of corruption and some great waste of money that had taken place previously, and an explanation requested, the reply is always: 'I was not here when that took place. That was before I got here. The records have gone to Washington.' And at Washington the details are unavailable." [28]

By the end of the fifth year the diversion of Alliance funds from the original objectives to purposes calculated more to jeopardize than to achieve the targets was continuing even more vigorously than it had in the first year.

"On nearly every front." The *Manchester Guardian* buttoned up the story well. "On nearly every front the Alliance has failed . . . the Alliance was in some degree a panic measure dreamt up in the aftermath of Castro's successful revolution in Cuba. . . . Behind the revolutionary slogans the reality (of the Alliance) is not very impressive." [29] It found quite correctly that the plans to accelerate economic and social development and to encourage programs of comprehensive agrarian reform had fared no better than the democratic institutions.

The fate of democratic institutions. "Seven years ago," a presidential candidate (John F. Kennedy) had shouted at San Antonio, Texas on September 12, 1960, "there were fifteen strongmen in Latin America dominating the life of their countries. Today there are only five. Three years from now, there won't be any."

Unfortunately the gap between rhetoric and reality was never greater than in this field. Political instability increased, shifts in control of the governments by "illegal procedures" multiplied, mil-

---

[27] Speech, November 19, 1965.
[28] *Congressional Record*, July 26, 1966, p. 16274.
[29] *Manchester Guardian Weekly*, September 1, 1966.

itary influence expanded. A dozen coups neatly distributed among eight countries found the five years ending with about half the population of the area under military rule. And the Administration found itself defending its position merely in terms of consistency as between the Kennedy and Johnson administrations: "In the case of Argentina," Assistant Secretary of State Gordon explained, "the recent coup (1966) took place on the 28th of June and recognition on the 15th of July. In March 1962 there was a coup in Argentina against President Frondizi and the Kennedy Administration recognized the new regime 19 days later instead of 18." Adding a note of practicality unusual for a theoretician of the Alliance, he drew on his experience in Brazil to note that "if a military is completely united in its will, obviously it can overthrow a government with ashtrays." [30]

Now the new thesis developed that Latin America is simply "not ready" for democracy. The thought had of course been present earlier. When the Alliance was coming into being, an Assistant Secretary of State had warned the Congress that "in most of Latin America there is so little experience with the benefits of political legitimacy that there is an insufficient body of opinion which has any reason to know its value and hence to defend it." Now Assistant Secretary Gordon lectured the Senate Foreign Relations Committee on the fact that "political development is a process in time," and that in Brazil for instance the military dictatorship which he had supported so vigorously demonstrated that the time for constitutional democracy still lay far in the future for Brazilians.[31] They were just "not ready" for such a mature concept. The influential Senator Hickenlooper, showing that his education by State Department witnesses before the Senate Foreign Relations Committee had not been in vain, urged that we avoid making "a fetish out of what we call democracy in countries that in many cases do not have the least conception of what community and state responsibility may mean for the individual." [32]   Again, Assistant Secretary Mann insisted that "the military is a force for

---

[30] *Meet the Press*, NBC TV Program, August 21, 1966, Transcript.

[31] *Hearings before the Senate Foreign Relations Committee on the Nomination of Lincoln Gordon to be Assistant Secretary of State*, February 7, 1966, p. 15.

[32] *Hearings before the Senate Foreign Relations Committee on Foreign Assistance 1965*, p. 231.

stability." [33] And to this, General O'Meara, U.S. Army, Commander-in-Chief, Southern Command, had an explanation to add: "The amenability of the military forces to suggestions from American forces can be very important in the future." [34]

The Liturgy. Even the patriotic liturgy which President Kennedy had invoked, that we must act "not because the communists may be doing it, not because we seek their votes, but because it is right. If a free society cannot help the many who are poor, it cannot save the few who are rich," could no longer be celebrated comfortably when at long last Senator Gore, inflamed by some particularly obnoxious operations in the field of investment calculated to win business support for the Alliance at the expense of the objectives orginally posed, protested that "the aid program has in large measure come to be a subsidy for American business and American exporters," and demanded a distinction between the profit motive and the eleemosnary, the selfish and the charitable." [35] And the increasingly shabby values of the Alliance prompted a British reporter to warn that "nothing is more likely to bolster the bogey of dollar imperialism than such a false dichotomy of values, which says that dictatorship is perfectly acceptable so long as it does not nationalize American oil refineries."

The Bugle Call. For Senator Robert Kennedy's speechwriters, the words came easy: "In every American land a revolution is coming, a revolution which will be peaceful if we are wise enough, compassionate if we care enough, successful if we are fortunate enough, but a revolution which will come whether we will it or not; we can affect its character, we cannot alter its inevitability."

"If *we* are wise enough and if *we* care enough and if *we* are fortunate enough," indeed.

From the day the Alliance was projected, the great question had been whether the bugle call sounding reveille is always welcome, whether the Latin Americans themselves were actually interested in making the changes whose inevitability the United States now confronted them with. A great newspaper summed up the record

---

[33] *Hearings before the House Foreign Affairs Committee on H.R. 7750,* p. 157.

[34] *Ibid.,* p. 351

[35] *Congressional Record,* July 22, 1966, p. 16041.

of the five years: "The future of the Alliance was put in the hands of those groups in society who would suffer the most if there were really to be a revolution. Consequently it has had the reverse effect from what was intended. Far from alleviating the misery of those below, it has reinforced the power of those set in authority. The lid of the powder keg has been battened down yet more firmly." [36]

The utter failure of the bugle call could be read in the criticism of a brilliant ambassador to the Organization of American States: "In Latin America the bulk of the public still continues to look on the Alliance as a U.S. aid program instead of as a grand inter-American revolutionary undertaking in which the major effort must be made by each of the Latin American countries themselves. . . . Almost all the criticism of the Alliance that is made in our countries is based on the erroneous conception that this is simply a special loan (sic) program of the United States rather than a joint revolutionary undertaking." [37]

And the debasement which the Latin Americans seemed to suffer gladly as they grubbed for scraps from the table infuriated many who remembered the days when individual dignity and national honor were treasured in Latin America. Such was the former Minister of Finance of Argentina who grieved that "there is no international assembly at which our delegates neglect to assert our 'super-honorable' condition of under-development or neglect to assert that we feel identified with the aspirations of our 'twin brothers' of Togo, Ruanda, Burundi, Jordan and Thailand rather than with the advanced nations with which we formerly associated." He even refused to share the exultation of the new bureaucracy in the fact that "the Secretary-General of the United Nations has been kind enough pursuant to this self-downgrading to include Argentina as one of the countries linked by destiny and aspirations with two-thirds of humanity whose annual per-capita income was $136." [38]

Five years after President Kennedy had sounded the call for a

---

[36] *Manchester Guardian Weekly,* September 1, 1966.

[37] Ambassador of Costa Rica. *The Evening Star* (Washington), February 10, 1965.

[38] Dr. Federico Pinedo, *Economic Survey* (Buenos Aires), August 24, 1965.

decade which at its close "will mark the beginning of a new era in the American experience," it appeared that the more the United States was willing to escalate the effort to meet the challenge that it perceived in Latin America, the more the Latin Americans seemed willing to leave the battle to the North Americans. There was no lack of Latin Americans ready to accept the U.S. doctrine depicted by a cartoonist: "If we cannot solve the problem, we can always subsidize it." After all, the priestcraft of the Alliance—the bureaucracy, the "consultants", the U.S. university community, and the business leaders—were living well off the corpse.

If after five year the rather lugubrious prospect repelled decent-minded citizens who had once viewed the Alliance as a crusade for "a new era in the American experience", the prescriptions being brought forth for the next five seemed even more self-serving and certain to defeat the purposes of the Alliance. Prescriptioneering in the United States for improvement of relations with Latin America has as long a history as sloganeering has in Latin America as a substitute for meaningful appraisal and action. Let us next examine some of the emerging prescriptions.

Chapter II
The Prescriptions

"Más acción concreta y menos palabras" was the cry of the Latin American delegates when the Second Inter-American Conference of Ministers of Labor opened in Caracas in May 1966. It was a slogan in fitting sequence to that which had prevailed before the Alliance: "Más divisas, menos sonrisas." And it recognized what even the White House conceded, namely, that "reality did not match the rhetoric which flowed about the Alliance on both sides of the Rio Grande." [1]

The core of the slogan, however, rested in the question: More action *by whom?* We have seen that the United States had carried out its pledge faithfully. Even so enthusiastic a believer in the free flow of dollars as Walt W. Rostow, special adviser to both President Kennedy and President Johnson, insisted that U.S. action had been adequate: "By and large, as far as public capital is concerned, requirements have been met. . . . In the Inter-American Committee on the Alliance for Progress we make an annual review of the requirements for external assistance from all sources for each Latin American country. . . . This objective analysis, which results in a statement of requirements, has by and large been met." [2]

But the frustration of the wild hopes built up by the rhetoric of the Alliance tolerated no such definition. And it would have been entirely out of character for Latin American politicians to analyze *why* the effort was failing, much less to accept responsibility for the failures. Indeed, there was a steady deterioration in the extent to which the Latin Americans were willing to face up to the experience with the Alliance.

---

[1] Theodore C. Sorensen, *Kennedy* (Harper & Row, New York, 1965), p. 604.

[2] NBC, *The Today Show*, September 23, 1966.

First, there was the continuing protest at the simple inadequacy of the funds committed by the United States, even though the data clearly revealed full compliance with the pledge. In Chile, the incoming president (Eduardo Frei) insisted that the "Alliance is simply inoperative," and warned against relying on the "mirage" of foreign aid. Mirage indeed! $471 million in actual disbursements of donations and concealed donations, 16% of the total such disbursements made by the United States and in a country with only 3.8% of the population, and already having the third highest per-capita gross national product in the area. In Brazil, where his regime had been characterized by utter disregard for proper priorities in the use of national resources and by corruption so conspicuous that it shocked even Latin Americans, ex-President Kubitschek had the gall to voice suspicions that "we have seen the United States too often undertake commitments and then not fulfill them." In Bolivia, when almost $400 million had gone down the drain in a decade of mendicancy, the Minister of Economy protested that "the Alliance is an engine that is idling." And well into the fifth year of the Alliance, the Argentine Foreign Minister, whose country was engaged in a decade-long demonstration of "how to run a richly endowed country into the ground", pouted that "the Alliance cannot succeed unless it provides the resources that have been promised."

From dissatisfaction with the loot and particularly with the share of the loot each was getting, the Latin Americans heated up the protest with demands for less conditions and restrictions on the use made of the funds. Here there was a statistical sticker in the annual data on funds in the pipeline which grew and became an affront to every politician who dreamed of what he could do with such money if only it were made available without the "silly" proviso that it must contribute effectively to the objectives of the Alliance for Progress. By June 30, 1966, the Agency for International Development was reporting that it alone had $1.6 billion in unexpended balances awaiting use by Latin America in suitable manner. (See Table XI). And this did not include the many other spigots (calculated by the House Appropriations Committee as numbering at least sixteen) through which the blessings flowed from Washington. That they should have to complement U.S. efforts with their own self-help measures, or that they should have to wait until there was some assurance that the money would

Table XI

AGENCY FOR INTERNATIONAL DEVELOPMENT
ESTIMATED UNEXPENDED BALANCES
JUNE 30, 1966
(millions of dollars)

Argentina	$ 56.1	Honduras	$ 14.5
Bolivia	64.6	Mexico	41.2
Brazil	456.0	Nicaragua	29.4
Chile	134.9	Panama	25.2
Colombia	94.2	Paraguay	10.1
Costa Rica	23.9	Peru	44.2
Dom. Rep.	55.9	Uruguay	4.1
Ecuador	44.6	Venezuela	19.9
El Salvador	20.8	IDB Trust Fund	284.0
Guatemala	18.2	Unitemized	125.0
Haiti	0.6		

not be wholly wasted, misdirected or simply stolen, was a shocking discovery for the Latin Americans.

Argentina's President protested that "the conditions imposed deprive the Alliance of dynamism and force." Bolivia's Minister for Rural Affairs worried that the "United States finances only areas which are found to warrant high priority for the economy." Juan Bosch's party in the Dominican Republic objected to the idea that "a dreamy bureaucracy imposing conditions would stand in the way of the needs of the people." In Brazil, Governor Brizola, confronted with objections to the expropriation without compensation of certain U.S. properties, argued that actually such expropriations "are a favorable movement for the Alliance for Progress. . . . We have two elements holding back our programs—one is the latifundistas and the other the foreign economic group. Unless we get rid of both, the Alliance will not work. They will eat all the dollars provided for aid and in less than ten years if these groups remain, all the dollars will be back in the United States." The imposition of conditions seeking to assure effective use of U.S. funds brought a challenge of U.S. motives. One of Bolivia's better minds concluded that the Alliance had actually been concocted by the United States in response to the "circumstances of the strategic expansion of U.S. capitalism, i.e., the need for new markets for its exports," [3] and when the Bolivian delegate returned to the attack at the subsequent meeting of the board of governors of the Inter-American Development Bank, the press reported that he was charging that "Washington may have ulterior imperialistic motives." [4] This after a decade in which the United States had literally kept the Bolivian population alive by counteracting the policies of the revolutionary government which had wrecked the country economically, politically, and financially!

A spokesman for Peru sounded off for the whole area: "The qualifications for aid cannot be adapted to our environment. We are asking for a policy more adapted to reality."

It is true that on his disastrous mission to Latin America (June 4-22, 1961) the President's Special Emissary, Adlai Stevenson, had stupidly told the Latin Americans that it would be "both hard and wrong for the United States to impose conditions" on the flow of funds from Washington. But the legislative history of this program, and the discussions with the Latin Americans from which the program developed, clearly indicate, as Senator Fulbright put it, the position that "if a country is not willing to make firm commitments for undertaking specific reforms, we should say we are not interested."

It is illustrative perhaps of the deterioration of the U.S. position in the face of the prescription which the Latin Americans were insisting upon that in the first year of the Alliance, the State Department cravenly at the insistence of the Chilean government withdrew a U.S. diplomat from its embassy in Chile because of that government's charges that he had allegedly "pressed in *private* conversations for the reforms which the U.S. Congress had clearly indicated must complement the flow of U.S. funds." By the fifth year, on the other hand, a high officer of the American Embassy in Chile was apologizing to the Chileans for the findings of the U.S. Government Accounting Office regarding the waste—and worse—that it had uncovered and publicized in its investigations of outlays of U.S. funds in Chile, and was urging them to disregard the criticism.

---

[3] Guillermo Bedregal, "Problemas de infra-estructura, regimen monetario,, y desarrollo económico de Bolivia," *Mundo Económico,* Marzo-Abril, 1962, p. 53.

[4] See *Washington Post,* May 20, 1962.

The amount dubbed unsatisfactory, the restrictions on use intolerable when linked with the objectives of the Alliance, it was a short step to the third prescription of the Latin Americans: that U.S. donations under the Alliance must be considered a "right" so that any recurring question of how much would be forthcoming and under what conditions could be eliminated. Throughout the five years, as the immense flow of funds continued, there was always the suspicion in Latin America that no nation, not even the United States, could be so stupid as to permit indefinitely this drain on its resources when the results were so clearly unsatisfactory. The Chileans therefore led Latin America to a demand that "the right" of access to the Treasury of the United States be recognized in a new international agreement or treaty.

The rationale was mixed. The Brazilian Ambassador to Washington voiced the regret at the "humiliation" the Latin Americans experienced when they had to ask for aid or prove that they intended to use funds raised from the U.S. taxpayers effectively.[5] From London, the *Sunday Times* reported an Argentine professor's protest that "the flaw in the Alliance is that it patronises us. . . . We will never be content unless we are allowed to be ourselves." [6]

But there was an easy way to avoid this humiliation. Let us look at a case in point. Late in 1966, with disbursements of donations and concealed donations to Peru proceeding at a $38 million per year pace, the Government of Peru begged Washington for an additional $383,200 of food for the starving *campesinos* in the Department of Puno which had been badly hit by adverse weather. The request was of course granted. And a week later the Peruvian Congress voted $33 million for the purchase of sophisticated military equipment overseas!

It so happens that Peru was enjoying an extremely prosperous year both on internal accounts and on balance of payments. It could have avoided the humiliation of begging for aid simply by accepting the feeding of its starving people as a top priority for its budget. And surely, it could have avoided the humiliation by cutting down the pending purchase of military aircraft and other military items to the extent of $383,200! Instead it chose to beg. What better way could there be to eliminate what the Brazilian

---

[5] Speech, November 13, 1963.

[6] April 12, 1964.

Ambassador called "the lingering feeling of humiliation" on the part of the Latins and the "self-righteous attitude of resentment at what they consider a rather lax or even ungrateful behavior" on the part of the United States than to adopt suitable priorities in the use of resources at their command.

Chile provided another typical case of the "humiliation" which accompanied the system of drawing on Alliance funds. Since thousands died annually from measles in Chile, the government asked for $800,000 for a mass immunization campaign against measles. The experience was particularly humiliating because at the time the government was negotiating for guided missiles for its naval vessels with which to set off a costly rivalry among the naval powers in Latin America, and presumably to have to devote time to pleas for assistance for children was a strain on a bureaucracy whose "Plan" called for expansion into sophisticated and wholly unneeded military equipment using scarce exchange resources. No Chilean official, apparently, asked whether in the hundreds of millions of dollars budgeted annually by Chile the campaign against measles might not have been given higher priority, without resort to mendicancy abroad. Instead, there was the demand that this "humiliation" created by the self-imposed status of mendicant cease.

Nor was there any improvement after five years of such "humiliation". A few months into the sixth year, Chile placed an order for $20 million of British jet fighter planes which roused even the *New York Times* to ask: "Why spend $20 million in fighter planes and then seek help from the Agency for International Development for Chile's internal economic and social needs?" [7]

The answer provided by the Chilean Ambassador in Washington illustrates how hopelessly lost the Latin Americans are in their conception of the problems the Alliance was supposed to attack. The Ambassador wrote the *New York Times* that the funds for the sophisticated aircraft having already been appropriated for the special purpose, "the law itself specifically forbids" use for any other purpose.[8] The inability to comprehend the initial error in

---

[7] October 25, 1966. "Chile is not facing a war threat. Arms are for internal security and for nothing else. Chile simply can not afford millions spent on toys for the Chilean Air Force and Navy."

[8] *November 7, 1966.* The Ambassador claimed that the planes were needed "to fulfil Chile's share in continental defense plans." This was promptly denied by U.S. officials.

appropriating funds for such purposes when the nation was a mendicant plying the charity lanes, and the inability to understand that if the funds had remained unused for the aircraft they might eventually have been reallocated by a government seriously interested in economic and social progress, must shatter any illusions one might have regarding achievement of the objectives of the Alliance.

Still, the Latin Americans chose to insist on their "right" to figure in the budget of the United States in the manner they might jointly decide. This was their way to end the humiliation, to make access to the U.S. Treasury a "right." And they found a ridiculous justification: "The Alliance for Progress is not a crusade for charity," the conservative newspaper *El Mercurio* in Santiago shamed itself by saying, "but instead simply a payment to Latin America for the benefits which the United States had derived from its historic association with Latin America." [9]

Assistant Secretary of State Gordon disposed of this effectively: "I have occasionally heard it argued by Latin Americans that the inter-American system should be conceived as a sort of bargain in which Latin American support for United States strategic and security interests is balanced against American support for Latin American economic interests. This strikes me as a singularly erroneous view. When German and Italian agents were seeking before and during World War II to subvert Latin regimes to the purposes of fascism, the security of Latin America was engaged no less than our own. When only six years ago, the agents of Trujillo sought to assassinate a Venezuelan president, and more recently the agents of Fidel Castro sought to capture Caracas in a lightning coup d'état, the security of Latin America was even more directly engaged than our own." [10]

But once the Frei regime entered office, it took up the argument and advanced it to the degrading status of blackmail.

The Chileans announced that they would press for compensation for support of political measures for which the United States might seek backing in the Organization of American States. The one important thing, the Chileans argued in effect, is that money be paid them without any binding relationship to achievement of the

---

[9] UPI dispatch slugged Santiago, March 3, 1962.
[10] *Christian Science Monitor*, October 19, 1966, p. 9.

goals of the Alliance for Progress such as had prompted the United States thus far to tie strings to the flow of cash, however weak the knots might be. As the Chileans put it formally: ". . . una compensación ha de ser de caracter económico . . . auxilio permanente y no voluntario, ni con fecha fija." [11]   A shamed Latin American writer of integrity was moved to warn of the direction of policy: "Convertir a la política exterior del continente en un mercado de extorsiones o de chantajes por todo lo alto." [12]   Latin America under this prescription was to have a "right" to have the U.S. Treasury underwrite its corruption, its disregard for social justice, its inequitable tax systems, its faulty distribution of land and of the national income, in the same manner that individual Latin American governments had a "right" to expect the United States to hold them in power by a flow of arms while the same governments noisily proclaimed their hatred of "intervention," even though they had succeeded to office precisely through overthrows of constitutional government.

Sometimes a Latin American leader had the self-respect to recoil from the implications of blackmail. In October 1966, for instance, President Castelo Branco rejoiced aloud that Brazil now seemed to have sufficient foreign exchange to abandon "recourse to political blackmail." [13]   But in general, the Latin Americans supported Chile vigorously in the effort to institutionalize the combination of mendicancy and blackmail.

On the part of the United States, the Senate Foreign Relations Committee had rejected flatly the notion that Latin America has a "right" to access to the U.S. Treasury. In the *Report on the Foreign Assistance Act of 1965*, the Committee insisted that these countries be informed that "they have no inherent 'right' to assistance from the United States and that such aid depends in part on the maintenance of a climate of mutual cooperation." After five years, Senator Morse reported, "some countries have taken the surprising position that they are entitled to aid as a matter of right. There was a conference in Latin America where they wanted to write into the OAS Charter the commitment in treaty form. We had an informal meeting of the Committee on Foreign Relations

---

[11] *Diario las Americas,* March 25, 1965.
[12] *Diario las Americas,* March 28, 1965.
[13] Brazilian Embassy, *News from Brazil,* October 17, 1966.

and the State Department was left with no room for doubt that the Committee was not going to make that commitment." [14]   The *Washington Post,* summing up the accomplishments of five years, editorialized correctly that "self-help has yet to replace moaning in some of the countries." [15]   In fact, in most of the countries.

Reform. Not all Latin Americans saw the problem in terms simply of an inflow of capital for redistribution to safe havens abroad or to enable delay in the obviously needed reforms by further bolstering the oligarchies.

Early in the program Archbishop Helder Camara proclaimed that "the Alliance for Progress is dead, although I wish its resurrection. The first reason for its failure is that it was necessary to establish a strict connection between aid from the Alliance and basic reforms; but unfortunately, the wealthy people in Latin America talk a lot about basic reforms but brand as communists those who decide to put them into practice." [16]   As it became more and more clear that reforms called for were being honored in the breach, a fine scholar, Josué de Castro, addressing himself to the Brazilian Northeast which the Kennedy family had discovered in 1960 and adopted as its own political punching-bag, warned that "all aid from the Alliance for Progress (is) irremediably doomed to fail unless . . . accompanied by basic domestic reforms . . . the first of which must be to abolish the feudal agrarian system. . . . The Alliance, instead of helping the Brazilian people, will actually help their enemies. The end result of these inadequate efforts of relief would be to foment revolution." He conceded that the United States had tried to help but found that not much of the aid had reached the people. "Everything has been tried . . . all have failed and must fail again since at bottom they are employed to preserve the status quo and the privileges of the few." [17]   Significantly, perhaps, he was writing in exile, having had his civil rights cancelled by the Brazilian military government which the United States had helped bring into office and continued to underwrite heavily.

[14] *Congressional Record,* July 25, 1966, p. 16173.

[15] August 18, 1966.

[16] TV broadcast, February 21, 1963.

[17] *Death in the Northeast* (New York, 1966).

But it is significant that the Latin Americans themselves were not prepared to execute the commitment to reform, without which external aid must fail. Was this too a function of the United States? In the very geographic area to which Josué de Castro was addressing his remarks, U.S. officials protested that "they can do little to improve social and economic conditions without effective cooperation from local authorities and so far they have not had it in agriculture."[18] This did not free the United States from its responsibility to expend money effectively, of course. And when a U.S. official identified as "the biggest disaster of the Alliance program the experience in northeast Brazil in which we had built 2,000 classrooms at the urgent request of the local authorities only to discover that the government did not have teachers, books or the organizations to make good use of them," obviously blame had to be shared. Senator Robert Kennedy would undoubtedly repeat many times his assertion that "as long as there is a Kennedy in public life in the United States there will be a friend of northeast Brazil,"[19] but this would remain rhetoric as long as there was no serious intent by the Brazilians themselves to execute the commitment to reform.

The Confederation of Christian Trade Unionists (CLASC), which was challenging the AFL-CIO for leadership of the labor movement in Latin America, protested that the Alliance is too dependent on existing governments which are oligarchies. But its prescription seemed to be that the United States would have to *force* the Latin American governments to include a representative popular base in the planning of the expenditure of Alliance booty. It protested that for five years the "reforms" such as they were had been handed down to the workers from above whereas the individual worker should be participating directly in the planning of any reform that affects him. To an outsider, familiar with the old Latin plaint of U.S. intervention, nothing could seem more exclusively the task of the Latin Americans themselves than the determining of the make up of the decision-making personnel in their own individual countries.

Everywhere the supreme dilemma of the Alliance emerged:

[18] NBC, TV Program, December 25, 1966, "The Frank McGee Report." The quotation that follows in this paragraph is also from this Report.
[19] *Saturday Evening Post,* April 23, 1966, p. 43.

Latin America's ambivalence toward the United States, which had not been changed a bit by the launching of the Alliance. (1) The demand to be rid of U.S. influence and (2) the whining sense of neglect. Or, (1) the demand that the United States help Latin America solve its problems, but (2) only by throwing the money over the transom and going away rather than interfering in the decision-making process which in the hands of the Latins doomed U.S. aid to futility. And then (1) the protest that U.S. aid has been rendered futile because (2) the U.S. has not interfered sufficiently to assure effective use toward the stated objectives.

The noted historian, Arnold Toynbee, predicting a series of violent revolutions because it had proved so hard "to get through to direct relations with the real mass of the people who need the Alliance for Progress so much," put it well: "If America doesn't lay down any conditions, then all the money will go into the pockets of the rich and the situation will be worse than before. But if she does lay down conditions, people immediately beat the drum and say their independence is being threatened." [20]

The dead-end inspired a new series of prescriptions. The *London Times* published an extraordinarly perceptive commentary on "Washington's Error in South America." In its weakest section the author suggested that "the idea of Spanish Americans as backward and yearning to advance reflects the Anglo-American assumption of the prime merits of action, results and progress. The Spanish mind esteems these at a lower value and inclines rather to abstractions and the speculative aspect of performance. *For the most part they are as developed as they wish to be.* (Italics added). Outwardly they may deplore the visible symptoms of arrested development because its poor showing shames their ego, but inwardly they are seeking economic, political, social and cultural forms in harmony with their peculiar quality as a people."

This notion rejecting the "revolution of rising expectations" was hardly a suitable guide to policy in the 1960s. Ambassador Gordon was more nearly correct when he argued that the desire for "accelerated economic and social progress under free institutions clearly exists in Latin America. . . . I would guess that taken together the minorities (in opposition to this underlying will)

---

[20] *U.S. News and World Report*, March 30, 1964.

account for no more than 15 to 20 percent of the peoples of Latin America. The problem is to find and encourage articulate and effective leadership for the aspirations of the great majority and to relate a political mystique to the technical problems that must be objectively diagnosed and solved. . . . That sort of leadership cannot come from outside." [21]

Unfortunately it was at that point that the prescription broke down. For, in five years the Latin Americans proved that they were unable to grasp the conception of a strategically central objective. Unlike the politicians of Africa or Asia who had a plain clearcut objective of political revolution to free them from European rule, the Latin American politicians and their sycophant technicians spread themselves over a wide range of frustrations, resentments, grievances (real or imaginary) and embarrassments.

Typically there was the grievance against foreign capital. Should not the United States make available the Alliance commitment to enable them to buy out foreign enterprises? This might not contribute to growth, for it would leave the capital-short area no better off than before. But it would make fine political capital for a regime in power the day the money flowed in with which to chase the gringo out. Could some price-fixing commodity agreement be achieved which would increase the gains of the richest element in the community and enlarge the hoard of funds held abroad? It might result too in discouraging consumption and further complicating the problem of excesses of production over world consumption, and it might not contribute to social amelioration or help in the pressure on per-capita growth imposed by the rapid growth in population. But it would make fine political capital among the supporters in the oligarchy.

What, for instance, was the preoccupation of the area's most skilled economists when they advocated LAFTA, the Latin American common market? Was it the greater availability of goods and the more effective use of manpower and the larger number of jobs? Of course not. The ink was hardly dry on the documents when there arose concern lest the increased availability of goods and the more effective employment be accompanied by increased prosperity for foreign-owned firms capitalizing on the new incentive to ef-

---

[21] Lincoln Gordon, *A New Deal for Latin America* (Cambridge, 1963), p. 100.

ficiency. It would apparently be better to have less goods, and a distribution marked by greater inequality and inequity than to have advantage simultaneously accrue to foreign-owned firms as well. Even the voice of the area's great economist, Raúl Prebisch, rang loud: "Some apprehension is felt lest the benefits of the common market be reaped mainly by foreign instead of domestic enterprise. . . . I share these misgivings." Could it be that even this fine economist did not know that ninety-nine out of one hundred overseas workers employed by U.S. firms are of local origin and that the proportion is being increased as rapidly as men can be trained for the remaining posts? Or that the tax contributions (one-fifth of all government revenues in Latin America) and the labor policies of U.S. firms compare most favorably with those of the local enterprises? Or that the import of modern technology is greatly facilitated by maximum association with the fountains of the newer technology? Or that the deficiency of the area's capital is so great that the mobilization of capital must be maximized if expectations are to be realized? Or that one-third of the area's exports originated with the risk-taking foreign enterprises assuming risks that were unacceptable to local capital?

The point is that Latin America was concerned and preoccupied with goals having little or nothing to do with the central objectives of the Alliance for Progress. Senator Fulbright put it well: "If they insist on the right to make their own mistakes, there is not much we can do. . . . When a country shows it does not want to make these reforms, then I don't think we can be successful if we try to force *either* aid *or* reforms on them." [22] (Note well: *either* aid *or* reforms. In other words, the justification for the appropriations would fall flat in the Congress if in the judgment of the U.S. officials the likelihood of effective use was fatally jeopardized). Obviously the right to commit suicide is inherent in the policy-making apparatus of an independent nation. But there is no corollary obligation on the part of the United States to compensate it for the mistakes.

A bright Brazilian economist shaped *his* prescription to certain operational limitations. "The objective of accelerating institutional reforms such as agrarian or tax reforms may in the short run be incompatible with other desirable objectives such as creation of a

---

[22] *Christian Science Monitor,* March 10, 1965.

favorable climate for private investment or the stabilization of price levels. The reason is clear. The more drastic the pace of fiscal and agrarian reform, the greater the likelihood that the propertied classes now forming the bulk of private entrepreneurial and investor groups will feel fretful, aggravated and suspicious of the winds of change. The prescription of social justice is likely to stimulate wage and welfare revindications which complicate the task of inflation control and price stabilization. This does not mean the objectives of social reform and social justice are postponable or incorrect, for in the long run all objectives are compatible and self-reinforcing mutually. But not in the short run." [23]

This prescription would seem to be calling essentially for restraint rather than the bombastic rhetoric which had characterized the Alliance. For there could be no challenging the Director of Studies of the Royal Institute of International Affairs in his judgment that "rising expectations frustrated are a more effective breeding ground for revolution than mere static misery.".

Unfortunately the political values of sounding the alarm were such in the United States for those who had to push for appropriations that they were certain to defeat any effort at restraint, even though it had become a question whether the sense of panic or emergency could be sustained for decade on decade.

Conscious of the frustrating of rising expectations, Juan Bosch, former President of the Dominican Republic, warned the House Banking and Currency Committee that "there are no prospects for political stability in Latin America over the next several years, but to the contrary. All seems to indicate in the next fifteen years that we will have violent revolutions, probably some of them Communist revolutions." [24] This was offered not as a prescription but as a forecast.

Former President of Brazil, Juscelino Kubitschek, gloomed that "the Alliance seems to have been only a temporary expression of the willingness of the United States to design a better world, like

---

[23] Roberto de Oliveira Campos, Speech, November 13, 1963.

[24] *Hearings before the House Banking and Currency Subcommittee,* "Inter-American Development Bank's Role in Agricultural Development," (1966), p. 117. Bosch was asked to give the Committee the benefit of his judgment. He replied August 24, 1966.

Wilson's League of Nations and Roosevelt's Good Neighbor Policy. . . . The Alliance has not succeeded in accelerating social and economic development through free governments and so has fallen short of the chief objective—the consolidation of representative democracy." His prescription was incorporated in his protest "against the support given totalitarian substitutes for democracy which had undercut the Alliance . . . democracy had been so altered that it is not democracy at all." [25] It did no good for President Johnson to insist that "the United States has no mandate to interfere wherever government falls short of our specifications." [26] The Latin Americans would reject interference and then protest that lack of effective interference on the part of the United States.

Slogans. Essentially the Latin Americans sought an instant-mix formula for their social and economic problems, just as their forebears had believed there was an instant-mix for the political problems.

Once the Latin American leaders had believed that it was possible to *import* "the basic political skills and the arts of freedom." And if the truth be conceded, once many leaders of Europe and North America had believed that it was possible to *export* the basic political skills and the arts of freedom to the hundreds of millions who were ready to acclaim the name of freedom and democracy without any significant understanding of the matter. Indeed as late as 1961 the novices who had suddenly become Latin American "experts" in Washington believed in this capacity to export. The traffic in constitutions, in forms, the transplanting of political institutions and forms had flourished. But it had failed. And the Latin Americans were left desperately remote from political democracy, subject to unending constitutional crisis, a victim at home of chaos illuminated from time to time by coups d'état and a victim abroad of derision as the dictators enthusiastically subscribed to the recited words of democracy and "respect for the fundamental freedoms of men" at successive inter-American conferences, even as they trampled on these freedoms and made a mockery of democracy.

And now after more than a hundred years, effective govern-

---

[25] *The Evening Star* (Washington), May 13, 1966.
[26] *New York Times,* August 27, 1966. Speech at Denver August 26, 1966.

ment still absent, literacy unachieved, administrative capacity unavailable, the new sophisticates believed that there is an instant-
mix formula for social and economic problems, again echoing the
new "experts" in Washington. There was the brief-case brigade
proceeding from Washington, hastily mobilized in large part from
the cream of academic mediocrity to bring the "message" to their
colleagues in Latin America. There was the constant call to international conferences whose primary achievement was the establishment of still more bureaucratic organizations to feed on the
misery of the member countries. There was the appealing new
feature of the presidency in Latin America — the travel to visit
with other presidents — as a help in avoiding the issues and problems confronting the individual countries. There were the hastily
trained technicians, with their glib pseudo-sophistication of capital-
output ratios and marginal capital-output ratios, sought out and
offered up as a substitute for wisdom. There was the new economics
of planning, contemptuous of competitive capacity and relative
productivity and managerial performance, and concentrating on
simple additions to capacity. There was the *political* economist
flaunting his measures designed to discourage the inflow of capital
and to keep industry inefficient and to hold down production.

For five years the area searched for a slogan upon which it
could seize as an earlier generation had seized on the slogan
"democracy." Now, it seemed to have found it for the economic
sphere—hemisphere integration, or better, Latin American integration. In virtually every nation there were key decisions to make
on national problems, but unable to face up to the decision-making
function, the leaders now adopted integration as a means of avoiding national decisions, always with an eye to the appeal of a slogan
to the audience which the U.S. State Department had to satisfy
if it was to keep the money flowing. Everywhere the major countries were desperately failing in the handling of the railway problems, but rather than make the hard decisions, the slogan might
permit diversion of attention to integrating the transportation
systems of several nations, which could not possibly meet the local
transport problems which begged for effective local attention.
Everywhere there were key decisions to be made at the local
national level if the nation was not to be faced with disaster in
food supply as the population grew rapidly. But the slogan
"integration" might divert attention from these local decisions and
bring in some donations to boot. Everywhere local decisions had

brought major industries to crisis conditions for lack of competitive efficiency, but rather than cope with problems such as the error in one country of stimulating 22 companies to come in to make automobiles for a market for only 190,000 cars annually, it was easier to talk integration. At least that would put off the problem for a while. Or would it?

This is not to argue the merits of integration, the possible gains from economic integration. Instead, there is the fact that no slogan of this kind could long serve as a means of avoiding the *hard* national decisions.

Position papers: Economic. Two position papers by typical Latin American leaders need to be cited, one as an explanation of where the prescriptions of the Latins went wrong, the other as an illustration of those prescriptions.

Early in the history of the Alliance, the Minister of Finance of Colombia told the board of governors of the Inter-American Development Bank (April 23, 1962) that "the Alliance which was a carefully weighed plan to sustain our exports of primary products as a cornerstone of all proposed development and to provide additional financing assistance to expedite it, has not been able to maintain a steady measured pace and this irregularity continues to impoverish our people, deepen economic differences between classes and trigger crises, devaluations and unemployment, such as we have witnessed in several countries in the past few months. That these phenomena are still occurring frequently is a sign that the Alliance, at the end of the first year, has not yet been able to reverse the downward trends in our economies that motivated its creation. One thing we can do in its behalf is to examine its shortcomings."

The Minister went on:

"The first and most fundamental shortcoming is the little it has been possible to do in support of markets and prices for our primary export commodities. As far as Colombia—as well as most Latin American countries—is concerned, the greatest contribution the Alliance could make would be to establish a world coffee agreement on a long term basis. As long as this is not achieved, any help that may be given to us, however, generous, will not be new blood and fresh life for our economy, as had been planned, but will merely act as a palliative to prevent a total collapse. . . .

"The prices of our exportable raw materials drop, those of manufactured goods continue to increase, thus widening the gap between the terms of interchange. Most Latin American countries have made commendable efforts to diversify their production for export by seeking new and more favorable trade outlets. But this Latin American awakening coincides with the appearance of a series of restrictions, prohibitions, preferences and tax and customs barriers in large world markets which are apparently more like fortresses aimed at total isolation than of exchange.

"The Alliance should be used as additional support to accelerate development and not as insufficient compensation for losses caused by situations which we can remedy. If this is not done, we shall come to the end of our ten-year program only to find these same peoples even poorer than they are today, and still worse, deprived of all hope for the future. It is necessary to act at once if we want to prevent this very noble effort of a people and of a continent which has definitely dwarfed the great altruistic feats of all times from becoming the greatest tragedy in history." [27]

The paper had no sooner been delivered than even journalists perceived the misconception which assured failure of the Alliance: "Washington had touted the Alliance during its formation as a great new bulwark against communism. Mejia sees it as an opportunity for Colombia and friends to obtain dollars and other benefits without effort. . . . *Nowhere did he mention the self-help measures such nations as his agreed to undertake as their contribution to the Alliance for Progress.*" (Italics added).

It is particularly significant that Colombia should have been the source of this position paper, because Colombia was one of the succession of "showcase" countries selected to demonstrate the possibilities of the Alliance for Progress. The coffee agreement which the Minister of Finance sought as the "greatest contribution" the Alliance could make *was* entered into by the United States. *And* Colombia found itself the beneficiary of the $80 million per year which the State Department's implementation in defiance of congressional authority assured it. *And* Colombia *in addition* was given disproportionate sums of assistance. Yet, nowhere was the failure of the Alliance so complete as in the collapse of this "showcase." Oddly enough, real wages fell even for the workers in the coffee industry which was profiting so handsomely by the world coffee agreement. "Self-help" had been ignored in the original

---

[27] See *Inter-American Economic Affairs,* Volume 16 No. 1, pp. 84-89, for the text of the paper made available to the U.S. press by the World Coffee Information Center.

conception displayed by the Colombians and it continued to be absent. Meanwhile, the moaning regarding the terms of trade never ceased.

Position papers: General. Much more perceptive was the brilliant ambassador of Costa Rica when he appraised the Alliance after four years. He found the constant criticism of the Alliance that is made in Latin America to be based, "almost all of it," on the "erroneous conception that this is simply a special loan program of the United States, rather than a joint revolutionary undertaking." And he had a prescription deriving from the shortcomings:

> "We have not yet succeeded in having the programs of the Alliance supported by 'all energies of the peoples and the governments' as the Charter of Punta del Este demands. A clear awareness of full national participation in the great inter-American cooperative effort to which our governments committed themselves on August 17, 1961 has not yet been developed.

> "This is because the Alliance has not yet been equipped with a true political mystique. Perhaps too much emphasis has been placed on the technical approach. The Alliance has been presented as a complicated group of economic plans intended to satisfy physical needs. All that, of course, is very important, but not sufficient. For the Alliance to be successful, for the technical conceptions to be carried into practice, it is necessary to arouse the hope of our peoples, it is necessary to conduct a veritable crusade of political and social redemption that will capture the intellectual and emotional adherence of those who must give form to the new society. This includes not only the elites but also the masses." [28]

Early in the history of the Alliance, our Ambassador to Brazil had made precisely the same point, that "a political mystique is indispensable to the success of the Alliance for Progress." And he had underlined the even more important fact that "leadership in the creation of this political mystique must come from Latin America. . . . Unless the pursuit of economic and social progress, in the terms of the Charter of Punta del Este, becomes a major part of the national political life of participating country, and unless the great majority of people and organized groups and

---

[28] See *Inter-American Economic Affairs,* Volume 20, No. 4, pp. 91-96, which reprints a section of an important paper delivered by the Ambassador of Costa Rica, September 8, 1965, in which he explained to the Council of the OAS why his government opposes the proposal of CIAP that the IA-ECOSOC hold a meeting simultaneously with the Second Special Inter-American Conference.

leaders of influence feel themselves involved and committed to these goals, the Alliance for Progress will not succeed regardless of the technical soundness of individual projects and the amounts of foreign financial support made available to Latin America. The Alliance then will become simply another American aid program but not a cooperative process for bringing about a real change in the actual standards of living, in the prospects for their further rapid improvement, in the sense of participation in progress by all classes and regions of the national communities, and in the security of civil liberties and the institutions of representative democracy." [29]

After five years there was no sign of the development of the indispensable mystique. The area was prepared to moan more loudly, it was inspired to "demand" more boldly, but it was essentially a prisoner of the economic philosophy which it had happily developed to avoid facing up to its problems.

Economic Philosophy. It is not surprising that the two position papers cited, even though one represented a total misconception of the objective of the Alliance and the other a brilliant explanation of the failure, had something in common, namely, the invoking of the terms of trade thesis.

Probably no piece of economic thinking ever did more damage to the developmental aspirations of an area than the thesis propounded by Raúl Prebisch, Latin America's first internationally recognized economist, regarding the terms of trade. The notion that countries on the periphery are being *victimized* by the more developed countries, the notion that countries producing primary goods suffer worsening terms of trade, had never had a satisfactory basis in historical experience. And certainly the "law" which Myrdal purported to see in the form of a "tendency inherent in the free play of market forces to create regional inequalities, the tendency becoming the more dominant the poorer the country," the "law" which finds the normal result of unhampered trade between an industrialized country and an under-developed nation to be a cumulative process toward impoverishment of the latter, did not warrant acceptance on its economic merits by Latin American political leaders.

But so attractive was the whine regarding "victimization" to

---

[29] Lincoln Gordon, *A New Deal for Latin America* (Cambridge, 1963), p. 111.

leaders who wished to avoid serious internal adjustments that Prebisch had inadvertently provided the means of avoiding the attention to problems which he must have known require *internal* solutions. How easy to avoid the hard decisions when everything could be blamed on the foreigner and *his* improving terms of trade! How particularly attractive the doctrine when the ruling class actually did not want the end results of greater social equality and accelerated economic development at which the hard decisions must be directed! But it was significant that even after five years of the Alliance, when lip-service to the new objectives was freely given, the area remained a prisoner of the indolence in public-policy decision making which Prebisch's thesis permitted. Thus we have the Venezuelan Ambassador to the United States still preaching the nonsense that "the mechanism of exploitation (sic) consists in selling at increasingly higher prices for industrial products, and paying at increasingly lower prices for the products of the poorer nations." [30] We find the President of Argentina, after an administration which had virtually written the book on what *not* to do to promote economic and social progress, complaining that "the western world is not paying enough for Argentine products." [31] And no international conference could be free of the plaint of the Latin Americans that they were being "victimized" and "exploited" by the terms of trade. Of course, when the show-case (Colombia) collapsed under the "burden" of immense donations from the Alliance *plus* a fantastic improvement in the terms of trade, it was difficult to invoke the thesis, but sitll it was enunciated shamelessly for political advantage to a people who had suffered a generation of such deception.

No counter-attack by even the most eminent economists could sway the Latins from this easy way to avoid the hard public-policy decisions. Professor Viner could argue that the terms of trade mean little without reference to cost, he could discuss the tendency for the quality and productiveness of capital goods to rise relative to primary products, he could argue that qualitative changes give a bag of coffee more than it had gotten previously in terms of productivity of capital goods. But there was no audience. Economists of similar eminence could repeat endlessly that the problem was the failure to adopt suitable internal policies, and the excessive

---

[30] *Diario las Americas,* March 24, 1966.
[31] AP wire, April 20, 1966.

rate of population growth, and the low efficiency of agriculture, and the failure to stimulate efficient manufacturing processes, etc., but there was no interesting the Latin Americans. For the "victimization" theory made it possible to avoid unpopular decisions at home. So, the problems remained unsolved, the distribution of income deteriorated steadily, the growth rate remained unsatisfactory, by the Latin Americans' own wishes.

Among those who tried to shake the Latin Americans loose from their misguided reliance on the Prebisch thesis was the American Ambassador to Brazil. In perhaps the best presentation of the central issues on Brazilian-American relations ever made by an American official in public, he urged the National Economic Council to accept these facts: (1) That the thesis of a long-term trend in prices of primary goods necessarily unfavorable to such countries as Brazil, which was long advanced by the ECLA Secretariat, was based largely on nineteenth century British data which did not allow for reductions in shipping costs or for inherent difficulties in any long-term measurement of comparative prices for manufactured goods. (2) That "most serious scholars today are very skeptical as to the validity of any long-generalizations about inherent trends in the terms of trade." (3) That the tendency in less professional circles in Latin America to charge that adverse price changes are part of a so-called "process of spoilation" is without foundation. As for instance the Brazilian who talked about Brazil producing five million tons of merchandise to give away free to the richer countries of the world. (4) That talk about Brazil's "losses" in potential export earnings are simply ingenuous. (5) And he even went on to what became the second standard plaint—the stagnation in exports. He said that if Brazilians want to talk of making presents, they should look at the present that Brazilian coffee policy had made to its competitors in Africa and other producing countries.

The Ambassador even invoked the testimony of a very fine Mexican economist with a worldwide reputation, Dr. Victor L. Urquidi, who had written: "The custom of computing what Latin America 'loses' every time the prices fall does not appear to be a useful analytical method, since what one 'fails to gain' is not always 'lost', and an economic analysis would have to include estimates of the effect which having maintained the previous prices at a higher level would have had on the volumes of production and export.

The damage caused by the fluctuations in export prices is registered not only when they fall but also when they rise too much and provoke inflationary disturbances or create incentives to production which later will not be justified." [32]

Oddly enough, the over-worked "victimization" thesis, understandably attractive to the Latin American politician, won over some North Americans too who should have known better. For instance, Walter Lippman came back from his briefings in Latin America spouting childish prattle about "the terms of trade are such that the prices the countries receive for their exports are extremely low as against the prices they must pay for imported manufacturers. No wonder there is a chronic deficit in the balance of payments and that what they lose (sic) in world trade by selling cheap and buying dear just about nullifies the benefit of the capital they acquire from foreign aid." He could be answered publicly, and in fact was by Professor Theodore Morgan but to no avail: "Such deterioration has been true only if you take the 'right' period. It has for example been true in the main since the peak of the Korean boom in primary products in 1951. But it is not true if you take as your starting point 1938 and it is not true if you look at a still longer period following the considerable data back into the nineteenth century. A better generalization for this more adequate time perspective is that there have been wide swings in the terms of trade and sharply diverse experience for individual commodities and countries." [33]

Congressman Curtis, coming away from the Joint Economic Committee hearings, insisted quite correctly that "there are serious flaws" in the Prebisch thesis that "render it questionable as a basis for formulating U.S. economic foreign policy," and urged the Latin Americans to strive to maximize their total export earnings rather than resting their aspirations on the flawed "victimization" thesis, only to find that the Latin Americans had devised still another "victimization" thesis to use in avoiding the hard decisions required for social and economic progress, namely, that their share of world trade seems to decline automatically.[34]

---

[32] Speech by Ambassador Lincoln Gordon, January 29, 1963. The citation from Urquidi's work is from *Viabilidad Económica de América Latina*.

[33] *Washington Post*, August 23, 1965.

[34] See *Congressional Record*, April 6, 1966, p. 7425-6.

Orchestration of the new plaint went forward promptly with the launching of the Alliance for Progress. It was "found" that "Latin America's share of world exports had declined from 11.1% in 1950 to 6.7% in 1960." It was "found" that while "world exports of manufactured goods were increasing 103% from 1928 to 1955-57, Latin America's exports of basic commodities excluding petroleum had risen only 14%." It was "found" in 1965 that "while the developed countries have increased exports over the past decade by 130%, the less-developed countries have not even attained a 50% rise. The area with the lowest growth was Latin America, with a gain of only 35%."

Here surely was a God-given "justification" for politicians explaining the misery to which Latin America saw itself consigned while other nations were developing actively and achieving social progress. What in the world could the Chilean Ambassador in Washington have been thinking of when he said that *there is no excuse* for the intolerable incapacity Latin America has so far demonstrated for liberating the vast multitude of its people from their misery and suffering, from their ignorance and their sickness, from their oppression and frustration?" [35] Had he forgotten the "victimization" by the terms of trade? And now this new "victimization" by export stagnation? Could any Latin American politician ably abetted by his so-called economists *lack an excuse* with this "victimization" so "clearly demonstrated"?

It was almost useless for Professor W. Arthur Lewis to tell an international conference on inflation and development in Rio de Janeiro in 1963 that world trade is growing at a faster pace than ever and that if under-developed nations, Latin American ones in particular, do not know how to profit or cannot profit from this situation, the fault is with supply and not demand; and that nothing has been so prejudicial to export growth as over-valued rates of exchange. [36] It was almost useless for Gottfried Habeler to suggest how negative had been the effects of their export policy on exports and to advise that "one of the reasons for the low rate of growth in the trade of the less developed countries is to be found in the

---

[35] UP wire, August 19, 1965.

[36] Committee for Economic Development, *How Low Income Countries Can Advance Their Own Growth* (New York, 1966) pp. 36-37. Other quotations in this paragraph are from the same source.

highly protectionist policy they follow and which goes far beyond what would be justifiable on the basis of infant-industries argument, terms of trade, or any other national reason. In this way, productive resources related to exports have been diverted to protected industries which in turn has been harmful to exports." And it was almost useless for Professor Nicholas Kaldor to state that "there can be no doubt that the majority of underdeveloped countries would benefit considerably, both in terms of efficiency and real income, as well as in flexibility, if they concentrate their efforts on raising their exports instead of finding substitutes for their imports."

It was almost useless, for to have abandoned the protest against terms of trade "victimization" and export stagnation "victimization" would have meant facing up to the hard decisions that needed to be made. Obviously whatever might be occurring in export markets need not have deterred an effort to correct the many internal policies which stood in the way of social progress. And obviously the mere recitation of the statistical data failed to explain *why* this deterioration in relative export position was occurring, why export stagnation relatively had set in. Any serious examination of the causes would have exploded the myth of "victimization." Could that be risked, as long as there was an alternative, namely, mendicancy, assignment of all responsibility for all ills to the United States, and blackmail?

Some illustrations may be in order. Coffee had long supplied one-fifth to one-quarter of the area's external purchasing power created by exports, and much more in many countries. In 1947-49 it had achieved a per-capita consumption in the United States of 18.2 pounds, the trend was upward, and this was clearly one commodity in which stagnation did not seem in prospect. But within a short period, Latin America was able to reverse the upward trend and set the industry on a permanently downward course. Despite the extreme profitability of coffee production in Latin America, the Latins made decisions on pricing which reversed the trend of consumption. By 1957-59 they could boast they had been able to reduce consumption per-capita in the United States to 15.7 pounds. But this did not suffice. When in 1963-64-65 the United States as consequence of the exuberant ignorance of the Alliance phrasemakers allowed the Latin Americans to write their own prices in London through cartel manipulation of the market, they set prices so high that they were able to achieve immediately a reduction in consumption to 14.7 pounds, with the trend splendidly downward. A staff report of the Federal Trade Commission reported that the Latin Americans had been able to cut consumption from the 1946 peak by some 25%.[37] Was it a "law" of export stagnation "victimizing" the coffee producing countries or was it merely irresponsibility in policy making which thus doomed the developmental aspirations of the area? Was it an accident that as part of this price-fixing policy the distribution of income tended to become even more inequitable, the hoard of funds shipped abroad for safe-keeping was enabled to increase, and real wages for workers in the coffee-growing areas actually declined? Nor does the story end there.

Not only were the Latin Americans able to achieve a decline in per-capita consumption in their major market, to slow consumption elsewhere, and to confront themselves domestically with the fruits of over-production, but they were able simultaneously, by making production of coffee so attractive at the prices, to induce expanded cultivation in Africa so as to enable them to surrender a great portion of the market to Africa. Indeed, from 1955-56 to 1959-60 (average) to 1965-66, they were able to induce a doubling of the export capacity of Africa. Some achievement! Some policy-makers!

Another example may be cited. Chile has had bitter experience with the "substitution" process in its export list. Its once potent monopoly of nitrates broke down in the face of the competition of synthetics, and for a generation the core complaint to the United States was that the U.S. must in some way arrest the rise of the competitive synthetics. In fact, during World War II and there-after, the primary demand in Chilean-American relations was the insistance that in some way the United States prevent technological developments from disturbing Chilean trade.

But it was too much to expect Chile to learn anything from its experience. Well into the fifth year of the Alliance, the Chileans perceived an opportunity to make a quick killing in the copper market and at one stroke raised the price of copper by 47%. Every independent authority in the field cautioned Chile that there is an

---

[37] Staff Report, April 26, 1966, "Cents-off promotions in the coffee industry."

area of potential substitution of materials for copper which could if invoked hurt copper badly, and that experience has shown that once substitution occurs it tends to become permanent, and that a price boost of this magnitude in itself and as a token of recurring policy attitudes was virtually a challenge to search out substitutes for copper. But Chile rejected these pleas. Again the privilege of making its own mistakes must be stressed. But to this privilege attaches responsibility. And it is precisely this responsibility that Chile believes it can shed in the curious ambivalence of its policy approach. There was in fact a precedent. In the early 1950s Chile had similarly kicked over the traces with an attempt to play the copper market. When it found it had erred (as always against the best advice) and saw its copper piling up in unsalable amounts, it turned to the United States and *demanded* that the United States acquire for stockpile strategically-*unneeded* supplies in order to bail out the Chilean Government for its mistake.[38]

It must be reiterated, lest we be accused of thinking in terms of surrender of policy-making authority unbecoming the relationship between independent nations, that Chile has the full privilege of making any decision it wishes on copper, just as Brazil had in the series of unwise decisions on coffee that doomed its export potential. What *is* at issue here is the privilege of asking the United States taxpayer under cover of the Alliance for Progress to pay for the mistakes. *This* privilege Chile and Brazil do not have. If the political process in independent countries is to have any validity at all, it calls for a judgment by the voters of the particular Latin country of the wisdom of a particular regime's action, rather than a bailout by the United States to reward the error-makers and to keep them in office despite the damage they have done to their own people.

---

[38] The industrial editor of *The Financial Times* (London) wrote on April 26, 1966: "In an increasing number of markets which had previously been regarded as tied to copper, there is evidence that consumers are now prepared to undertake the research to overcome technical problems such as jointing and welding and to install the new plant. The unreliability of copper both in price and in adequacy of supply inevitably encourages the manufacturers to look for alternative materials. . . . Past experience suggests that the technical problems involved in switching out of copper are not nearly as formidable as they appear. In the case of copper the need for a new marketing orientation is even more vital to overcome the reputation for unreliability which the material has now acquired."

The list of illustrations that might be cited in the field of "relative export stagnation" is endless.[39]   A different category of decision might perhaps be added at this point.   A generation of Brazilians have suffered a lower standard of living than they need have suffered because their governments chose as a major political decision to retard the development of their fabulous iron-ore reserves and to force the development of major resources elsewhere in the world.   The privilege of making this decision, suicidal as it was, cannot be challenged except by the political process in Brazil itself.   But even under the loosest determination of the meaning of the Alliance for Progress, the United States cannot be expected to compensate for such errors.   There simply is not enough money in the world that can be mobilized for such a purpose.

Similarly, the Chileans in the late 1950s and early 1960s had delayed for at least five years an expansion of their copper industry which would have had enduring impact on their external earnings position.   Instead, they chose mendicancy.   It is true that the Chileans have always had an extraordinary sense of smell regarding Washington money, ever since Fomento was first created. But for the United States, there is an important element of policy here. To the extent that the response to mendicancy under the label "Alliance for Progress" made it possible for Chile to delay decisions that might have freed it from mendicancy and also accelerated its development, the Alliance apparatus must be judged self-defeating.

In any event, it is clear that the second aspect of the "victimization" theory on which Latin American policy makers have relied to enable them to delay the vital internal policy adjustments simply has no basis in fact.

---

[39] It might be noted that even with petroleum being found in places where hope had previously been abandoned in exploration, the same disregard for long-range outlook was to be found among the Latin Americans and their associates in the permanently under-developed areas.   For instance, in April 1966, the National Coal Board (U.K.) in a summary of Europe's energy requirements prepared in association with European analysts argued that a sound and vigorous coal industry during the next twenty or thirty years would be an indispensable precondition of economic well-being partly because "the efforts by the Organization of Petroleum Exporting Countries to obtain higher prices, *if necessary by pro-rationing output,* must cast doubts on all assurances about the future of oil supplies."

Yet, partly from this thesis of self-pity, there evolved in the fourth year and expanded in the fifth year of the Alliance still another field of mythology similarly without economic basis and similarly calculated to defeat the purposes of the Alliance for Progress. This dealt with the problem of debt service

Concern for the Latin Americans' handling of their borrowing problems is not new in the executive branch of the United States government. More than fifty years ago, Woodrow Wilson was deeply disturbed by the belief that "they (the Latin Americans) have had harder bargains driven with them in the matter of loans than any other peoples in the world. Interest has been exacted of them that was not exacted of anybody else because the risk was said to be greater, and then securities were taken that destroyed that risk." [40]

It is of course true that nowhere is the Latin American capacity for corruption in public life, disregard for the public interest in the use of public funds, and lack of integrity in meeting obligations, so marked as in the history of its external debt. It is true also that historically intermediaries were prepared to milk these qualities to the detriment alike of creditor and debtor. Indeed in November 1966, a professional liberal, the much respected ex-President José Figueres of Costa Rica, was still lamenting that "la historia de América Latina en sus relaciones con el capital mundial de inversión es triste," and was protesting that there had been cases where three-fourths of the face value of loans remained abroad.[41] He might even have cited the case where the eagerness of speculators to accept Latin American bonds was such that a British banking house once floated successfully an issue for a country in Latin America that did not even exist!

But the misfortune is that while upheavals in world money markets completely altered the conditions affecting the supply of such funds, conditions in Latin America with respect to corruption, misuse of public funds, and lack of integrity toward obligations hardly changed over a century and a half.[42]

---

[40] Ray Stannard Baker, *Woodrow Wilson: Life and Letters* (New York 1931), Volume IV, p. 284.

[41] Diario las Americas, November 2, 1966.

[42] It should be noted that the term Latin America is being applied for the bulk of the area. Argentina has shown unusual respect for obligations in such times as the great depression. And in recent years Mexico has mobilized both integrity and more effective use of borrowed funds.

Oddly enough, even back to Wilson's time, the United States sought an answer to the problem by its own action, rather than comprehending that the solution lies with the Latin Americans themselves. In the summer of 1913, William Jennings Bryan brooding over Latin American foreign debts then totaling over 2.25 billion dollars, wrote Woodrow Wilson:

> "They (the Latin Americans) are now compelled to pay a high rate of interest and to sell their bonds at a discount. . . . If the United States offers to loan them its credit to the extent that such a loan is safe, the bonds could be made to draw four and a half percent, which would be an immediate saving to them in the way of interest and the difference of a percent and a half between their bonds and ours could go into a sinking fund which in a reasonable time at compound interest could pay off the debt and leave them free. We could in this way relieve them of the debts which embarrass them and enable them to construct such railroads as are imperatively necessary for the development of their countries. The second advantage would be that the plan would give our country such an increased influence . . . that we could prevent revolutions, promote education, and advance stable and just government. . . . We would in the end profit, negatively, by not having to insure expense in guarding our own and other foreign interests there, and positively, by the increase in trade that would come from development and from the friendship which would follow the conferring of the benefits named." [43]

Bryan could not have foreseen the road down which he planned to take the United States. The United States first indirectly made its credit available by extending loans with reasonable prospect of repayment through the Export-Import Bank, once the private money market had been virtually closed due to failure to meet obligations on the part of Latin America. Then, after a decade of criticism that dollar bonds had been used needlessly to defray local-currency expenditures when they should have been limited to external requirements, the U.S. began to edge into local-currency financing. Then it began the long orgy with "soft-loans" which were nothing but concealed grants, and then to herald the failure of the Alliance in its fifth year, there began the campaign virtually to put Latin America on a dole openly.

"Prevailing (sic) conditions of international trade deny our countries the possibility of overcoming the limiting characteristics of underdevelopment," the President (of Chilean origin) of the

---

[43] Baker, *op. cit.,* p. 433.

Inter-American Development Bank shamed himself by saying at the plenary session of the Conference of Foreign Ministers in Rio. "The weakness of our export position has been reflected in growing international indebtedness." He went on: "Latin America's long-term foreign public debt payable in foreign exchange has climbed from $4.3 billion at the end of 1956 to $11 billion at the end of 1964. Service on this debt, in principal and interest, increased over the same period from $425 million to $1.6 billion."-[44] He had another set of figures too: "Between 1956 and 1964 the region's external long-term public debt payable in hard currencies increased 147% from $4.3 billion to $10.6 billion. During the same period, payments for principal and interest virtually tripled from $455 million to $1.36 billion dollars. The foreign-debt servicing burden rose from 5.5% on balance of payments receipts on current account in 1956 to 15.4% in 1964. In the latter year this level stood at more than 20% for four Latin American countries."[45] But the conclusion was always the same: More concealed-donations from the United States.

The chorus was quickly mobilized: The Assistant Secretary for Economic and Social Affairs at the Pan American Union insisted that "something be done about the onerous Latin American foreign debt service." And he added his bit: "The blame for this is as much the creditor countries' as that of Latin American borrowers. If the latter occasionally (sic) might have been imprudent in contracting some of these debts, the former at times urged borrowers to accept loans they should not have contracted and imposed rather harsh terms and other conditions." [46]

The Inter-American Committee on the Alliance for Progress (CIAP) could not be expected to stay out of the act: "In part, the problem results from the insufficiency of control over the contracting of foreign debts. But of equal importance have been the inclination of certain lending countries to grant credits basically for the purpose of promoting their exports and their inability to

---

[44] Felipe Herrera, Speech at the Plenary Session of the Second Special Inter-American Conference of Foreign Ministers at Rio de Janeiro, November 23, 1965.
[45] Felipe Herrera, Remarks at the Roundtable Conference on Capital Movements of the International Economic Association, Washington, July 21, 1965.
[46] *Journal of Commerce*, April 16, 1966.

adapt themselves to loan policies that would have assured loan terms more appropriate to the development needs and the capacity to pay of the Latin American debtor countries." [47]   In other words, the "creditors" (read donors) should have known that concealed donations were the order of the day.

And its findings were as expected: "Move toward forms of financing where the terms of repayment conform to the character of the project being undertaken and the borrowing country's ability to service the debt."   In other words, concealed or open donations.

Now it was time for the Agency for International Development to get into the act.   In a document titled "A Study on Loan Terms, Debt Burden and Development," the Agency reported that the average annual rate in increase of public debt from 1955 to 1962 had been 12%, a rate obviously out of line with external earnings trends, ratios of changes in gross national product, etc.[48]   And it moved swiftly to the thesis that real loans must be replaced by donations in some form, whether open or concealed, to fool the U.S. Congress: (1) "The ability of these countries to alter the structure of their economies so as to increase exports and reduce the need for outside capital is severely limited in the short run." (2) "The fundamental advantage of soft loans (concealed donations) is that they make possible an orderly and responsible (sic) flow of needed resources without choking the flow in the early stages through too rapid an increase in the debt service burden." (3) "For most of these countries either existing modest targets of growth rates for development must be largely given up or they will need more than one or two annual shots in the arm in the form of a net flow of real resources beyond their immediate ability to pay for such resources."

"One measure widely looked at by potential lenders is this debt service ratio—the ration of debt service payments due in a particular year to actual or prospective export earnings. . . . The global estimate for less-developed countries indicates that debt-service payments rose from 3.7% of export earnings in 1959 to 9.1% in 1963. Considerable softening of terms by all lenders would be needed to keep the overall debt service ratio from exceeding 10%."

---

[47] See *Hearings before the Senate Foreign Relations Committee,* "Foreign Assistance 1965," p. 285.

[48] Staff Study released to the press April 1965 for propaganda purposes.

The Agency conceded that the so-called development loans contain a subsidy element in the form of low interest rates and maturities: "If we discount the future flow of payments at 4%, roughly the current Treasury borrowing rate, the value of the subsidy element amounts to about one-third of the total face value of the loan." And then it fumbled itself into contradiction with its central thesis before congressional committees. The Administrator of AID had pledged to the Congress emphatically that "we are not in the business of making aid available to bail out creditors of a given country." [49] This in testimony on the protest by the International Economic Policy Association that "A reading of the studies of the Inter-American Committee on the Alliance for Progress makes it clear that servicing of past debts is one of the primary functions of our aid under the Alliance. To use aid money to repay past debts of these countries is not contributing to economic development but financing past and to some extent current consumption beyond their means." [50]

Nevertheless, the Agency for International Development now went on record to favor soft loans (concealed donations) because "soft loans facilitate the flow of resources by others, by maintaining the creditworthiness (sic) of developing countries in the eyes of others." And turning specifically to the case of Brazil, it supported concealed donations because they enable Brazil to service credits previously arranged and any new credits that might be arranged. In other words, that U.S. donations should be used to bail out existing creditors and service new obligations to European banks and other creditors.

To underscore the position as one that had been determined at the highest level of this government, the Secretary of State now appeared before congressional committees to warn that "the level of external public debt of these nations has been steadily increasing and in some cases alarmingly so." [51] And accordingly that the *United States* must do something about it.

---

[49] *Hearings before the Senate Foreign Relations Committee,* "Foreign Assistance 1965," p. 598.

[50] *Hearings before the House Foreign Affairs Committee* on "Foreign Assistance Act of 1965," H.R. 7750, p. 1222.

[51] *Hearings before the Senate Foreign Relations Committee,* "Foreign Assistance 1965," p. 9.

A discussion of the new mythology, the third leg in the structure being built to avoid facing up to internal problems and to make mendicancy a permanent doctrine in inter-American relations, can take a variety of lines: First, there is the point that none of the discussions of the great rise in foreign public debt probe seriously into the causes of the rise and into the causes of the relative ineffectiveness of the flow of this great mass of money. Until the lessons of the failure of this great flow to achieve results consistent with the aims of the Alliance are learned, it would be foolish to expect any better results from a new flow. Second, all of this great accumulation of debt went forward originally without any guarantee by the United States that it would provide service in the event Latin American governments claimed incapacity to pay. To expect the United States as part of the Alliance for Progress program to provide retroactive insurance for careless creditors is thus utter nonsense. And it is particularly dangerous because the whole effort goes forward with an understanding shared alike by the bureaucrats and by those concerned with the best interests of the United States that there is a definite limit on the amount of money that can be wrested from the Congress for the purpose of the Alliance for Progress. In other words, to divert funds to retroactive insurance for European creditors means that much less for effective social progress activity. So that the well-being of Latin America is directly involved.

It must be remembered that financial indigestion is not a new phase of Latin American life. Over generations, when borrowing was a function performed in the private money markets, Latin American countries had over-extended themselves frequently and sometimes as during the Great Depression the condition applied to virtually all countries. There was then no question of retroactive insurance to be provided by the taxpayers of the creditor country whether it be the United States, Britain or France. It is true that creditors sometimes challenged the readiness to declare a moratorium on external obligations and insisted that if a country really had integrity and self-respect it could so interpret minimum essential import requirements that funds would still be available to meet external bond obligations. Nevertheless, the moratorium was a common experience, and it was the familiar sequence for demands to be made thereafter for equal treatment for all creditors, and for governments of the creditor countries to be saddled with diplomatic negotiations assuring equal treatment.

But now, thanks to the Alliance for Progress and the kitty that had been provided by the U.S. Congress, when the Latin Americans found themselves "over-burdened" with debt and in keeping with the looseness of the times seized on such inflated definition of minimum essential import requirements as to make it appear that service is impossible, the world experienced the thesis that moratorium is a bad word.

Moratorium for Brazil? The *New York Times* was shaken and almost shocked out of its mind. Why, its editors declared, "a moratorium would be a confession of financial bankruptcy." [52] It never occurred to them that the declaration by Brazil that it was unable and unwilling to meet its obligations, which had preceded the need for a painful choice by creditors of how to proceed, was the real point at which the bankruptcy had been confessed. And this had already occurred. The *New York Times* went on: "The fear that Washington will refuse to come to the rescue" with vast donations to service the debt "has provoked rumors that the Brazilian Government is contemplating a moratorium." Obviously the editors had read some AID study which insisted that unless U.S. donations were forthcoming to service obligations previously incured, the "creditworthiness" of Brazil would be subject to challenge. What greater burlesque than to speak in the same breath of "creditworthiness" and then to assert that the country is unable and unwilling to meet its obligations? What "creditworthiness"?

It must be clear that for creditors, who had over-extended themselves by their own greed and who had no claim whatsoever on the U.S. taxpayer, to be given a great proportion of funds intended for social progress in the Americas would fatally affect the Alliance. But so lacking in any seriousness of objective was the bureaucratic colony that administered the program that in the five years of the Alliance well over one-fourth of disbursements was absorbed in precisely such an operation.

The head of the Bankers Trust Company asserted that "European policy as regards exports to Latin America is based upon the assumption that the United States Government will continue to hold an umbrella over the solvency of that area of the world. It is

[52] August 31, 1964.

inconsistent to provide an umbrella for Europeans and to deprive Americans of protection equal to that given Europeans." [53]

In so saying, of course, he missed the point completely. There was no justification whatever, to provide *anybody*, European *or* American, with retroactive cost-free insurance. There was no justification to reward carelessness in appraising creditworthiness. And there was no long-range benefit accruing to Latin America from this policy which so unfairly penalized the U.S. taxpayer.

It may immediately be asked: Why should the Latin Americans care about which section in the United States community profited from the Alliance? The answer is simple. If there is one issue on which there is general agreement, it is that the funds available for the Alliance and likely to be available in the foreseeable future are limited. Therefore, any misuse of Alliance money, any diversion from the economic and social purposes for which it is appropriated, works against the best interest of Latin America. A moratorium involving ultimately a scaledown of principal consistent with the conditions alleged to exist in the debtor country could then have been followed by a fruitful use of the same amount of donations to the benefit of Latin America. Instead, under the misconception that they were in effect gypping the U.S. taxpayer, rather than hurting themselvs, the Latins in effect underwrote their affluent creditors to their own lasting disadvantage.

Just as there is agreement on the limitation on funds available from the United States, there is also agreement that Latin America is a capital-deficient area, which means that any diversion of capital to low priority or political purposes involves a net loss and perhaps an irreparable loss in meeting requirements for high priority purposes. Yet, the Latin Americans during the five years perceived the opportunity to realize their long-stand political objective of "chasing out the gringo" and so fell neatly into the hands of foreign investors who were ready to shed certain unporfitable investments. Knowing well that each dollar used merely to substitute for an existing investment was a dollar taken from new productive uses, the Latin Americans proceeded to dissipate a large proportion of the Alliance financing for takeovers of foreign-owned investments. The Alliance became a bailout apparatus for certain shrewd foreign investors. But it must be stressed that this

---

[53] *Journal of Commerce,* April 18, 1966.

could not have happened if the Latin Americans had not been prisoners of their ancient political slogans. And of course it could not have happened if the bureaucracy of the Alliance had not had such contempt for the professed objectives of the Alliance.

A matter of attitudes. Five years of preaching self-help and simultaneously encouraging mendicancy as public policy obviously could not have been expected to succeed, on the part of the United States. And obviously until there was a fundamental change in Latin American attitudes accepting the primacy of the objectives enunciated under the Alliance for Progress banner, no effort of the United States could succeed.

A British observer for *Encounter* immediately sensed this on his first journey into Latin America: "What the failure of the Alliance proved is that "to develop" is a reflexive verb. No rich country can 'develop' a poor one. Only the will of the people in the poor country can do that, even though they may need help from the rich in the process. What is lacking in much of Latin America is the effective will to develop—to change the old system and to break up the many existing profitable arrangements in order to speed up economic growth and to spread the wealth more widely."

A distinguished U.S. economist, self-labeled a "one-month" expert on Latin America," spotted the trouble with equal ease. He found that the Alliance might be "mistaking the symptoms for the disease." He suggested: "The Latin American problem has to be approached in the direction of modifying popular conceptions of what is economically and politically just . . . the proper diagnosis for Latin America is not capital malnutrition and income maldistribution. Rather, it is a combination of endemic economic miscomprehensions, a widespread acceptance of certain notions of social justice that do not square with the economic realities, and a high degree of inertia. If one accepts this diagnosis, it is obvious that high on the list of remedies must be one that will stimulate a reformation of ideas and of spirit." [54]

But he qualified as well as a prophet when he suggested that "the remedial task is so staggering that there is a strong temptation

---

[54] J. L. Robertson, member, Board of Governors of the Federal Reserve System, "Remarks before the National and State Bank Divisions of the American Bankers Association, December 10, 1962.

to throw up one's hands and look for diagnoses that call for simpler remedies, remedies for example that can be provided from an open pocketbook."

After five years, even the new director of the Agency for International Development claimed that he now understood. "You could drown people in dollars but that would not do the job. . . . Money is the least important element of foreign aid. Aid is a matter of attitudes." [55]

But after five years there was an immense and growing bureaucracy that had to maintain itself. It had a vested interest in only one matter—the maximum rapidity in expenditure of as much money as possible. Any change in the U.S. outlook on the Alliance looking to results rather than to simple appropriation and disbursement had to be viewed suspiciously. And after five years there was a political stake in the Alliance: errors must not be admitted. Thus, we find Senator Robert Kennedy's speech-writers, well after the close of the five years, recounting the tale of the proportion of the U.S. gross national product that was being expended in such aid programs as compared with the figure of a decade previous, and insisting that this showed that "we should *increase* the resources" made available. [56]

At take-off, the noted Raúl Prebisch had predicted that "the Latin Americans can be on their own and moving ahead fast within a period of approximately ten years." [57] But after five years, there was no sign that the Latin Americans were willing even to recognize the requirements of public policy on their part, and they were increasingly turning to a policy of permanent mendicancy coupled with blackmail to avoid the hard domestic decisions.

Where had the United States erred?

---

[55] William S. Gaud, *Christian Science Monitor*, July 7, 1966.

[56] Robert F. Kennedy, "Latin America and the Demands of Justice." *Diplomat*, November 1966, p. 44.

[57] *U.S. News and World Report*, August 14, 1961.

Chapter III

The Concept

The Alliance for Progress was conceived in ignorance. The American Ambassador's description of how Kennedy's advisers became "experts" overnight: "I'm going to be appointed to a high Latin American post. Can you suggest some good books I ought to read?"[1] The night club wit visualizing President Kennedy's thinking: "Caroline is a nice kid alright but this is the last time I let her plan an invasion." The *Sunday Times* (London) description of the eager-beaver American Ambassador, another overnight expert, entertaining the Chileans with his Spanish: "It's a great privilege for you that I'm here today."[2] The assignment of policy direction to a man of whom it was written that "before May 1961 Latin America for him was scarcely more than a geographical expression." The gaggle of pundits, fresh from their instant-knowledge briefings in all the discredited theories, protesting as the press put it that "it's not that we don't have the solution . . . it's just that none of the problems seem to fit the solutions." In such a

---

[1] De Lesseps S. Morrison, *Latin American Mission* (New York 1965), pp. 28-29. "I had been told that so improvised, so Alice-in-Wonderland were those first New Frontier days that Goodwin was quite taken back to find himself a Latin American expert helping make policy in a part of the world he had never visited. Shortly after coming to the White House he had accosted a newspaperman. 'I'm going to be appointed to a high Latin American post,' he told him. 'Can you suggest some good books I ought to read?' "

[2] *The Sunday Times Magazine*, May 1, 1966, p. 24. "After nearly a year in Chile, Ambassador Dungan still spoke little Spanish and with an awful accent. 'It's a great privilege for you that I'm here today,' he told a group of astonished schoolchildren, and his only certain phrase is 'very interesting' which he will use even in answer to pleas from beggars. When an aggrieved old man thrust a petition at him once, Dungan smiled, said 'very interesting' and then snapped out in English 'what did that guy want?' "

climate, success in public policy would have taken a miracle. The miracle was not forthcoming.

The central expression of the ignorance on which the Alliance was based rests in the concept of "conscience money." José Figueres, former president of Costa Rica, whose ideas greatly influenced the new experts, laid the groundwork for this concept: "To compensate for the long period of exploitation, capital must be injected from the countries that have accumulated most of the wealth into the countries that have accumulated practically nothing but needs." [3] President Kennedy eagerly accepted this concept of U.S. exploitation of Latin America. He told a newsman: "The United States now has the possibility of doing as much good in Latin America as it had done wrong in the past." [4]

It was understandable that Mrs. Eleanor Roosevelt, so well-intentioned and so free of understanding of economics, should write: "For a long time it has seemed to me that our real trouble in Latin America has been that we have never taken enough time to sit down and seriously consider the economic problems of the people. If a country could grow coffee easily, we (sic) never protested if it became a one-crop country." [5] But for a great nation to build policy destined to last generations on such utter ignorance was shocking. To accept as a consequence of U.S. action or inaction the Latin Americans' inability to govern themselves and their unwillingness to alter their attitudes toward social and economic problems was inexcusable. This was a prime example of what Sir Denis Brogan has called "the first and greatest American illusion", namely, that "where there is trouble in the world it was caused by something which the United States did or did not do." Less elegantly Harry Golden had put the point even better: "America ain't what's wrong with the world." And the United States certainly was not what was wrong with Latin America.

Indeed, Roberto Campos, who was among the first to comment on the use of the term "conscience money," spoke of its use in Latin America only as an "extreme manifestation," in which *"hostile-minded* groups in the receiving countries see in aid pro-

---

[3] *The New Leader,* October 10, 1960.

[4] Jean Daniel, *The New Republic,* December 14, 1963.

[5] *New York Post,* December 14, 1960.

grams a form of conscience money." (Italics added). And he urged the avoidance of even a very limited application of the thesis: "Aid must not be conscience money paid by the industrial countries to eschew the anguishing decision to open their markets for exports of the poor countries." [6]

The damage done by accepting the charge that the United States had "exploited" Latin America and now must make amends by unlimited donations was irreparable. For, it deprived the United States of the capacity to demand effectively the self-help measures without which the Alliance must inevitably fail. It made the United States a prisoner of the Alliance rather than a participant. It was odd that a President who had voiced such strong suspicions of mythology which "distracts us everywhere—in government as in business, in politics as in economics, in foreign affairs as in domestic government" should have fallen victim to the hoariest myth of inter-American relations—the notion that the United States had exploited Latin America. But perhaps the inexperience of the advisers may explain it.

As if this were not enough, there was in addition the eager acceptance of Latin America's perennial lamentation—of neglect by the United States. "Those of us who had the privilege of advising President Kennedy on policy toward Latin America in the early development of the Alliance," wrote a trusted adviser, "were moved by a deep conviction that the United States had made a serious error during the previous fifteen years—an error shared by both our major political parties. That error was an undue concentration on other regions of the world while Latin America was being taken too much for granted. The Alliance remedied that error." [7] We had, the Assistant Secretary charged, "taken for granted the sympathy and cooperation of our Latin American neighbors." [8]

This too was part of the mythology of inter-American relations.

---

[6] Speech November 13, 1963. This Brazilian economist delivered a number of papers on the Alliance which should be in any important collection dealing with the Alliance for Progress.

[7] Lincoln Gordon, *Congressional Record*, June 16, 1966, pp. 12753-12754.

[8] Address by Lincoln Gordon given before The Pan American Society of New England, November 10, 1966.

It had been answered effectively at inter-American conferences at which the United States pointed to the urgency of the task of rebuilding war-torn Europe and the immediate demands of the effort toward a just and stable peace. The Latin Americans had even been paid the tribute of assuming that with their pockets bulging with their profits on World War II they too had an interest in the recovery of Europe and a responsibility in the task of achieving a just and stable peace.

The error in accepting the charge of neglect could be seen five years later (1966) in the protest of the Colombian Foreign Minister that "the United States still does not devote enough attention to our problems and fails to grasp our needs." [9] By that time Presidential Adviser Rostow and Assistant Secretary Gordon were arguing that the Latin Americans were getting all they could handle for the moment, and that increased aid must depend on development of a capacity and willingness to use it effectively. But there could be no acceptance of this view by the Latins, having tasted blood in the acceptance of the joint myths of exploitation and neglect. Of course it could be shown that Colombia had profited disproportionately from the Alliance during its period as a showcase and had sat on its hands refusing to take the action needed until the collapse. But it was more profitable to pursue the myth of neglect which Kennedy had been persuaded to accept, to intensify the charge of "exploitation," and above all to warn of the danger to the *United States:* "Your leaders must realize the enormous importance of Latin America as a peaceful and democratic neighbor, especially after the developments in Cuba and the Dominican Republic."

Now, the requirements of public policy were relatively simple: It was imperative that the Latin Americans understand or be made to understand that the threat symbolized by Cuba or the Dominican Republic and the warnings of ultimate violent revolutions were in the first instance a threat and a warning to *them,* not to the United States. It was imperative that the Latin Americans be made to understand that their growing inability to govern and their unwillingness to accept modern conceptions of social justice threatened *them* in the first instance, and not the United States. It was imperative that they be made to understand that with proper

---

[9] June 12, 1966.

economic policies they could long since have enjoyed more productive economies capable of supporting their people at much higher levels of income, and that the absence of such policies was a failing of their own, rather than something that could be blamed on or corrected by the United States.

If, as Senator Robert Kennedy argued, "the American people are ready to recognize that aid is a moral obligation;" if, as the President had argued, "if a free society cannot help the many who are poor it cannot save the few who are rich;" it was equally clear that U.S. aid could not be effective or decisive for those who refused to help themselves. And it was, in terms of policy decisions, even more significant that there were areas begging for such an effort *within* the United States where surely the claims on the U.S. Treasury were more easily justified if for no reason other than that the effort was likely to be more effective.

Some twenty-five years previously, a prominent Mexican banker-economist, Eduardo Villaseñor, had argued that the choice rested with the United States whether it wanted to be linked with a poor Latin America or with a rich Latin America, in the course of a plea for a larger flow of U.S. capital. "Get rid of your treasure—lend it, give it, throw it away—if you do not want to perish in the midst of plenty." [10] But even though Latin American problems were then increasingly engaging the sympathies of the United States there was an understandable reluctance to be an international fatboy as long as the Latin Americans assured failure to achieve goals by their lag in modifying domestic policies that tended to perpetuate and deepen the weaknesses of their economies.

Now, the diplomats who commuted from the Waldorf Astoria to the Mayflower in Washington, to deplore the miserable living conditions in their countries, and the new class of bureaucrats, the most highly paid the world had ever known and following close on their heels in the first fruits of personal affluence, were still not aware of alternatives of policy on the decision to "get rid of your treasure."

When Nelson Rockefeller blasted the Alliance for Progress as "representing neither an Alliance nor Progress," the Senate Ma-

---

[10] "Inter-American Trade and Financial Problems" (Reprinted for private circulation from *Inter-American Solidarity* (Chicago, 1941) p. 94.

jority Leader smarting under the criticism lashed out at him to remind Rockefeller that "in your own backyard, so to speak, in New York City you have a microcosm of the immense problems of poverty, human neglect, and inequity which are at the root of the ills of Latin America." Mansfield obviously was correct. The United States had taken the political decision to solve in Latin America in an incredibly short time at great cost to itself, problems that it could not solve at home or found too costly to solve at home. It had based this political decision on the economic reasoning that it requires only an identification of the stereotypes of Latin American society to produce the solutions.

Thus, the new "experts" read up on the stereotype of the Roman Catholic Church, the reactionary fat torpid unconcerned guardian of the status quo, quickly accepted the "achievements" of the Mexican Revolution (unaware that there had been increased inequality and increased inequity in distribution and an infliction of social injustice) as stemming as one of their sources claimed from "the severing of the relations with the church and the firing of the priests out of the schools," and felt they had found one target. Yet, New York's dominant religious group was perhaps the most socially conscious body of its size in the world, and its Catholic community too was socially conscious and alert and concerned with community problems and still, as Senator Mansfield noted, no solution could be found for the microcosm of the problems that the Alliance was expected to solve in a decade in Latin America.

Again, the "experts" discovered that the Latin American economic organization was faulty and cited the consequence that personal incomes were below $400 per capita and big blocs were left below $100 per capita. But New York with its median family income of $6,100 and an effective organization into a community of economic affluence and civilized taste was found to have a higher ratio of persons over 15 incapable of writing a simple message in English or some other language than all but fifteen of our states, it failed to reach the national average for adults who have completed high school, and the ratio of functional illiteracy was high. In New York, one person in twenty was on relief, mere statistics as some critics protested in the compilations of the living dead, and 220,000 children were preparing in the institutionalized slums to survive as a scandal to the affluent society. And instead of making progress, the city had grown poorer, until half of its families were classified as "deprived," and one-quarter as "poor." In New York City, the Board of Education revealed in 1966, "a majority of the city's pupils read more poorly than their counterparts throughout the country, and the gap is widening; one out of every five pupils in the city's elementary and junior high schools in the spring of 1966 was behind two years or more in reading." In New York City, the *New York Times* caculated, 585,696 people make up the "welfare family."

The new experts luxuriated in their "discovery" of the carapace over the rich in Latin America which made them incurious, unconcerned, content to avoid taxes and avoid social responsibility. But in New York where people "think" and are concerned and are socially responsible, where the rich largely do not evade taxes nor shift them to those least able to bear them, and where there are no latifundia and no land reform problems, nor terms of trade headaches, New York seemed to do no better with its microcosm of Latin American problems, all of which the Alliance was to master in the critical decade.

While President Johnson was pledging that the U.S. taxpayer would not cease to be burdened "until every *campesino,* every worker (in Latin America) is freed from the crushing weight of poverty, disease and illiteracy and ignorance,"[11] in our own country, with an achievement in affluence such as the world had never seen or even envisaged, some 0.5 million persons in New York City alone were on the relief rolls at the very peak of the boom and the number swelled by 10,000 per month. The Assistant Secretary of the U.S. Department of Health, Education and Welfare mourned that "you can go to Cook County Illinois tomorrow and find three generations receiving public assistance." Twenty-four million Americans were "poor" by the yardstick that they can qualify for welfare assistance under the laws of the states in which they live. And in the decade ending 1964 the number of persons on relief in the United States had increased some forty percent, far outdistancing the rise in population. When President Johnson brought in his education program, he reported that school districts in 95% of the counties in the United States could qualify for aid under a formula which required that either 3% or 100 of

---

[11] May 11, 1964, address to the Latin American ambassadors in Washington.

its school-age children come from families with annual incomes of less than $2,000. Poverty, he found, was national, not regional.

Secretary of Agriculture Freeman reminded the country of its four million rural homes that need major repairs or should be condemned as unfit; of the fact that a fourth of all farm homes and a fifth of rural non-farm homes have no running water; that fifteen to thirty thousand rural communities have no water systems; that in county after county across this land, almost every single well is contaminated, partly because the people who live there do not have sewer systems either. And he, a liberal of sound qualifications himself, asked the professional liberals to realize that "the typical farmer is not one who drives a Cadillac which he bought with federal subsidies . . . in vast reaches of this country, the rural dweller either has no faucet at all or if he has one, the water that flows out of it is unsafe to drink." [12]

While Senator Kennedy was deploring the condition of the Peruvian Indians who "had never heard of President Kennedy or President Johnson . . . and spoke no Spanish" (surely not to be attributed to U.S. exploitation or neglect), the Senate Committee on Interior and Insular Affairs was reporting that almost 400,000 U.S. Indians maintain a special relationship with the government of the United States, as they had for well over a hundred years, that in the last dozen years alone $1.5 billion had been available for Indian programs, and yet "adult Indians as a group are only half as well educated as other citizens of the United States, they receive one-third to one-fourth as much income per capita, their life expectancy is only two-thirds that of the rest of the population," and as Senator McGovern put it "I have had the experience of visiting Indian reservations where the level of living is not one whit better than in some of the most severely under-developed countries of the globe." We had been unable to solve a problem involving 400,000 persons within our borders, but were joyously embarked on a program to solve in the same manner problems involving 200 million people overseas.

The point of this recitation of facts is that the logical conclusion that the Senate Majority Leader should have reached from his counterblast at the microcosm of Latin America's problems that

---

[12] April 3, 1965, Address before the 18th convention of the Americans for Democratic Action.

could be found within our borders was the need to abandon rhetoric in favor of an approach to realism. True, the existence of unsolved problems in the United States or in New York City did not serve as an excuse properly for Latin America to ignore its own problems. But it should have sobered the "experts" who were expecting structural reforms in a decade in Latin America and who balked at the insistence of the Congress that there be an orderly pursuit of goals, rather than the wasteful emergency-task-force approach, involving a frantic effort to throw money at the problem in the largest possible quantities. Nothing militated against success for the Alliance more than the establishment of wholly impossible goals, and the determination to proceed with the largest avalanche of money conceivable, subject only to increases as the failures mounted. And always, with a premium on haste and a deprecating of the merits of understanding where the failures were coming from. "We cannot afford to waste time by thinking about whether we shall succeed," cried the U.S. Coordinator for the Alliance. Indeed! Benjamin Franklin at a Constitutional convention launching a much greater experience in government had offered better advice: "To get the bad customs of a country changed, and new ones, though better, introduced, it is necessary first to remove the prejudices of the people, enlighten their ignorance, and convince them that their interests will be promoted by the proposed changes; and this is not the work of a day."

"Money is the best persuasive force available," Kennedy's best friend among the journalists came away from his excellent briefings to say. "The policy makers consider it the only force of diplomacy that will accelerate the acceptance of internal reforms in countries like Brazil or Peru. . . . The money does not buy friends and it does not always achieve persuasion but it is the best persuasive force available." [13] FDR had had that same confidence in the power of money in Latin America, when, discussing lend-lease with noted author John Gunther, he had winked that "money talks" and indicated his assurance that the money was going to help all along the line in Latin America. But five years of the Alliance found the Administrator of the Agency for International Development announcing *his* discovery: "Money is the least important element in foreign aid. Aid is a matter of attitudes, of helping other people solve their own problems. It must be tied to self-help,

---

[13] *Christian Science Monitor*, July 7, 1966.

to performance. You could drown people in dollars but that would not do the job."

What the United States had done, thus, in the innocence of its new advisers, was to accept the blame for Latin America's lack of social and economic progress and anxiously try to convince the Latin Americans that *we* would now correct our error, in apology for which the Alliance had been entered into. And "we" meant simply money. For *we* knew nothing else.

And the more panic the United States displayed in seeking to convince Latin America that we regretted having made the area "a society without noble aims, a slobbering mess of irresponsibility and mean devices," and were now embarked belatedly on an effort to correct the wrong we had done Latin America, the less the necessary attitudes and decisions were forthcoming from Latin America. Even the appreciation which some U.S. taxpayers might have liked to hear expressed was absent, although common sense would have warranted anticipating this. As a famed U.S. labor leader put it in the language of the street quite effectively: "We support whatever bum they have down there, but you give a bum a dollar every day and he'll hate you for it. You cannot buy friendship. Everybody knows that except the government." [14]

"What we are really asking for," the unhappy administrator of the Agency for International Development explained to the House Foreign Affairs Committee, "is a bigger size of bait. We think it will dramatize the interest of the United States in really working with these Latin American countries . . . and we think as a result of that that they will be more forthcoming in working with us.'

"Psychologically," asked Congresswoman Church, "might it not be helpful for you to be able to say that you have to have these reforms *before* the U.S. Congress will go ahead with the plan, thus giving you another safeguard?"

"It is arguable," the honest administrator replied. "The advice we get is that given the temperament of the people with whom we are dealing, if we are in a position to say to them that here is this very substantial sum of money, the American people are seriously interested in this, we are not just trying to butter you up and go

---

[14] James Hoffa.

away, they say that would be the most effective way to do it. It is arguable." [15]

After five years, the combination of (1) policy based on apology for non-existent wrongdoing, and (2) implementation based on convincing the mendicants that the donor would continue to protest his sincerity and continue the flow of money even when the beneficiary failed to do his part, had left the United States a prisoner of the Alliance.

This situation actually had been foreseen by Allan Sproul of the Wells Fargo Bank as early as March 28, 1962: "The technically competent people in Latin America have always been adept in devising economic plans and the politicians have been equally adept in promising social justice. The pinch will come, if and when plans are not carried out and reforms are not moved toward consummation, or when the political behavior of the country seems to run counter to our national interests. In such circumstances have we the criteria for deciding whether or not to go forward with our aid programs? Will we have a real choice or will we continue to be victims of pressures growing out of the political and military requirements of the world struggle in which we are engaged? Experience sheds a dubious light on the experiment."

Former Secretary of State Dean Acheson thought optimistically that it would be possible to disengage ourselves from the hopeless battle, that sooner or later we shall find, in Browning's term, that the 'kissing had to stop.' "

> "One may be pardoned for doubting that the Alliance for Progress promises a cure. . . . Periodically, the United States is presented with demands for loans to meet chronic balance of payments deficits, and to refund prior loans. These loans grow in almost arithmetical progression. The alternative presented is the depression caused by a country's going through the wringer, popular suffering, social unrest, political upheaval, the surfacing of the communist underground, and so on. So far the United States has succumbed and paid. But sooner or later one suspects we shall find, in Browning's term, that 'the kissing had to stop.' " [16]

There is evidence, however, that Acheson underestimated the rapidity with which effective vested interests for their own preser-

---

[15] *Hearings on Foreign Assistance Act of 1962,* Part 3, p. 416.
[16] *Chicago Daily News,* December 7, 1963.

vation would be built up under the Alliance slogan to make it impossible to redirect the effort to its original objectives. No international bureaucrat was going to relinquish the potent weapon handed him when Kennedy accepted the myth of U.S. guilt for past exploitation of Latin America. And no bureaucrat in Washington was going to let facts reach the Congress when justifications for appropriations could be written in fraudulent terms.

The former president of the World Bank, Eugene Black, has done well to note that "the way we justify these programs, both within the government and before the Congress, often burdens the conduct of foreign affairs unnecessarily. The process of official self-justification often forces us to claim credit publicly and officially for our actions overseas when to do so can only thwart the ends of our diplomacy. *Our procedures often force us to detail results and accomplishments long before we have any right to promise results and accomplishments at all.* In these ways, we encourage dangerously unrealistic expectations among people abroad and sow the seeds of disillusionment here at home." [17]

Put in practical terms: Once the State Department felt that it must conceal the deficiencies of the program in conception and implementation from the Congress lest the appropriations have tough sledding, it lost its bargaining power on the other end—with the Latin Americans. It could not argue in Latin America effectively against faulty response to self-help requirements when simultaneously it had to tell the Congress, under its program of deception, "that everything is proceeding according to plan."

The device chosen by the Executive Branch was "optimisme de commande." There was an arrogant almost insolent belief that the growing failures could be talked away and the vast bureaucratic machine protected by continued protestations of satisfaction and expectation and by endless claims of achievement before congressional committees. At the end of the first year, the Department adopted the "one more year will do it" technique, counting on its ability to deceive the Congress annually by promising that *just one more year* is needed to show the promised results. After the first year, the U.S. Coordinator for the Alliance for Progress asked for another year — "the Alliance stands at a watershed today. 1963

---

[17] *Congressional Record,* June 9, 1966, p. 12119.

will be decisive." By April 1963 the Secretary of State was telling the House Foreign Affairs Committee that "I feel encouraged." By May 1963 the State Department claimed "marked improvements" which on close examination turned out to be mounting political instability, expanding military interference with democratically constituted governments, decisive falling off in business investments, rising inequality of distribution of income, increasing flight of domestic capital to safe havens abroad, shocking maldistribution of public funds in the form of low-priority expenditures, and record levels of graft and corruption. Utterly contemptuous of the Congress, the State Department demanded that the Alliance for Progress be given credit for these "marked improvements."

Fraud became the central relationship between the Executive and the Congress, between the Executive and the people. Fraud in presentation of data to the congressional committees, fraud in the outlining of objectives, fraud in appraising the experience, fraud in playing on the generosity of the American people.

Thus, no presentation was attempted without citing Mexico as the very symbol of achievement under the Alliance. But Mexican land reform had preceded the Alliance although it was now cited as one of the three successes of the Alliance in this field. Mexico had actually suffered incredible discrimination against it in the distribution of the "loot" of the Alliance. Only 3.2% of the disbursements of donations and concealed donations in the five years went to Mexico although it had some 17.4% of the population, and although half of its population with a per-capita income under $150 was living far below the average level of the Latin American countries. See Table XII. Curiously, Mexico had met the requirement of self-help better than any of the more-favored nations, and a dollar of U.S. funds went farther in social and economic progress in Mexico than anywhere else in the area for that very reason. Yet, it was discriminated against and at the end of the period had been told it must now go it alone without such easy financing. Yet, Mexico was the symbol to which all the "statesmen" referred when they sought an illustration of what the Alliance had achieved. Elsewhere there had been a failure to establish a climate of investment that would attract at least the minimum of private foreign investment considered by President Kennedy the key to success or failure of the Alliance and there had been a frantic effort to devise means whereby the risks could be shouldered by the

Table XII

Proportion of disbursements of donations
and concealed donations given certain
countries compared with their proportion
of the Latin American population affected

| | Proportion of Disbursements | | | | | Share of the Population |
	Fiscal 1966	Fiscal 1965	Fiscal 1964	Fiscal 1963	Fiscal 1962	
Mexico	2.6%	4.8%	3.7%	2.8%	1.3%	17.4%
Argentina	2.4	3.1	1.3	4.1	0.2	9.9
Bolivia	3.8	4.8	7.9	5.5	6.2	1.9
Brazil	27.7	35.3	18.7	20.8	36.6	35.8
Chile	14.9	12.5	14.8	18.8	20.6	3.8
Colombia	8.3	10.4	14.4	10.1	12.0	7.5
Guatemala	1.0	8.2	1.8	1.1	1.7	1.9
Peru	5.5	4.3	5.1	2.9	2.7	5.5
Uruguay	0.3	0.05	0.4	1.4	0.9	1.4
Venezuela	3.7	4.2	6.9	3.4	0.4	3.8

United States Government to avert total disaster. In Mexico the climate was a matter of considered policy and it was such that investment was attracted in volume to prevent a totally dismal picture in the annual summaries of private investment. And despite the discrimination against it, it was the Mexican growth rate that helped keep the area's record from being wholly disastrous, when the appeal for funds reached the Congress. Indeed, one-third of the increase in gross national product in the area during the five years came in Mexico with its roughly one-sixth of the population and its meager assistance from the Alliance for Progress.

The Mexican achievement contrasted so sharply with that of the area generally that Senator Fulbright at one point was moved to ask whether, instead of using Mexico as the symbol of achievement of the Alliance, it should not more properly be used to show what can be done without what certain authors he had quoted called the Alliance's "subsidies to client states and political bribery." Is it purely coincidental, Fulbright asked, that our relations with Mexico are very good and Mexico has participated less in the Alliance than any other major country? The State Department replied hastily with factual inexactness that Mexico has received a lot of assistance too.[18]

Again, the fraud took the form of the annual recitation of houses built and textbooks printed. "We can point," said the Secretary-General of the OAS at the ceremony commemorating the fifth anniversary of the Alliance, "to 400,000 homes built, 100,000 teachers trained, 18 million free textbooks distributed, 23 million people fed, 1,000 hospitals and health centers built, 2500 urban water-supply systems installed." But this misses the point of the Alliance completely. The Alliance for Progress was not a test of whether a hundred dollars from the U.S. Treasury could be converted into a dozen textbooks, or whether ten thousand dollars could be converted into an apartment, or whether a million dollars could be converted into a hospital or health center. The recitation annually of these data totally missed the point.

As the Senate Committee on Government Operations noted when it was told that "thousands of housing units have been constructed, several airports have been improved, hundreds of miles of road have been built, thousands of loans have been made," the fundamental test must be conducted in quite different terms unless the objectives of the Alliance have been totally abandoned:

> "Has U.S. assistance really served as an incentive and support for self-help measures or has the availability of substantial external aid actually reduced incentive for reforms? Are the funds provided spurring economic and social development? Are the projects undertaken those which will induce the vigorous and sustained development that it needs in order eventually to reduce its dependence upon external assistance: Are the projects conducted in a reasonably efficient manner?" [19]

Again, there was the fraud of persuading the Congress to underwrite enormous additions to Alliance donations through such devices as the International Coffee Agreement, as it became clear that the Congress would eventually see through the fraud being perpetrated in the annual resort to the appropriation process directly. Here there was a display of complete dishonesty as to the objectives of the agreement and as to its cost to the United States. And what

---

[18] Senate Foreign Relations Committee, *Hearings on S. 2859,* May 2, 1966.

[19] *United States Foreign Aid in Action: A Case Study* (Washington, 1966), p. 49.

is more, a central tragedy—not just the breakdown in integrity in our government which was a high enough price to pay—but the fact that the beneficiaries of such improper aid represented in no fashion the social reform which was sought from the Alliance. Quite contrary!

Senator Paul Douglas was one of those who spotted the fraudulent path that our aid was taking:

> "We (the Congress) get led on step by step and even though we may be legally free to retreat and withdraw at any time, the pressures against us doing so become overwhelming and then in the cause of the good neighbors it is said that we should not exercise our legal rights. . . . In the embassies and the cocktail parties and the tea parties we will be acclaimed for following out the good-neighbor policy, but this is the superficial crust of Latin American life. The real volcano is found underneath. . . . The articulate, educated wealthy groups will prosper. There is no surety that the families down at the bottom who live on a miserably low scale will benefit appreciably." [20]

Again, the need to separate performance from renewal of the appropriations had become so great that increasingly there was pressure to find some way to internationalize the vehicle for distribution of the funds, so that the Congress might be stripped of its power to scrutinize each year's performance.

Now, fraud was not new in inter-American relations. Long before the Alliance, the inter-American highway project had emerged as a classic fraud in the deception which characterized the annual presentations before the Congress.[21] Well before the Alliance, the Bolivian aid program with its technique of "just one more year and we shall have the job done and the country moving effectively" had constituted a degrading exhibit of the depths to

---

[20] *Hearings on H.R. 8864*, Senate Finance Committee, 1964, pp. 98-100.

[21] "Some twenty years ago," reminded Senator Gruening," a treaty was entered into with the Central American countries in which it was agreed that Uncle Sam would carry ⅔ of the cost of the construction of the highway and the beneficiaries would pay one-third (the Central American countries). When I was in Central America two years ago, I found that with one exception all the Central American countries were paying their share out of U.S. foreign aid funds. In other words, they were using our money to pay us back." *Congressional Record*, August 11, 1964, p. 18430. See also Report by the Comptroller General of the United States, "Unnecessary costs resulting from inadequacies in administration of Inter-American Highway in Costa Rica." (Washington, May 1964).

which the government had sunk at the hands of the all-powerful State Department bureaucracy. Even as Secretary of State Rusk sought the appreciation of the Congress for "the stronger spirit of solidarity (which the Latin Americans were showing) with respect to the Castro regime, the Congress was being informed by its foreign relations experts that despite the great volume of money being poured into Latin America, the area's capacity to act in principle or in gratitude was so small that "I doubt very much the value of the sanctions voted against Cuba if today we turn down the coffee agreement." And Senator Wayne Morse even went to the floor of the Senate to voice the belief that never again would we be able to get the cooperation of Latin America on principles at conferences unless we are prepared to pay for votes by such devices as the $500 million per year subsidy to plantation owners. The fraud had even been perpetrated on the Latin Americans when first Adlai Stevenson assured them that "their attitude toward Cuba" could not be allowed to have any relationship with the extent to which U.S. economic and financial cooperation is forthcoming for individual countries, and when Secretary Rusk hung over Punta del Este the threat that the U.S. Congress might balk at the Alliance appropriation if the countries did not sign on the dotted line presented them, and when the United States sinking lower purchased outright a vote from as dismal a dictatorship as the hemisphere had seen, a living symbol of everything the Alliance for Progress does *not* stand for. Small wonder that what Kennedy had called "an expression of the noblest goal of our society" should have reduced to a sordid grubbing for spoils where a dictatorship could cry out: "We supported the U.S. on Cuban sanctions, on the Hungarian question, on admission of Red China to the UN (so) we feel we are entitled to assistance from the United States and do not hesitate to appeal for it." The price tag in that case: $100 million!

The simple fact was that the conception of "conscience money" provided no serious guidelines to policy. The *London Times* had suggested early in the game that "a great deal of muddled thinking still clouds the immediate prospects (of foreign aid). Why are the industrial nations giving aid? Is it simply part of the cold war? Is it promoted by purely altruistic motives? Or is it a way of giving a boost to exports?" The Congress sought a handle to the problem but since "conscience money" was not calculated to have much mileage, it was necessary to appeal to the threat of communism, to the example of Castro, to what Senator Kennedy chose to call "the inevitability of revolution."

Secretary of Defense McNamara even argued that "certain small expenditures might well have been all that were necessary" to save the Batista regime, "to prevent Cuba from being taken over." [22] The Congress could be quickly mobilized to support of a plan to buy or support friends in the great crusade against communism and when in fact the House Foreign Affairs Committee some four years too late bethought itself to inquire why actually funds were being voted for the Alliance, it came up with the finding that "it is the sense of the Congress that in the administration of these funds greater attention and consideration be given those countries which share the view of the United States on the world situation." [23] But by that time the Department of State felt it need not concern itself with the views of the Congress. An Assistant Secretary of State had an answer: "I am not sure that the objective of the Alliance is specifically to combat communism." [24] Thus the Latin Americans could be assured that they need not waste time concerning themselves with the Congressional notion that it would be nice to be on the same side as their benefactors. DeLesseps Morrison only a few weeks after Punta del Este, when the phrasemakers had arranged specially favorable treatment for Chile because unlike thirteen other Latin American countries Chile had *not* gone along with the United States, had pointed out that he was met thereafter with "sardonic comments of colleagues that the way to get favorable action from the United States was to rebuff her publicly." [25] But the Congress had been persuaded by the State Department to ignore such considerations as representing only the personal view of a U.S. politician who merely happened to know more about Latin America and international politics than the phrasemakers around the President. And implementation after Punta del Este had precisely reflected the point about which Morrison worried, except where votes were bought directly for cash as needed at in-

---

[22] *Hearings on S. 1983*, Senate Foreign Relations Committee, p. 658.

[23] *Report of the House Foreign Affairs Committee on H.R. 7750*, pp. 38-39.

[24] *Hearings before the Subcommittee on Inter-American Affairs of the House Foreign Affairs Committee*, "Communism in Latin America, 1965," p. 95.

[25] *Latin American Mission* (New York, 1965), p. 221.

ternational conferences. The State Department had become convinced that support for the U.S. position would never reflect conviction but merely the expediency arising from donation-applica-
tions in the "In" box, and the deference to this creditor's position.
In mounting contempt for Latin America the Department insisted
that the countries could be relied upon only as political toadies,
their self-respect surrendered in the truckling for donations.

This down-grading of the Latins had been building steadily. It
showed itself early in the adoption of the thesis that the Latin
Americans were "not ready" for democracy. This was not a new
thesis obviously. When the Alliance was being born, an Assistant
Secretary had warned the Congress that "in most of Latin America
there is so little experience with the benefits of political legitimacy
that there is an insufficient body of opinion which has any reason
to know its value and hence to defend it." It flowered in Assistant
Secretary Gordon's lecture to the Senate Foreign Relations Committee on the fact that "political development is a process in time,"
and that in Brazil for instance the military dictatorship which he
had supported so vigorously demonstrated that the time for con-
stittutional democracy still lay far ahead for Brazilians.[26] They
were just "not ready" for such a mature concept. And as we have
noted, the influential Senator Hickenlooper, eager to show how
much he had learned at the feet of the State Department witnesses
before the Foreign Relations Committee, pontificated that "These
countries still have to have a strong-man government. I think we
made a mistake in making a fetish out of what we call democracy
in countries that in many cases do not have the least concept of
what community and state responsibility may mean for the individual." [27] An Assistant Secretary of State (Vaughn) chimed in:
"I don't think the Dominican Republic and its people were ready
for democracy. . . . I am not sure they are today." [28]

One easy conclusion could have been expected. Assistant Secretary of State Mann hoped the Congress would understand that "I
am not one of those who are anti-military in Latin America. I

---

[26] See *Hearings on Nomination to be Assistant Secretary of State,* February 7, 1966, p. 8.

[27] *Hearings before the Senate Foreign Relations Committee on Foreign
Assistance Act 1965,* p. 213.

[28] *Hearings on the Nomination of Jack Hood Vaughn to be Director of
the Peace Corps,* February 9, 1966, pp. 2-3.

think the military is a force for stability." [29]   And to this, General O'Meara, U.S. Army, Commander-in-Chief, Southern Command, had an explanation to add: "The amenability of the military forces to suggestions from American forces can be very important in the future." [30]   We repeat these quotations because· of their importance.

Small wonder that the press fell in with such "experting." Jenkin Lloyd Jones, one of the very best of the newspapermen, typically wrote: "Latin Americans generally are not honest enough to make popular government work. The upperdogs are callous to the underdogs, and the underdogs increasingly dream of the good day when they can rob the upperdogs. This is not the way you build great nations." [31]

To all this downgrading of the Latin American capacity for democratic government, the *New York Times,* aghast at the disclosures regarding the Pentagon's "political study programs" in Latin America which arose precisely from the process of downgrading, was moved to dissent: "The truly extraordinary misjudgment lies in the premise that the Latin American governments cannot take care of their own internal political problems and need the U.S. Defense Department to help them out."

It was now a short distance to the next step. How easy to reach the judgment that there need no longer be scrupulous adherence to treaties and international law, and to announce cynically that an emergency, so defined by the United States unilaterally, justified intervention (in the Dominican Republic) in disregard of international law. How easy to arouse the House of Representatives to support Resolution 560 looking to the introduction of U.S. armed forces to forestall alleged subversive threats self-defined in the Pentagon. How easy to dismiss the OAS as a collection of mendicant states waiting to be bribed.

But the fault did not lie with the United States alone, it must quickly be noted. As a former ambassador to the OAS from one of the few remaining independent nations in Latin America said: "It is unpardonable for the powerful to abuse their strength but

---

[29] *Hearings before the House Foreign Affairs Committee on H.R. 7750,* p. 157.

[30] *Ibid.,* p. 351.

[31] *The Evening Star* (Washington), May 29, 1965.

it is also unpardonable for the weak through convenience or cowardice to renounce their own dignity." [32]

After five years, perhaps the most discouraging aspect of the failure was the unwillingness of the original phrasemakers of the Alliance to learn anything from the experience, their continuing belief that rhetoric alone sufficed. Great newspapers could yield: For instance, the *Washington Post,* a vigorous and very influential supporter of the objectives of the Alliance, could concede that "it is a good thing for the country periodically to re-examine the premises of the aid program," particularly presumably now that "the old hopeful rhetoric of the Alliance and its emphasis on Latin reform are gone and in their place is a more modest perspective tailored to the short-range possibilities in Latin America."[33] Prominent congressional leaders could concede shortcomings: For instance, Senator Javits, a liberal deeply devoted to the objectives of the Alliance, could come to realize that "broad social reforms had been pushed more for the impression they would make on the liberal mind than for what could actually be accomplished." [34] And Senator Morse could take to the floor of the Senate his discovery that money alone is not the key.

But typically, Richard Goodwin, perhaps the best speech-writer the White House had housed in a generation and probably the most influential and certainly the best of the "fresh minds" that had been brought to the Latin American problem, continued to protest that "there were those who said that the Alianza was a fine statement of faith but as a policy it was unrealistic idealism run wild, the blunder of a novice administration, blinded by its own moral fervor or, less creditably, by its own campaign rhetoric. But they were wrong then; and they are wrong still." [35] He was content with the rhetoric, and preferred to ignore the facts. Thus, he insisted that "the greatest progress (of the Alliance) has been political." He rejected the notion that "the Alliance is simply an aid program or an anti-communist program." He insisted that the Alliance is "an ideology of development combined with concrete

---

[32] Luis Quintanilla, quoted in *Chicago Tribune,* June 9, 1965.

[33] December 22, 1966.

[34] *Congressional Record,* February 23, 1964.

[35] *Congressional Record,* April 13, 1966, p. 7709 "The Future of the New World," remarks to the Women's National Democratic Club.

instruments to transform ideas into action and action into results. . . . It not only praised social justice but it demanded social justice, providing funds for the job, and reserving special support for those who want to do it. It set an ambitious target of steady economic growth. . . . It promised full support and enthusiasm only for those countries dedicated to political democracy, the liberty of man, and the freedom of each nation to chart its own course."

Not for him concern with the fact that half of the people of the hemisphere had fallen to dictatorships which had broken down existing constitutional order, that the military were increasingly arrogating to themselves the exercise of constituent power, that the principle of representative government was being abandoned. Not for him examination of the data on economic growth, not for him sober appraisal of the growing gap between the rich and the poor, as the distribution of income became steadily more unsatisfactory. Not for him consideration of the fact that the Alliance was in reality rewarding precisely those countries and governments which *avoided* the objectives of the Alliance rather than being guided by them. Indeed, not for him (and it must be understood that here we are using him merely as typical of the establishment's approach) an examination of the premises of the program, which actually should have preceded the launching of the Alliance. For, it so happens that even the glib recitation of the "premises of the Alliance" had been faulty in the extreme.

The fact is, as a wise policy-maker of long standing (Adolf Berle) has pointed out, one of the major obstacles to economic growth is sheer ignorance as to the nature of the process. There has been no real breakthrough in the problem of how economic growth can be planned and brought off. We are not even close to a theory of development. We must still learn what engenders economic development and we must learn what development is *good*. It is entirely likely that the remarkable amalgam of values with which the United States proceeded, the amalgam which represented the promise of American life and brought forth this unique society, is not duplicated in Latin America, and we have yet to learn what the peculiar configuration of values in each Latin American country holds out for each emerging society.

In this sense, Lincoln Gordon did well to emphasize to the Congress that "aid for development is still a highly experimental business. When we have medical research or research in trying to get on the moon, everybody expects a lot of money to be wasted in failures. In the case of development, which is really a much more complicated business than getting to the moon, people seem to expect a record of 100% success. What we do is to try to see where the failures are, to learn lessons from them, to correct these particular failures and to get on." [36]

The vital criticism here is that a great deal was known of individual failures in the developmental process in many of the Latin American countries *before* the Alliance was launched, and the novice administration preferred to ignore the fund of knowledge rather than build on it. Perhaps the administration should have known that nations in capital-deficient areas that prefer to use the "loot" of the Alliance to buy out existing physical properties so as to achieve the political benefits of anti-Yanqui sentiments were disqualifying themselves from serious consideration as participants in a great effort to raise standards of living. For, if there was one continuing thesis that had to be emphasized it was that of limited resources to accomplish a task never before undertaken by any nation, and the diversion of limited resources to programs or activities counter to the objectives sought inevitably doomed the effort to failure.[37]

Again, perhaps the administration should have known that the program must fail if the recipient country could not take an order of priorities seriously. Twenty years previous to the Alliance, the Coordinator's office in Washington had had experience with Bolivia that was very pertinent: The Bolivian government had been offered a small sum for technical assistance in public health, and its prompt response was that this was fine, a parallel sum would now be deducted from the budget for public health that must be covered with Bolivian taxes, leaving the amount spent on public health unchanged. The lack of comprehension of the basic problem remained unchanged. But there was a difference: In the climate prevailing during the days of the Office of the Coordinator, the Rockefeller Office had explained and demanded that

---

[36] TV, *Meet the Press,* August 21, 1966.

[37] Walter Lippman has noted that the Alliance was an attempt to do "something that is really unheard of in human history. We are trying to help a whole continent do what would be accomplished by a big revolution without having the revolution." It was an attempt to achieve unlimited aims with limited means.

foreign aid is intended as a stimulant to better mobilization of local resources and would be forthcoming only when it serves that purpose. Now, the zeal of the bureaucrats to do business was such that it sufficed to get the Latins to accept the money, and for the bureaucrats the zeal to do business overwhelmed the imperative of doing business wisely.

Argentina provided a good example of the complete failure to achieve comprehension of the importance of priorities. Generations of Argentines and generations of Argentine-U.S. policy had focussed on the problem of hoof-and-mouth disease in the Plate. Literally billions of dollars were earned from meat exports and the protests focussed on the capacity to expand the billions if only the United States would overlook the presence of foot-and-mouth disease. Yet, when finally the Argentines were able to presuade themselves that maybe they should take a look at the situation seriously (as other markets became threatened) it was necessary to bribe them by providing the financing for the experts from Washington. This great country with its billions of dollars and its standard of living literally stemming from meat, and with its enormous annual governmental outlays in the hundreds of millions of dollars, could not comprehend the priorities of national interest that dictated use of its own funds *in the thousands* for this purpose. Who can fail to despair of success for the Alliance when such a mentality persists in one of the three leading countries of the hemisphere?

If it was deplorable that the Alliance should have gotten under way with deliberate decision to ignore the accumulated body of knowledge of the developmental experience, it was even more regrettable that from day to day the primary concern came to be with covering up the failures (lest they jeopardize the continuing flow of largesse) rather than with learning from them by open analysis and appraisal.

Returning to the recitation of premises of the program, the fact is, as the *London Times* had suggested, that while the desire to help Latin America springs from the best traditions of the West, the effects are unpredictable. That "as a country grows more prosperous, it does not necessarily grow more socially content or more politically stable." That, as the Latin Americans take over our jargon of technical progress there is no guarantee that they will continue to look to us for inspiration rather than to other ideologies. Thus, the continuing emphasis to the Congress, as a gimmick for wresting money from it in the form of a blank check, that prosperity will avert the threat of communism, might itself be faulty, for communists have sought for revolutionary material in the more advanced states, toward whose level the Alliance sought to raise the Latins, rather than in the feudal or primitive stage countries.[38]

David E. Bell, Administrator of the Agency for International Development, had this in mind when he balked at the notion that "economic assistance is a sure recipe for democracy." He said that the question is often asked whether U.S. aid helps the growth of democratic attitudes and institutions and that he for one was not sure of the answer. His own view was that aid is substantially helpful because of the thousands who are impressed by the freedom and mobility of our society, by the manner in which we foster democratic institutions like the savings and loan associations and democratic trade unions and the like where people learn at first hand how a pluralistic society functions and experiences the need for responsible choice, and by policies designed to broaden economic participation and spread the powers of economic decision. But even in his official position he hesitated to find a justification for ignoring failures in economic assistance programs just because of the myth that anything expended by the United States in Latin America contributes to democracy, which was essentially the ideology of the Alliance.

From its editorial pages the *New York Times* protested the administration's practice of over-selling the Alliance, the Administration blasts that anyone who objects to the volume of foreign aid projected is in effect indicating that he considers these countries unimportant and that he considers the threat of a communist takeover unimportant; and the reverse side of the coin, the insistence that if the amount determined by the bureaucrats by some form of magic to be exactly right is voted, the countries will preserve their independence, poverty will cease, and victory over communism will be assured.

Even the notion that the poverty and misery of the continent was the breeding ground of revolution, with which Senator Robert Kennedy continued to threaten those who demanded more effective

---

[38] "The Bread and Butter Fallacy," January 27, 1955.

use of Alliance funds, demanded examination. The *Manchester Guardian* dared suggest that "where people are oppressed by poverty, they suffer. They do not rebel. If peaceful change is not on the agenda, violent revolution at present seems equally improbable." [39] Adolf Berle, chairman of the original Kennedy Task Force on Latin America, suggested that the Alliance settle for something less than the original phrase-makers contemplated: "To those of us who knew the area forty years ago and survey it now, it is clear that in most areas transformation is in fact going forward about as rapidly as history allows. . . . It is fashionable to say here that Latin American progress requires social revolution. But it does not lie in the mouth of an American to prescribe the horrors of civil or class war for other nations." [40]

What had happened essentially was that the "novice administration", to use the words of Mr. Goodwin, had started with the conviction that nothing of consequence had occurred before it arrived on the scene, that if indeed something had taken place it was of no value, and that all history started with the advent of the Alliance's proponents. Indeed, *Fortune* Magazine even published a feature article suggesting that development was a new concept and hailing the feverish activity of some three hundred consulting firms that had seized on the promotion of development, a new field of human activity. To anyone who knew Latin American economic history, this was a fearful libel. Latin American development has a long and impressive history. A study of the history of the Argentine or Brazilian or Chilean railway systems, or an examination of the great developmental activity of the mining and petroleum companies, or a study of the adaption to market of certain export commodities like meat, or indeed a study of the financial history of overseas loans, could have provided both information and instruction to the "novice administration" that might well have prevented many of the errors suffered in the five years of the Alliance. How ridiculous to say that "economic development in the under-developed world is a quite new concern of mankind, it traces back only to 1949." And how ridiculous to assert

---

[39] *Manchester Guardian Weekly,* September 1, 1966.

[40] In the early days of the New Frontier, Berle had been considered the real hope for achievement of effective policy since he knew Latin America and knew public policy. He seems however quickly to have been edged out from the policy-making machinery.

that interest in development came only in the seventeen years that saw a buildup of 100,000 "professional developers", the new bureaucracy whose contribution so far had been to slow rather than accelerate development. What did these phrase-makers think had produced the flow of technology and the flow of billions of dollars into Latin American development and the raising of standards of living in the generations before the Alliance for Progress and its related programs? [41]

The fact was that the Alliance, contrary to Mr. Goodwin's rhetoric, had no ideology of development, it had neither capacity nor intent in implementation to demand social justice, and inevitably it moved farther and farther from the principle of supporting political democracy through devices of implementation. There was only the basic thesis: That affluence is the *right* of every Latin American nation and of all Latin Americans. And importantly, that affluence is a right whether created through the efforts of these nations and their people, or whether exacted from the Treasury of the United States through a combination of political blackmail and shameless mendicancy. And the buildup of the bureaucracy proceeded under the assumption that not only would the right to affluence be exercised but also that it would be exercised in conformity with a fundamental law of human behavior, namely, that most men seek to satisfy their needs with the minimum of exertion. This law, in the eyes of the Latin Americans, led them to the U.S. Treasury.

In the prescriptioneering of the time, there was no shortage of perception on the part of Latins as well as of North Americans. Assis Chateaubriand, Brazil's press lord, for instance insisted that the Latin Americans have a greater need to be lifted from their present level of immaturity of intelligence than for material support from the Alliance.[42] And one of the most brilliant of Mexico's exceptional corps of fine economists, Victor L. Urquidi, lamented that "secondary political considerations stand in the way of clearly defined policy and good administration, and virtual paralysis grips both government and private initiative." [43]

---

[41] See *Fortune,* October 1966, "There's Plenty of Promise in the Underdeveloped Land, p. 150.

[42] *The Evening Star* (Washington), October 1, 1965.

[43] *Encounter,* September 1965, "Rediscovering Latin America," p. 27.

But it remained for a spokesman for the Inter-American Committee on the Alliance for Progress (CIAP) to provide uninten-
tionally the reason why no prescriptioneering based on the hard
facts need be invoked. After the years of disillusionment and
failure, he proclaimed that "the future continues bright because
the United States has agreed to extend the period in which it will
provide financial support for the Alliance."

Why worry about performance, achievements, results? Why
worry about objectives, goals? Why be concerned with the
premises of aid? The pork barrel was being replenished. For
the bureaucrats this was an end in itself.

There would presumably continue to be protests on the part of
the Latin Americans that our aid is too slow, the bureaucratic maze
of Washington too complicated, the laws governing the flow of
funds too insistent on discouraging waste. Indeed, former President
Figueres of Costa Rica had complained almost from the start that
since the Alliance itself is ten years late, if you want to save a continent and it is late in the game you cannot run the rescue operation
like a banking operation, and you should be prepared to waste
some money. To this, Teodoro Moscoso, administering the Alliance program for the United States, had apologized that "it is
true that often we cannot act as quickly as we would like, but the
requirements of the law must be met." In fact, he dared suggest
that even if the laws had not been so drafted and their legislative
history of protest against waste and ineffective expenditure so
clear, critics would still properly have had to keep in mind that
even in the United States "we with all our technicians, techniques
and capital abundance need time to carry out our own projects.
. . . We cannot gainsay mature judgment and technical soundness
in investing the tax dollars of the American people." [44]

Nevertheless, it was possible to compromise and to waste a very
large proportion of the funds taken from the taxpayer. The disbursement of funds became an end in itself. A case study will at
this point serve to point up this fact.

---

[44] Speech delivered by Teodoro Moscoso at Marquette University, Sept.
29, 1962.

Chapter IV

A Case Study

"Intellectually," Teodoro Moscoso explained to the appropriations committees early in the game, "I think the Chileans are one of the superior people. . . . Some people believe that perhaps they have the best trained human resources in Latin America. They are well educated. Chile is a modern society in many ways. They have been very resourceful in many ways: Despite the fact that they are surrounded by the Andes on one side, the Pacific on the other, deserts on the north and rain forests down to the south, they have been able to get for their people perhaps one of the highest standards of living in Latin America." [1]

The committees were suitably impressed and sought more details on what seemed to be a "natural" to become the show-case of the Alliance for Progress:

> *Congressman Minshall:* "You told the Chairman that the Chilean people were able to make their own decisions and handle their own affairs. However, right here in your own statement, you imply they cannot make the proper decisions."
>
> *Mr. Moscoso:* "I will explain that the latent capacity of a person is not utilizable unless you can give him the necessary skills, and even if you might be born with a very high IQ, unless you get the necessary training and the necessary experience . . ."
>
> *Congressman Minshall:* "They do not amongst themselves have the necessary decision-making ability today?"
>
> *Mr Moscoso:* "I said they needed our assistance to be able to develop that capability."

---

[1] See *Hearings on H.R. 9499* (Senate Appropriations Committee), p. 711; and *Hearings on Foreign Operations Appropriations for 1964* (House Appropriations Committee, p. 2384, 2415.

Mr. Moscoso, an extremely able man, was then assistant administrator of the Agency for International Development, charged with coordinating U.S. efforts in the Alliance for Progress.

Mr. Moscoso then added what should have been the clincher, in the climate of the early days of the Alliance: "Chile was one of the first countries to present their Plan, their national and social development plan."

And if this were not enough, he could reinforce the argument with a quid pro quo:

> *Mr. Moscoso:* "If we give them the help that I hope we will give them, they will be able to help us, and they are already helping us in certain ways."
>
> *Congressman Passman:* "In what ways?"
> *Mr. Moscoso:* "The President of the Inter-American Development Bank is a Chilean."

For many congressmen, the fact that Chile had allowed one of its citizens to accept the post from which the goodies would be ladled out, a post which paid extremely well, carried immense prestige, and one from which any country could not fail to profit by having a special friend at court, seemed something less than an argument for U.S. assistance.

In any event, in five years the United States committed $685 million to Chile and actually disbursed $606 million. Of the commitments, $600 million consisted of donations and concealed donations. Every week for five years the United States disbursed in donations and concealed donations almost $2 million. Over 45% of U.S. exports to Chile were covered by the donations and concealed donations. The flow of funds was utterly disproportionate relative to the population of the country and particularly so as compared with the money going to countries with much lower standards of living.

But when the disbursements had been completed, Senator Robert Kennedy rose to inform his colleagues that "in the last year, I have travelled to Chile where there is no joy, but only day that follows day, with death the only goal." [2]

This "modern society," with its "best trained human resources," and "well educated," and above all with its early adoption of a "Plan" which after all was the magic word in the Alliance, this virile forward-looking intelligent democratic people had become a pitiful mass, a joyless mass looking forward to death as its goal.

---

[2] July 21, 1966.

At about the same time, Senator Kennedy's colleagues released a report on the situation which related the Alliance effort to the conditions Kennedy so vividly described: "There is little to indicate," a report prepared for the Senate Committee on Government Operations concluded, "that U.S. assistance is having a meaningful impact upon Chilean economic and social development." [3] The report was submitted by Senator Ernest Gruening as the outgrowth of apprehensions he had felt with respect to the operation of the Alliance as a result of two study trips to Latin America. Gruening was a liberal of unchallengeable credentials and had been an expert on Latin America when Kennedy was still learning to read.

If both Kennedy and Gruening appeared dissatisfied with conditions in Chile, there was nevertheless an important difference in approach. With his strong uninformed preconceptions, Kennedy concluded that the United States was simply not spending a large enough percentage of its gross national product to aid Chile and similar countries. He was not concerned with the experience in flooding Chile with so much money in the preceding five years. He had no serious interest in what had been done with the money. Gruening on the other hand sought a clue to the failure in the manner in which such disproportionate allocations had been disbursed. The Gruening Report concluded from the Chilean case that "the magnitude of assistance has little connection with the results obtained. Rather it is clear that an excessive infusion of funds overburdens fragile institutions, creates a profusion of new activities for which trained manpower is not available, and ends by dissipating efforts to the point where virtually no permanent benefits result. Furthermore, large-scale assistance vitiates the host country's initiative to attack basic problems. Meanwhile, after a time, recipient nations come to depend upon concessionary aid and to regard it as their 'right', thus multiplying the economic and political risks of eventual disengagement." [4] Gorging the Chileans with cash and concepts they were not prepared to handle had been a failure.

Shortly before the Committee on Government Operations pub-

---

[3] "U.S. Foreign Aid in Action, A Case Study," submitted by Senator Ernest Gruening to the Subcommittee on Foreign Aid Expenditures of the Committee on Government Operations, p. 121. Referred to hereinafter as the Gruening Report.

[4] p. 121.

lished the Gruening Report, the Agency for International Development sought to blunt the impact of the findings on public opinion by issuing a special and very unusual statement praising its own efforts in Chile. The primary concern of the Agency obviously was that the flow of appropriations from the Congress be maintained rather than that objectives laid down by legislation be realized. The mere matter of spending the money, getting rid of it, had become an objective in itself, the central preoccupation of the bureaucrats. In this sense, the Gruening Report and any similar investigation endangered the bureaucracy. After all, the rate of per-capita growth in gross national product had *declined* significantly in the five years of the Alliance in Chile as compared with the previous five years.[5] The gap between the rich and the poor had widened to defeat what was surely an objective of the Alliance. There had been no really serious advance in land and agrarian reform. Private investment, which President Kennedy had defined as a key to effectiveness of the whole venture, had *declined* so sharply that in five years the net inflow of direct-investment money into Chile from the United States was less than in the three preceding years;[6] and throughout the period the "affluence" provided by the flood of donations and concealed donations had enabled Chilean officials to avoid the propositions made to the government for immense mining investments which might have yielded as much in "earnings" shortly as the country hoped to get from its mendicancy in Washington. It was obviously important for the bureaucracy that these points not become known too widely. And when finally the Gruening Report appeared, the press cooperated with the Agency for International Development by ignoring it. Nevertheless, the Committee in bringing out the Report had performed an immensely useful public service.

It so happens that two years before that Report was released, the Comptroller-General of the United States had handed the Congress a very disturbing analysis of the manner in which aid disbursements were being made in Chile. It was pointed out that (1) "the Agency did not adhere to accepted standards of pro-

---

[5] Official estimates given the Congress put the decrease in the pace of growth per capita at 15%.

[6] $58 million was the net inflow from the United States for direct investments in the five years; in the two years 1958-59 the amount was $58 million.

gramming and project planning for the large number of projects;" (2) "no meaningful review was made of the Government of Chile's plans, specifications, and cost estimates for the projects undertaken;" (3) "appropriate consideration was not given to the abilities of the various agencies of the Government of Chile to carry out their part of the program;" (4) "funds were used for a period of time to subsidize and help maintain the Chilean escudo at a rate that was known to be overvalued in relation to the dollar;" (5) and "Chilean imports from the United States had declined, despite the large disbursements, both in dollar value and in relation to total imports of Chile." [7]

Far from achieving improvement in the method of disbursing the funds of U.S. taxpayers, the Comptroller-General's recommendations were largely ignored. In fact, as soon as the findings reached Santiago, the Chileans reacted indignantly to the audacity of a U.S. agency questioning the manner in which U.S. funds had been wasted and objectives defeated. And even more regrettably, certain officials of the U.S. Embassy were than quoted in the press as having apologized to the Chileans for the findings of the Comptroller General, and presumably for his presumption in believing that the taxpayers have a right to proper expenditure of appropriations voted by the Congress. This was actually one of the central issues, as the Gruening Report saw it. Gruening insisted that if the purposes of the Alliance are to be achieved, we must examine continuously the experience, we must be ready to admit the failures, and above all we must profit from the experience so as to avoid repetition of the mistakes.

The findings of Senator Gruening, himself so deeply committed to the objectives of the Alliance for Progress, were disturbing in the extreme:

(1) "For several years AID justified its requests for assistance to Chile by pointing to the existence of the ten-year plan as an assurance that funds would be well spent for development purposes. Unfortunately, Chile's plan is not an action program, as AID has subsequently recognized. Rather, it is largely a series of projections exploring the inter-relationships of the major sectors of the econ-

---

[7] Comptroller General of the United States, *Report to the Congress of the United States: Deficiencies in Administration of the Earthquake Reconstruction and Rehabilitation Program for Chile* (June 1964).

omy under certain quantitative assumptions. As such it provides an analytical framework for Chile's economic development, but does not set forth clear priorities or definite projects. *In practice, the Chilean Government has made vital decisions with little reference to its plan."*

(2) "Chile's investment budget remains largely a random shopping list of unevaluated, unrelated projects submitted by various agencies and ministries. Even where the (AID) Mission finds a way to avoid the white elephants, it does not improve the quality of the program because it aggravates a bad situation by releasing Chile's domestic resources for financing the ill-conceived pork-barrel ventures on the list."

(3) "Assistance to Chile was no Marshall Plan operation." The Chilean government agencies lacked the capability to identify key projects; to formulate projects in terms of sufficient economic, financial and engineering detail to serve as the basis for programming investment; to make priority determinations; and to evaluate projects in process. In other words, funds could not simply be channeled in Chile's direction with any assurance that they would contribute to that country's long-range growth.

(4) To remedy this situation, AID had initiated a comprehensive inter-related program of technical assistance to the key Chilean agencies involved in planning and execution. But technical assistance to achieve any success must be welcomed and strongly supported by officials of the host government who are responsible for instituting innovations. AID deluded itself into believing that acquiescence to the initiation of projects meant backing for the activities. But projects languished for lack of interest and for hostility on the part of nationals of the host country. Some projects bogged down in the face of determined resistance when Chilean participants or bureaucrats felt their prestige and position threatened by innovations. Some had to be discarded because newly appointed Chilean officials did not consider them as important as had their predecessors. Written in June 1966, the Report concluded that "AID's original intention of strengthing Chile's capacity to administer an extensive development program has virtually collapsed. AID has been reduced to a piecemeal approach, standing ready to offer technical assistance to whatever agency appears receptive at the moment."

(5) Numerous projects were started in Chile in a burst of enthusiasm but without any real knowledge of the host country's capability to carry out its part of the bargain, or of the project's contribution to the long-range development of the country. In other words, having "won" the appropriations from the Congress by a variety of pleas, ranging from an "or else communism" threat to the more simple "their vote will be needed at some international conference", AID considered itself under pressure to unload the money in order to get back in time for more if the expanding bureaucratic structure were not to be allowed to collapse. The Report found "AID's evaluation of the merits of the overall program and of individual projects inadequate." It had little foundation for decisions in the way of objective research and analysis. Projects were often undertaken on the basis of a single technician's enthusiasm for his specialty, and a persuasive advocate was especially influential when those responsible for final selection had no way of *knowing* since no objective analyses were available. The Report detailed chapter and verse for a large number of operations, but no attempt will be made here to discuss all of the many illustrations. One such involved the enthusiasm with which AID entered into a small rural-industries project in 1963:

In November 1963 AID described the venture in glowing terms: Over 2,000 informal associations of small farmers exist in the rural communities, these groups can be *easily* transformed into cooperatives for developing and operating community canning centers, lack of capital has served to limit progress, the project will finance itself after the initial 1963 AID contribution, the project was initiated after a *careful study* of suitable locations where maximum benefit might accrue, operations will start in March 1964. AID noted that the project had met with *a very favorable response* from the Ministry of Agriculture and the rural communities visited in connection with selecting sites for the industries. In fact, the project enjoys *enviable* support from the government of Chile. . . . The fifty sites for canning industries have now been selected together with nine for other plants and units. (At this point the Gruening Report offers up a comment: "Any reader is likely to be impressed by the field description of the project. . . . It has all the elements of an Alliance for Progress success story.")

By August 1964, the Agency's reports were indicating that *forty* cannery sites had been selected, thus eliminating ten supposedly selected by November 1963. By October 1964, apology was being made in its official reports that "progress has not been as rapid as expected . . . due in part to internal problems in INDAP, difficulties inherent in seeking collaboration between individualistic and ill-trained farmers in dozens of communities . . ." And a staff member of the AID Mission had inspected twelve approved sites and found some unsuitable.

By February 1965 the AID group was seeking from the local authorities data on sites that must be relocated because of *a lack of local resources or enthusiasm.* (At this point the Gruening Report asks: "What had become of the 'enviable support' the project was said to enjoy locally? And by what alchemy had the 'over 2,000 informal associations *easily* transformed into cooperatives for developing and operating canning centers' been converted into 'individualistic and ill-trained farmers' resisting collaboration?"

By the end of 1965 only *two* canning plants were in operation, less than twenty of the fifty sites originally contemplated had been approved. And the concept of the program as one where farmers would assume a major portion of the initiative had been altered significantly.

(6) Not only was the ability of U.S. agencies to monitor and expedite on-going activities inadequate, but also any relinquishment of the monitoring responsibilities to the host government tended to be fatal since it assured inadequate controls. A housing project was cited where absentee landowners diverted to their personal advantage 38% of the funds intended to benefit their farm laborers, a misuse of funds that could have been averted by adequate controls. When Gruening dared suggest that given its monumental housing requirments for its rural population, Chile can ill afford the high incidence of diversion of scarce funds to unauthorized purposes, particularly where the misuse further widens the gap between the rich and the poor, AID replied that (1) rendering assistance to under-developed countries presupposes administrative imperfections, and if *efficient* management of U.S. outlays were to be insisted upon, much of the activity would have to be eliminated; and (2) Chilean sensibilities preclude too heavy an insistence on the presence of U.S. personnel with oversight responsibilities.

The issue is clearly joined, as the Gruening Report notes. If the recipient governments are sincere in their desire to achieve the objectives of the Alliance, they must be in the lead in demanding that abuses be ended wherein few benefits reach the people and instead the well-connected take advantage of weak government administration. This because at all time the concept of limited resources must be accepted. No country, not even the United States, can be conceived of as an inexhaustible fountain of resources for so many under-developed countries. This is essentially what is meant when it is insisted that the attitude of the under-developed country rather than the amount of money that can be extracted from us by mendicancy or blackmail is the key to the achievement of the objectives laid down by President Kennedy. This is the point which Senator Robert Kennedy failed to understand. And it is clear that in many Latin American countries the change in attitudes is going to come only slowly, and it is probable that the easier the mobilization of the funds from the U.S. Treasury, the slower will come the vital change in attitudes.

(7) The lack of gratitude on the part of the mendicants had long concerned the Congress, but most Americans have known that it would be too much to expect a beggar or even a blackmailer to be grateful for assistance rendered. The Gruening Report found that Chilean government officials had been reluctant to identify projects as being financed by U.S. funds or as being related to the Alliance for Progress. But it did not find this shortcoming serious only from the standpoint of a show of gratitude or an absence of gratitude. The important fact, the Report noted, is that "Latin American people, accustomed to high-sounding rhetoric and campaign promises which have not materialized, are understandably cynical. To gain their support, the Alliance must demonstrate its serious intentions with visible achievements. Structural changes and long-range development take time. In the meantime, public support must be generated for unpopular but necessary measures and impatience must be allayed. . . . To obtain this vital civic backing, a sense of hope must be engendered, a conviction that the Alliance does indeed hold promise for a better future." How could people take hope from the Alliance if a Chilean political party concealed the connection of the Alliance with current visible activity, such as it might be? So much for the effort to conceal the connection between the Alliance and the projects undertaken.

The effort to conceal the connection with U.S. financing involved an even more important point.

"There are sound reasons for publicizing the role of the United States in the Alliance. For almost two decades prior to the Alliance, Latin American leaders had hammered at the point in every inter-American meeting that their chances of a transition from stagnating to dynamic economies are slim without U.S. aid, while at home they decried the lack of interest of the United States in their problems. And they had warned that their people, despairing of solutions for their plight, might erupt in chaotic fury or seek redress by embracing communism; accumulated grivances regarding U.S. alleged indifference led to bitterness and misunderstanding, poisoning relations between the United States and its Latin American neighbors."

Obviously, if the people were now allowed to learn that U.S. help was already under way it might relieve the sense of hopelessness and abandonment by the United States. And far from being offensive to national pride, public awareness of sustained sympathetic support for their own efforts might give the Latin American common man encouragement.

The Gruening Report objected to the position of the State Department calling for a "consistent policy with respect to *not* pressing for identification." In this way, the State Department promoted the fiction that U.S. aid is something shameful or even a weapon in the hands of the extreme left with which to flay Latin Americans who accept U.S. cooperation. It was an absurd situation. On the one hand, the "experts" said anti-Americanism is rampant because of U.S. indifference. On the other hand, they said Chilean political leaders run the risk of unpopularity if they acknowledge U.S. assistance.

(8) Again and again, Gruening found that too little consideration had been taken of the recipient nation's ability to administer the aid rendered. The level of aid appeared to have been determined more by a country's aspirations (so often soaring) than by realistic appraisal of the capacity of local institutions to handle the infusion constructively. *"The magnitude of assistance in relation to Chilean capabilities had been excessive for effective utilization."* In the desire for rapid results, our mutual purposes have been defeated by overtaxing the capacity of Chilean agencies. The whole

Chilean effort had been replete with unmet objectives, failures due to ill-conceived projects, lack of trained manpower, misman-agement, inability or unwillingness of Chilean agencies to provide agreed-on local currency costs, flagging interest on the part of the Chileans themselves due to lack of interest or concern or hostility even because of the identification of the work with predecessors in the jobs.

(9) How to induce the Latin Americans to take seriously the problems which prompted the Alliance for Progress had continued to be the core problem. Had the Latin Americans regarded them-selves as active participants in the effort toward the goals, had they worked out a mystique of social and economic progress, in-stead of regarding the Alliance simply as a cover for transfer of funds from the U.S. Treasury, a large barrier to progress would have ceased to exist. But the challenge of finding means *to make* the Latins help themselves continued to be the basic problem. Was the carrot-and-the-stick the key?

At the start, Congressman Passman had protested that "if you tell people you will have to do this in order to get the money, and then you start giving them the money *before* they do it, it stands to reason it will become more difficult for you to withhold money in the future;" and this made such good sense that Teodoro Mos-coso was moved to cite an old Spanish saying in support of it: "A musician you have already paid does not play as well." [8]

This had touched off a continuing search by AID officials for evidence, spurious if necessary, of the self-help already under way, each time they came to the Congress for more funds.

The Gruening Report raised some serious questions about both the carrot and the stick. In the first place, it pointed out that the stick is a paper tiger. The donor can never very strongly insist on the conditions which accompanies the flow of funds, and in fact all too frequently the Latin officials do not allow the condi-tions to become known to their own citizens. Since the public does not know the circumstances and conditions which the govern-ment accepted when it secured the aid, any suspension or with-holding becomes doubly offensive when it occurs for what seems to the uninformed public to be no reason at all. *The Economist*

---

[8] *Hearings on Foreign Operations Appropriations for 1964*, p. 2415.

(London) may have had this in mind when it said that "to give money away and then to snatch it back again is guaranteed to win any prize offered for the policy least calculated to win, or to influence, friends." And the Latin Americans tend to feel secure in the fact that the "political fiasco that might result from a U.S. decision to terminate aid acts as an effective brake on the U.S. ever taking that step." In other words, the U.S. had become a prisoner of the Alliance, not the director with suitable powers.

In the second place, the thesis of the carrot is false because the desirable economic measures set forth as conditions for U.S. aid involve political determinations, and nothing in our experience gives us superior knowledge of the best political strategy to pursue in an alien environment. Only the government of the recipient nation can estimate the potential economic, social and political benefits or risks from its own domestic actions. "In these circumstances the prospect of U.S. assistance must be a very minor factor if any in a government decision to meet or not meet the commitments upon which program loans are conditioned."

What then was the alternative? Should funds move from the United States in despair of getting anything more than a 10% or 15% performance, and if so, could such a flow long be maintained in the face of alternatives of policy which confront the United States Congress, alternative priorities and uses of funds confronting the U.S. taxpayer? And if a billion dollars a year at best could narrowly do the job set forth, was there likely to be any serious impact on the problems the Alliance was directed at, if it was expended with only a 10 or 15 percent performance?

Again and again, Gruening came down to the bare fact that the Alliance cannot succeed until and unless the Latin Americans themselves are prepared to make the maximum effort of their own free will, until they were willing to concede that the menace to their continued national existence demanded efforts on their own part. As long as the Latin Americans felt they had to be paid to do something for themselves, and as long as the mechanics of the payment enabled them even to escape doing what they committed themselves to do, this was essentially a hopeless situation. When President Kennedy visited Bogotá, the U.S. Information Service found that "an understanding that the primary responsibility for the success of the Alliance lies in their own self-help does not yet obtain generally." After his visit, it found that the number of people who believed that success of the Alliance depended mainly on the U.S. effort had doubled! [9] After five years, when successive collapses for lack of an effort by the Colombians themselves had staggered proponents of the Alliance for Progress, it was clear that the bulk of the Colombians still considered the U.S. effort the vital ingredient and their leaders did nothing to disillusion them on this score.

(10) The Report conceded that measurement of the requisite self-help is difficult. It admitted that it was uncertain how to weigh good intentions against frustrating realities, when for instance, an administration succeeds in getting enactment of basic reforms only to find its efforts vitiated by incompetence or glacial resistance on the part of the bureaucracy responsible for carrying out the reforms. It admitted there was uncertainty on who was to judge what legislation is desirable and feasible and what actions are politically tenable, and that this left a need for a yardstick with which to appraise the overall effort, as for instance in the case of a country which takes aggressive action to correct bad situations in several major fields while completely neglecting others.

But the Report refused to accept the typical settlement of such issues made when AID, having no faith in the efficacy of monetary and fiscal tests and no expectation of fundamental reforms on the part of the Chilean Government, and knowing that U.S. aid would not serve developmental purposes, had nevertheless established essentially the same conditions for the 1964 program loan as in the previous year. And the Report objected to the long advocacy of the export of funds to Chile on the basis of capacity to use them effectively by Plan only to have AID assert on March 15, 1965 that it was not until now that there was an administration seriously interested in the Alliance. What credibility could attach to the Agency's statements when such deceit was conceded?

(11) The Report emphasized that "the Chileans have the sovereign right to spend or misspend their resources in any way they choose. The United States on the other hand has an equally sovereign right to choose not to be a party to folly." When AID

---

[9] House Foreign Affairs Committee, *Hearings on International Organizations and Movements,* "Winning the Cold War," Part VII, pp. 915-929, released March 31, 1964.

devised methods to enable the Chileans to be freed of legislative stipulations for the flow of funds, as in the case of the program-loan route escape from Section 611a (1) of the Foreign Assistance Act which required that no agreement or grant in excess of $100,000 be entered into if it requires substantive technical or financial planning until engineering, financing and other plans necessary to carry out such assistance and a reasonable estimate of the cost to the U.S. have been completed, the escape route was in a sense no service even to the Chileans. "For, capital was being frittered away without generating the development by which Chile could pay its mounting debt and attract fresh capital. . . . A time of reckoning must come. . . . When it does, no one should be surprised to have recriminations hurled at the United States for 'saddling Chile with a heavy debt.' "

(12) Every policy declaration by U.S. officials emphasized that the fundamental concept of the Alliance for Progress is timely and adequate U.S. aid to reinforce the Latin Americans' own efforts to make drastic changes in their antiquated economic and social systems. But each time the United States disregards this criterion, it throws into disarray the entire framework of the Alliance. The use of foreign-aid funds for foreign policy purposes other than developmental objectives undermines the concept of the Alliance. Some examples were cited: (a) Bailout operations entered into for political purposes had weakened the ability to make self-help criteria stick. For "not without logic" the Latins said that "you helped *them* without getting implementation of self-help commitments, why not *us* now?" (b) Emergency aid puts a premium on alleged political imperatives. Illustrated perhaps by the common joke that the best way to get money is to keep alive the communist scare. This either alone or in conjunction with the diatribe attributed by the press to Krishna Menon: "So far as the United States is concerned, you do not get money by sucking up. If you want aid, don't beg them, kick them." This seemed to have been illustrated by the Chileans themselves as early as the Punta del Este meetings. (c) It was widely believed that during the 1964 election campaign in Chile, the State Department had continued budget support and balance of payments assistance to prevent economic deterioration that might have sparked discontent and a swing to the far left, that the Department had deliberately papered over real conditions to prevent election of candidates to whom it was opposed. Admittedly there were many who believed that

Frei won on the merits of his program and was not substantially aided by U.S. efforts in his behalf. But the fact of the U.S. effort is usually accepted.

The Gruening Report found the confusion between economic and political objectives to have serious consequences. First, it created a climate of self-delusion within the Agency for International Development. "Examination of AID documents in the period when AID recognized assistance as being for political purposes reveals the tortuous reasoning to which the Agency had to resort to justify the funds on economic grounds. Unhappily the dubious justifications after constant reiteration began to acquire within the Agency an aura of truth, making realistic appraisal of programs impossible." Second, the confusion of political and economic objectives made the establishment of meaningful tests of achievement impossible. Third, it brought disillusionment to the people and the Congress because of the failure to achieve the economic results which admittedly had ceased to be the primary purpose of the assistance rendered.

(13) The Report stressed the crucial need for national leadership in each country, and the fact that only national leaders can make the fundamental political decisions vital to peaceful economic and social transformation. And it protested that U.S. assistance had continued to flow to countries impoverished in such leadership and that the State Department had apparently not yet learned the futility of aid under such circumstances. It warned that however commendable the desire of the American people to alleviate misery, the indiscriminate scattering of resources would bring at best ephemeral relief, and that a world dole was not the purpose of the U.S. aid program. And it sought emphasis on the harsh facts of development, that national leaders must be made to understand that there is no short-cut to economic growth, no 'instant' development, that they must cease grasping at panaceas to escape distasteful truths whether they be common-market schemes or commodity agreements or formulas assigning a fixed portion of every dollar earned by a U.S. citizen to the relief of the bureaucracies in Latin America.

A postscript to the Gruening Report is in order. The essentials for such a program as the Alliance for Progress were known at the start. Indeed, when the Alliance was launched, a spokesman for the State Department warned that "the effort for accelerated de-

velopment could be undermined by the squandering of limited resources on low priority uses, by the encouragement of inflationary
pressures, and by the incapacity of administrative machinery to do
what is needed." It had stated flatly that "development planning
cannot be merely on paper; it must be geared to the budget and to
the real centers of decision-making in the operating ministries and
other agencies controlling investment funds." [10]   And Roberto
Campos' call for a political mystique which would rally the great
majority of people and organized groups and leaders of influence
to the goals as a major part of the national political life of each
participating country had been laid down as vital.

What the Gruening Report did was to demonstrate clearly that
the essential mystique had been absent in Chile and that the requi-
sites for successful implementation of such a program had been
notably ignored.

What is shocking from the viewpoint of U.S. public policy is
the attempt of the bureaucrats to conceal the facts from the U.S.
Congress, to paper over the deficiencies lest their own jobs be
sacrificed in the failures.   Persistent prevarication by the Executive
to the Congress is a threat to the U.S. political system.   The annual
parade to the hill with demands for larger and larger appropriations on false justifications and on an "or else" basis of the most
spurious sort had after five years become a discredit to the nation.
If indeed this program was to endure, as President Johnson promised, until every worker, every *campesino,* had been effectively incorporated into the affluent society, it was imperative that it be
supported on its merits, or that it lose support on its proven deficiencies.

Meanwhile, the full implications of the program, which had
been accepted so carelessly because it seemed just another method
of milking the U.S. Treasury, began to concern the Latin Americans.   As the halting efforts of the United States to develop operating principles caused second thoughts on the subject, and some
sticky incidents, the London Times' correspondent in Mexico City,
writing from a country which alone had resisted a new doctrine of
intervention and had refused to be bribed into servility, reported
that "an important question of principle lies behind many of the in-

---

[10] Lincoln Gordon, *A New Deal for Latin America* (Cambridge, 1963),
p. 14.

cidents: Whether Mexico and the other Latin American countries
are to be permitted effective, and not merely nominal, autonomy;
whether in fact they are to be considered by the United States sufficiently adult to be allowed to develop and stand by their own
policies, both international and national."

Nowhere in the rhetoric to which the Alliance had been largely
confined for five years had there been a serious probing into such
subjects.   But reality inevitably intruded on the rhetoric now.

Chapter V

"Within a Framework of Democratic Institutions"

"There had been a time," Stebbins wrote in the annual review of the Council on Foreign Relations, "when the United States was widely suspected of favoring the power of military dictatorships in Latin American countries as the best way of heading off revolutions and safeguarding the profits of U.S. business concerns. To whatever extent this might have been true in the past, however, it had clearly ceased to be true by the time President Kennedy began to unfold his Latin American policy in the early weeks of 1961." [1] Nevertheless Kennedy had been advised that "resentment is so deep in Latin America that it will take a long time before the United States can expect to appear as a champion of democracy." [2] And for an administration which was making policy on the theory that the United States is what is wrong with Latin America, it was perhaps easier to accept this finding.

Still, Kennedy recognized, his biographer tells us, "that the military often represented more competence in administration and more sympathy with the U.S. than any other group in the country. To halt work on the Alliance in every nation not ruled by a genuine democracy would have paralyzed the whole program." [3]

True, the Alliance had been conceived as an "unfulfilled task to demonstrate . . . that man's unsatisfied aspiration for economic progress and social justice can best be achieved by free men working *within a framework of democratic institutions.*" (Italics

---

[1] Richard P. Stebbins, *The United States in World Affairs 1963* (Council on Foreign Relations, Harper & Row, New York, 1964), p. 270.

[2] José Figueres, *The New Leader,* October 10, 1960.

[3] Theodore C. Sorensen, *Kennedy* (Harper & Row, New York, 1965), pp. 599-604.

added). But beyond the rhetoric the administration had neither
conception nor method with which to approach the realities of
Latin American political life. There was "no discernible pattern"
of action, Sorensen concludes, "in a situation which itself had little
discernible pattern." Certainly the "fresh minds" of the Alliance
could find no pattern in the situation, weighed down as they were
with outdated myths of the area. And so, not surprisingly, Sorensen concedes that" reality did not match the rhetoric which flowed
about the Alliance."

After five years, Senator Robert Kennedy was still ticking off
the plaints: "During the years that followed World War II Latin
America was neglected and ignored. We gave medals to dictators,
praised backward regimes, and became steadily identified with
institutions and men who held their lands in poverty and fear." [4]

But now, what, after five years of the Alliance? Had there been
improvement? *Now* half of the people of the area were living
under dictators, and U.S. identification was closest with perhaps the
most dangerous of the political situations—Brazil—in which the
regime had enjoyed an unusual degree of blessing from the American Embassy when it destroyed representative government in Brazil
and was surviving now by incredible transfusions from the U.S.
Treasury of money that had been intended to achieve economic
progress and social justice "within a framework of democratic institutions." On its origins, the International Commission of Jurists
found that "any pretext of acting in the higher interests of the
Constitution or to protect the Constitution against the activities of

---

[4] "Latin America and the Demands of Social Justice," *Diplomat,* November 1966, p. 42.

[5] "It is perfectly clear that if the democratically-elected Legislature of
Brazil chose to reject President Goulart's proposals, or to accept them, it
would in either event be acting in accordance with its constitutional role.
It is difficult to find any justification for the overthrow of President
Goulart by the military without waiting for Congress to express its views
on his proposals. If Congress had rejected them, then presumably the
military would not have considered it necessary to intervene. If, on the
other hand, Congress had accepted the proposals, the pretext on which the
military intervened would have been less defensible than it actually was.
The Brazilian Constitution enables Congress to protect itself against en-
croachments of power by the President and it is precisely this role of Congress that the military took upon themselves. Whether or not President
Goulart was a good or bad executive, Left-wing or Right-wing, efficient or

President Goulart is self-evidently hollow." [5]   On its methods, the moderate *Jornal do Brasil* would describe the political situation underwritten by the United States in these terms: "Between the candidates who have been suspended and those who may be after the election, the voter goes to the polls with the sensation of performing a senseless act in the most melancholy and coerced election that has been carried out in this country." And on its character, the press the world over would label the new law abolishing freedom of the press as the final blow to the image of democracy in Brazil. But the State Department would not only underwrite the regime but also it would justify its action on the thesis that Brazil is "just not ready" for constitutional democracy, that it lacks political maturity, that "political development is a process in time," to repeat Assistant Secretary Gordon's words to the Senate Foreign Relations Committee. Was this the identification which Senator Kennedy sought from the Alliance for Progress? Had the substitution of $400 million package deals for medals been the great achievement of the Alliance in the continuing effort to discourage democratic government?

Now, the U.S. Coordinator, Alliance for Progress, was proclaiming that "the military dictatorships show an encouraging trend," [6] in answer to Senator Morse's protest that "we have been proving by our actions for three years that we have little interest in constitutionalism." [7] He did not need to depend on the Brazilian example. There was a better example in Argentina to show the "encouraging trend." Or, a body dedicated to the rule of law could do it for him: "The present (Argentine) government's attitude is that it is not provisional or transitory but permanent; the President is not provisional and the heads of the provincial governments are not appointed as caretakers but as full governors; this

---

inefficient, he was the constitutional president of Brazil and constitutional methods existed to restrain him from accomplishing any of the three things of which he was specifically accused by the military. The obvious conclusion to be drawn from the fact that the military did not wait for Congress to pronounce upon President Goulart's proposals is that they feared that Congress might accept them. Any pretext of acting in the higher interests of the Constitution or to protect the Constitution against the activities of President Goulart is self-evidently hollow." *Bulletin of the International Commission of Jurists,* September 1964, (Geneva, Switzerland), p. 2.

  [6] *The National Observer,* July 11, 1966, p. 12.

  [7] *Congressional Record,* July 18, 1966, p. 15301.

means in brief the pure and simple abandonment of the principle of representative government. The coup d'état was not directed against any tyranny and thus cannot lay claim to the right to resist oppression, a right admitted by some constitutional lawyers." [8]

Now, the United States had apparently accepted in Brazil the concept that the price of development is political authoritarianism. And when both objectives of U.S. policy were thereby defeated— development *and* democratic institutions—it would fall back on satisfaction with the achievement of political stability. Gone now was the notion that military regimes are more likely to breed communism than are civilian regimes, abandoned the idea that a U.S. frown in the form of recognition withheld or aid suspended could discourage military coups, and in their place the new guideline for policy, namely, the ability of a regime, *any* regime, civilian or military, constitutional or unconstitutional, to cope with the economic challenges facing all under-developed nations. Holding democracy in military tutelage had been the end product of five years of "no discernible pattern" of action.

Now, while the Assistant Secretary of State was protesting that "inevitably when we have gotten overtly involved in the politics of a nation the result was exactly the opposite of what we wanted." [9] the American Ambassador in Chile was insisting that "any ambassador who is not intervening today is not doing his job." [10] Both belonged to the original "fresh mind" clique which Kennedy had enlisted.

At the inception of the Alliance, no one could have been sure that it was possible to provide from Washington the essential political skills, the arts of freedom to people who acclaimed it without any serious understanding of the thing. But there had been no serious examination of the premises of policy. After all, rhetoric came easy, did it not?

But after five years, there was some uneasiness. Senator Javits posed one serious question: "One of the most interesting things about Argentina is that the whole military effort is directed toward

---

[8] *Bulletin of the International Commission of Jurists,* December 1966, pp. 53-56.
[9] *The National Observer,* July 11, 1966, p. 12.
[10] *Washington Post,* October 16, 1966.

blocking what many claim to be a majority of the people from electing a government which could be a Peronista government. It might be a Peronista government without Perón, which is the argument of about half of that movement now. Or it might be a Peronista government with Perón. Nevertheless it would be a government perhaps that a majority of the people, most of whom are workers and farmers, would want. There is a profound question for us as to what our attitude would be in this connection. We do not have to aid it. We can deny it aid if it became a government, but what shall we do about the processes which might conceivably bring it into being. . . . ?" [11]   And what could be done if the military prevented choice by a majority of the people?

Had U.S. subscription to the Alliance for Progress deprived the Latin Americans of the right to choose their own governments? Dare the Argentines select what the State Department considers to be an unsatisfactory government? Does the military earn U.S. favor by preventing a majority from choosing a government deemed unsatisfactory by the United States? One is reminded of the British representative to the United Nations protesting to Churchill regarding U.S. inconsistency in the Guatemalan case, where he felt that the United States "had supported the kind of policy in Guatemala which she had condemned as immoral when practiced by the Soviet Union in Greece or Korea. . . . It was the most flagrant act of aggression against a small state." And of Churchill's answer that "a great principle only carries weight when it is associated with movements of great force."[12]   How reconcile this with the U.S. position of relations among equals in the inter-American system and of the importance of free choice within each country? Was the Alliance for Progress a "movement of great force"?

In Chile, the question had been pointed up even more vividly. All through the campaign from which Frei emerged victorious, Washington held its breath lest the candidate of the extreme Left prevail, which would have confronted the State Department with a government less disturbed than Washington about Castro and determined to pursue an independent course of action politically.

---

[11] *Congressional Record*, July 21, 1966, p. 15789.

[12] *Churchill: Taken from the Diaries of Lord Moran* (Houghton Mifflin, Boston, 1966), p. 603.

The support given Frei by the United States during the campaign showed how disturbed Washington became at the possibility that a free choice might go against us. But the big question remained: Had U.S. subscription to the Alliance deprived the Latin Americans of the right to choose their own leaders? Was it fundamental to the Alliance that henceforth the U.S. would have a candidate of its own, in effect, running in each election in Latin America? Certainly the easy flow of rhetoric had avoided this important premise in the Alliance.

And quite apart from the matter of Peronism and communism, who was to judge the qualifications of the new governments? In the case of the Dominican Republic, popular sentiment long favored a candidate identified by official Washington as "ineffective," a "born loser," "indecisive," and "weak," to use some of the phrases attached to the public image of Juan Bosch.[13] What happens under the Alliance if the voters of a country seem to want a "born loser," a "bungler," or an "indecisive President?" Did such choices fall outside "the framework of democratic institutions?"

There were not lacking indications of what the United States wanted in a candidate or in a government. But all too often these were not the qualifications which the voters in the countries would have subscribed to. For instance, President Kennedy, on the occasion of the visit of Dr. Victor Paz Estenssoro, President of Bolivia, on October 22, 1963, said: "What you are attempting to do in your own country is what I hope all of us in all of our countries in this hemisphere would try to do for our people." The revelation came as a shock to many friends of the United States. Latin America's leading newspaper, *La Prensa* (Argentina) editorialized on the definition under the heading "Un Modelo Sorprendente." It was no secret that disproportionate financial assistance had been poured into Bolivia and that military assistance per capita had at one point reached the second largest per capita in the whole military assistance program. But were the Latins to understand that we wanted their countries to follow the Bolivian

---

[13] It might be noted that before State Department spokesmen "discovered" these qualities and lost their enthusiasm, the Department had boasted that "the spectacularly successful election in the Dominican Republic is an indication of what can be done with a certain amount of interest and help."

example, and was this the promise of the Alliance for Progress, as far as the U.S. was concerned?

The policy enunciation by Kennedy shocked congressmen on the right and the left alike.   Senator Goldwater protested that "if the President's words are to be taken at face value, if Bolivia is indeed his idea of an example to be followed by all Latin America, this administration is totally bankrupt in its Latin American policy." And Senator Morse who was already on the record after a careless on-the-spot study as considering Bolivia "an economic miracle of the twentieth century," now offered up his considered judgment:

> "The revolution that occurred in 1952 was a revolution of the extreme left, if not actually a communist revolution.   What useful purpose do we serve in sending her military aid now to seek to hold down by force the pressures that the revolution itself brought to Bolivia?   Bolivia remains one of the most unstable nations of the hemisphere both economically and politically.   The next largest recipients of military assistance next to the Dominican Republic per capita are Bolivia and Chile. Bolivia is the recipient of endless American financial aid.   She is beneficiary of the presidential contingency fund for contingencies that plague Bolivia but which do not threaten the vital interests of the United States.   She is the recipient of non-project money which means she gets it purely for budget support because the Bolivian budget must finance the nationalized tin mines. Because of the huge inflated payrolls of these tin mines her budget is grossly out of balance and the United States makes up the difference. Yet because of this tenuous economic condition there are those who believe Bolivia is threatened also by internal communism.   I suggest that the revolution that occurred in 1952 was a revolution of the extreme left wing, if not actually a communist revolution." [14]

The United States had intervened directly in the internal politics of Bolivia to hold a "constitutional government" in power.   The regime had achieved power by rigged elections.   It was admittedly corrupt.   It had concentration camps and the Gestapo-like Political Control which traced back to the guidance that the ruling party had originally taken from the Nazi regime in Germany, its modus operandi was ideological blackmail, it discouraged freedom of the press, and it had armed civilian groups to the teeth in the determination that if it were not allowed to rule, let chaos take Bolivia. To hold this regime in power the United States sent its ambassador to campaign with the head of the government, to share the obloquy for the rigged elections; it instructed the AID mission to ignore

---

[14] *Congressional Record,* November 14, 1963, p. 20777.

corruption in the use of public funds, to ignore violation of a free press, to disregard the destruction of human rights involved in the operations of the Political Control, and to yield regularly to each blackmail venture where the regime threatened to deal with the communists if U.S. money were not immediately made available in the form and amounts desired by the regime. What did the "born loser" lack, that the Bolivian regime had, to gain U.S. support? "The five concentration camps where flaming torches were applied to the bare feet of his political enemies?" [15]

In other words, if the Alliance meant that free choice had been surrendered by the Latin Americans, what was the basis on which the "satisfactory" candidates were to be named? Or was this to be a secret too? Or was it just too hard to define? Secretary of State Rusk, at the high point in the "credibility gap" in the United States, had pontificated that "The United States cannot act in secret. . . . This is a simple proposition which derives from the nature of our democracy, our power and influence outside our borders, and the presence of a vigorous and properly inquiring press. The bias, therefore, must be set against action in secret, and the policy officer is well advised to check his answer with the question: 'What if the American people knew about this tomorrow morning at nine o'clock?'" [16] Were the Latin Americans expected to put together the abolition of freedom of the press in the U.S.-supported Brazilian dictatorship, the concentration camps in the U.S.-supported Bolivian regime, the "encouraging trend"

---

[15] Even as the fraudulent elections and the nefarious conduct of the Political Control and the ideological blackmail and the corruption exfoliated, the State Department preferred to point to a press report in *The National Observer* (June 15, 1964): "Paz's experience in England had mellowed him. He was no longer the man who during his first administration had set up five concentration camps where flaming torches were applied to the bare feet of his political enemies." Indeed Paz could be quoted: "In England I learned how a civilized people can live." And so: "Thus reformed, Paz who had in the past flirted with Naziism and Communism, began flirting with Uncle Sam."

After the endless threats to embrace the communists if the U.S. did not yield to financial demands of the regime, it was shocking to read, when Paz was deposed in the fourth year of the Alliance, his pious protest that "the coup opens up conditions that could pave the way for communist exploitation." *Washington Post,* November 12, 1964.

[16] Paper delivered before American Political Science Association, September 7, 1965.

in the Argentine where there was not even the excuse of over-throwing a tyranny to prompt the rise of the dictatorship, in order to construct the model government for participation in an Alliance "within the framework of democratic institutions?"

Or was the model government merely one which "saved the country?" For "saving the country" had become the most gorgeous of generalities used to destroy free government. In Ecuador, the junta "saved the country" according to its manifesto from "the lack of integrity in the management of public funds, the predominance of extraneous or purely personal interests, the inertia and administrative disorientation that had become the common denominator of the government, and the national forces and international communism that took advantage of the chaos and governmental indifference to produce national disintegration." In Brazil the military "saved the country" from a leader who "violated the constitution, tried to introduce a dictatorship of the extreme left, increased his personal power at the expense of the power of the country." The military also saved the country from corruption, with which some of the leading supporters of the coup were themselves intimately associated! And this performance so impressed the American Embassy that it sought a message of warm wishes from the White House even before the deposed president had left the country. All of which gave point to the cartoon in *The New Yorker* showing a general, hot machine gun still in hand as he fought to overthrow the constitutional regime, receiving the cable of recognition of his "new government" from the Department of State. The cartoon followed in clear pattern that which appeared earlier in the *San Francisco Chronicle* showing a general standing before peons who said: "The Alliance for Progress is very successful; we're getting a much better class of military dictators." In Honduras and Guatemala the military "saved the country" from the threat of the coming to power of a popular leader who might disturb the status quo and with it particularly the position of the military itself.

Clearly the problem of definition of the conditions for the U.S. selection of Latin America's presidents was strenuous. As President Kennedy said: "We haven't got a consistent policy (on whether or not to recognize governments that take power by force) because the circumstances sometimes are inconsistent." [17] And it was re-

----

[17] Press conference, April 3, 1963.

called that when White House adviser Arthur Schlesinger Jr. was writing a newspaper column, he had suggested that what democracy needs is a new political spirit but "this need not mean intervention against dictators."

The chairman of the Senate Foreign Relations Committee fumbled for an answer: "We have allowed our fear of communism to drive us into supporting a number of governments whose policies are incompatible with the aims of the Alliance, and on three occasions — Guatemala in 1954, Cuba in 1961, and the Dominican Republic in 1965 — we resorted to force, illegally, unwisely — and inasmuch as each of these interventions almost certainly strengthened the appeal of communism in Latin America — unsuccessfully as well." He then offered up what was wholly unacceptable doctrine because it envisaged free choice by the Latin Americans themselves: "Maybe it would profit us to concentrate on our own democracy instead of trying to inflict our particular version of it on all those ungrateful Latin Americans who stubbornly oppose their North American benefactors instead of the "real" enemies whom we have so graciously chosen for them." [18]

What Fulbright was challenging was the premise of the Alliance that every Latin American country has the right to choose any type of government it pleases, *provided that* the government accepts the political and strategic concepts of the United States in so doing. He anticipated the theory that Ambassador Martin was later to develop from his experiences in the Dominican Republic, namely, that all violent revolts must through some automatic process turn communist, that since violence is almost inevitable for popular effective resistance to oligarchical regimes functioning by military dictatorship and police terror, the State Department must automatically go to the rescue of such regimes as soon as some revolutionary development threatens or is alleged to threaten them because the claim of violence automatically implies a communist revolt.

Boxed in in this fashion, he found the United States pursuing "two largely incompatible policies" under the Alliance: "discriminating support for social reform and undiscriminating anti-communism that often makes us a friend of corrupt and reactionary oligarchies." He faulted the administration for its failure or in-

[18] *The Two Americas,* p. 24.

ability to choose between accepting revolution and trying to suppress it.

The ease with which revolutionary activity became identified as communistic activity had long concerned the Congress: Early in the period Senator Fulbright had deplored the fact that "very often all the communists do is sympathize with the revolutionary movement and the first thing we know the movement is all communist which it was not originally. We tend to make them communists by our allegations. If we support obsolete governments and a revolution takes place, the revolution will inevitably identify itself with the communists whether the communists have anything to do with it at all. They may even have had nothing to do with it." [19] Senator Aiken protested that "any time a corrupt government is overthrown anywhere we give the communists credit, and three times out of four they probably are not responsible although they contribute what they can to overthrowing any government of any kind anywhere because communism is not built on sound government anywhere." [20]

After five years President Johnson found it advisable to restate the U.S. position: "The United States has no mandate to interfere wherever government falls short of our specifications. . . . In the Latin American countries we are on the side of those who want constitutional governments." [21] But operational guidelines were totally lacking. In five years it had been made abundantly clear that a "constitutional" government of Cuban form is not acceptable to the United States, and that if monetary and moral support could prevent the emergence of such a government from a free election, it would come freely from the Alliance for Progress porkbarrel. And if a government of such character arose by overthrow of a constitutional regime, however dictatorial and opposed to the concepts of social justice and free institutions that previous regime might be, it would not be countenanced by the United States. The policy definitions of President Johnson were thus quite unsatisfactory in operational problems. And it was particularly important because, as one observer has noted, "there is a general belief among students of Latin America that revolutionary up-

---

[19] *Hearings on S. 1983,* 1962, pp. 781-782

[20] *Hearings on S. 1983,* 1962, p. 45.

[21] Speech, August 26, 1966. *New York Times,* August 27, 1966.

heavals of a more profound nature than military coups d'état are likely to come in some of the Latin American countries during this decade." [22] What then? How would the U.S. react under the policy definitions?

When the Alliance was launched, the State Department offered a statement on the political requirements of the Alliance for Progress to the Senate Foreign Relations Committee:

> "For the United States the Alliance for Progress represents a much more intimate political contact with the course of events in Latin America than heretofore. We must support and work with groups who cherish democratic values and constitutional government. We must help them in the continuing contests with extremist factions and alien forces." [23]

Five years later, the Department put it differently: "The policy is clearly to try to support representative democracy as the ideal, the norm that we would like to see. The practice unfortunately falls short of the ideal." [24] And what interferes greatly with satisfactory practice? The necessity to reach political stability, lest challenges to governments involve violence, bringing forth the label communist, and the call for U.S. intervention.

When the Alliance had completed its first year, Heliodoro Gonzalez wrote: "The military assistance component of the Alliance had been converted by the end of the first year into an open effort by the United States to determine in each Latin American country what regime or party or political leader could contribute most to the political stability believed essential to realization of the social and economic objectives of the Alliance. And once the choice had been made in Washington, to render such military assistance as might best contribute to the assumption of political power by that regime or party or leader and the maintenance of the power thereafter. . . . It assumed on the part of the State Department an omniscience with respect to the future that it had never demonstrated in its analysis of political developments in Latin America. It assumed a degree of intervention in Latin American affairs that had never been acceptable to any self-

---

[22] Herbert L. Matthews, "Dissent over Cuba," *Encounter,* July 1964, p.82.

[23] *Hearings on the Foreign Assistance Act of 1962,* pp. 403-404. Senate Foreign Relations Committee. Remarks by Assistant Secretary of State Martin.

[24] Assistant Secretary Gordon, August 21, 1966. "Meet the Press".

respecting independent regime or party or political leader in Latin America." [25]   It should perhaps be added that to the military assistance would be added financial and propaganda support.

Now that the United States was setting itself up as the supreme arbiter of who can best provide the needed internal stability in Latin America, now that the State Department was in the words of its Acting Assistant Secretary "to make the selection of the government which we back and how we do it," [26] it became the thing to do to emphasize that the "Alliance represents for the United States a *new* form of intervention." The key word was "new." In the business field too, Secretary of State Rusk was simultaneously proclaiming the era of "dollar diplomacy—*modern* style. The key words were "new" and "modern". Liberals who once condemned intervention and dollar diplomacy now argued for them in the form even more drastic than the earlier advocates had dared envision and sometimes the curious shift provoked sufficient self-consciousness to cause efforts at re-examination and re-labelling. A liberal writer of great talent, William V. Shannon, was one who attempted it: "Intervention today," he wrote, "is not what was meant by intervention in the period from 1900 to 1930. No one is advocating the resumption of dollar diplomacy. Our intervention is not to protect the property of United Fruit Company or Standard Oil." [27] The difference was of course, as we shall note in the chapter on dollar diplomacy, that the great pool of dollars provided the Alliance made it possible to "protect" the investor at the same time that it "protected" the Latin American country from the benefits of developmental activities of the investor. Actually it was the very disregard for the lessons of dollar diplomacy of an earlier day, and the pragmatic opportunism of the Kennedy Administration which considered a dose of dollar diplomacy essential to the progress of the Alliance appropriations through the Congress that became still another measure of the failure. "We are intervening economically and militarily for the benefit of these countries through our Alliance for Progress," enthused the liberal Senator Gruening.[28] "Had manipulation in

---

25 "The First Year of the Alliance for Progress," *Inter-American Economic Affairs*, Volume 16, No. 1, p. 23.

26 *Hearings on S. 1983*, p. 784

27 *New York Post*, October 24, 1963.

28 *Congressional Record*, October 7, 1963, p. 17859.

Brazilian affairs by the United States brought the "victory" in Brazil?" the administrator of the Agency for International Development was asked. "The position we have maintained there may have been a contributory factor," he conceded happily.[29] The rejoicing on the success of the U.S. contribution to the Brazilian coup, in fact, was such that the *Evening Star* (Washington) was prompted to note that "diplomacy that is so hasty, exuberant and openly partisan in the internal affairs of another nation belies the definition of the word."

The search for policy led nowhere. As Sorensen puts it, "both economic aid and diplomatic relations were cut off, restored, or not cut off." But results were not forthcoming. Yet, even as the stigma of intervention became fastened to the Alliance, there were those who wanted more, not less intervention. After five years Senator Kennedy was demanding a cutoff in economic aid if any Latin American country had the independence or the impudence to buy arms abroad that the U.S. believed it did not need. After five years, Senator Javits wanted non-recognition to be coupled with a cutoff in financial aid. While Senator Gruening labored for return of a U.S. choice by naval force, Senator Javits and Morse demanded that "the President be given authority not only to deny recognition and to cut off military assistance, but also to come to the rescue of constitutionally elected governments when they request it *with all the resources at our disposal.*" [30]   (Italics added)

The idea of "all the resources at the disposal" of the most powerful military establishment and strongest economic power the world had even known being thrown automatically into a battle to hold regimes in office, whatever their character, in order to create more countries along the lines of the Bolivian regime, represented nothing short of a disaster.

Throughout the development of policy, there had been a clear strain of contempt for the Latin American. How else could an official believe that the people of a Latin American country would be so bereft of self-respect as to accept a politician maintained in power by a foreign country as anything but a puppet? How else interpret the belief that the Latin American is so apathetic that he

---

[29] *New York Journal-American,* May 3, 1964.
[30] October 15, 1963.

cannot conduct "liberating" revolutions because he just does not want to be liberated? How else interpret the belief that the Latin American is so corrupt that he will sell his sovereignty and independence for an allocation of foreign aid, that the economies are so dependent on the United States or that the officials who run them benefit so greatly from U.S. cooperation that the United States has only to withhold diplomatic recognition or economic aid to bring the political leaders to their knees? How else interpret the belief that the United States can impose democracy abroad? For, it was clear, we repeat, that the State Department had come to feel that Latin American support for a U.S. position would never reflect conviction but merely the expediency arising from donation applications in the IN box and the deference to this creditor's position, that the Latin Americans could be relied upon only as political toadies, their self-respect surrendered in the truckling for donations, or what Senator Dirksen was later to call their "wielding of the tin cup."

Admittedly, the Latin Americans had generated skepticism regarding their faith in democratic institutions and in the cause of freedom when, for instance, their central reaction to the rise of Castro and the communist regime in Cuba had been to use it as an instrument to get larger volumes of foreign aid for themselves, to fight for the Cuban sugar quota, and to disregard the refugees from Castro so desperately seeking a safe haven. Admittedly, they had generated skepticism when they demanded to be paid and paid in advance before agreeing to sanctions against the regime that was aggressively seeking to undermine thier governments and to spread communism into their countries as well.

But the United States had never found non-recognition a particularly effective instrument. The donations of the Alliance program in no case loomed so large that they were worth a sacrifice of sovereignty except in cases where the ruling group was so corrupt that it viewed the allocations not in terms of total balance of payments earnings or total budgetary expenditures but rather in terms of their own potential profit by way of safe havens in Switzerland or investment for their own account locally. Indeed, Secretary Rusk had insisted at one point that "you cannot buy these countries for 2% of their gross national product," [31] at a time when he was

---

[31] *Hearings on H.R. 9499*, Senate Appropriations Committee.

arguing that the proposed appropriations of less than 2% should be forthcoming more freely; whether his regret at the lack of result from such an expenditure was intended as a tribute to the integrity of the recipients or as an argument for expanding the purchase price was not clear. And direct military intervention still held out dangers so great to the United States that few Latin American political leaders were prepared to do more than yawn at the threat of "the full resources" of this nation being thrown against them.

With all its delusions of managerial omnicompetence Washington was still confronted with the fact that democracy is not built up by outside pressures, that it cannot be imposed on a nation overnight. And certainly the inclination of the Latin American to demand intervention when his rule was being threatened and his noisy resistance to intervention when he was solidly in power was not calculated to create an impression of leadership concerned with principle and as such entitled to respect.

No discernible pattern? Perhaps the real pattern — the series of "spectacles" by the fumbling giant — was a pattern of the failure of rhetoric:

In Haiti, the regime that the U.S. had excommunicated persisted in office. The State Department intervened to rid the hemisphere of the obnoxious dictator and fared so poorly as to humiliate the United States. Propaganda, a show of military force, manipulation of grants in aid, diplomatic pressure, all having failed, the State Department came to hope and pray and even quietly promise aid for a military uprising that would overthrow Duvalier. The Washington *Evening Star* told the story of this failure well:

> "The United States performance in the case of Haiti has been nothing short of ludicrous. First came an intensive propaganda buildup about the hatefulness of Duvalier's regime. Then, taking our lead from the neighboring Dominican Republic, we shook our fist at the two-bit voodoo dictator, assembled an invasion fleet against him, evacuated American dependents from his capital city, sailed a fleet up and down his coast, and put out the word he was about to flee the country. An absurd moment of truth ensued. Duvalier called a press conference: There must be some mistake, he said. He was not planning to run away. At which, if you please, the U.S. Government in effect now throws up its hands and says: Oh, well, if he wants to stay, of course there is nothing more to be said about it." [32]

[32] June 9, 1963.

In Guatemala, the State Department faced the threat of interference with our intervention in internal affairs, in the form of a Guatemalan citizen who might conceivably win the presidency if allowed to run for office. Once this unacceptable threat had been eliminated by a military coup, there was the by-now ritualistic display of indignation at the overthrow of a government by a junta, but the interruption in the flow of aid funds was limited to a short seventeen days.

> *Congressman Passman:* "Did we accept the Ydigoras government of Guatemala as a friendly government to the United States in what we were trying to do in Latin America? There was a friendly and anti-communist government duly elected in power, was there not?"
>
> *Mr. Moscoso* (AID): "Friendly and anti-communist."
>
> *Congressman Passman:* "These people came in and threw them out and said they were taking over?"
>
> *Mr. Moscoso:* "The reason for the takeover is rather well known in the press. The reason is that the friendly government in power apparently was not willing to prevent Mr. Arevalo from running in the elections. This group of military in order to avoid a communist-dominated government in Guatemala decided to take over the government."
>
> *Congressman Passman:* "That was an assumption." (That is, a free election would result in a communist dominated regime).[33]

A deposed President of Guatemala had some observations to make on the basis of Guatemalan developments:

> "The whole history of Latin America is one of constant and bitter struggle between democrats and those who negate the effective exercise of representative democracy. It is not unusual to see freely elected governments, civilian in outlook and democratic in character, such as the one over which I had the honor of presiding, defending themselves against extremist elements of the right and the left. It is indeed ironic that as soon as the Alliance for Progress began to make some headway, nearly ten constitutional regimes were forcibly overthrown by the military. The simple truth is that in most of these cases the people adversely affected by the social measures contemplated in the Charter of Punta del Este sided with the most reactionary members of the armed forces to depose those freely elected, legitimate and democratic governments. The so-called Betancourt Doctrine should be applied against totalitarian governments. I refer specifically to non-recognition of de facto regimes. It is saddening to note that when-

---

[33] *Hearings before the House Appropriations Sub-Committee on Foreign Operations 1964,* July 30, 1963, p. 2359.

ever measures of this type should be adopted, it is almost impossible to do so due to the large number of de facto governments; and that whenever democracies are in the majority, the situation does not seem to warrant such action." [34]

In Peru the U.S. Embassy entered an election directly by making sure that every Peruvian voter knew which candidate the Embassy supported. And on the eve of the election the U.S. Senate Democratic Whip was mobilized to deliver a public warning from Washington as to what might happen if the U.S. candidate failed to take office. After all, under the new political formula, a candidate with one-third of the voters behind him must be considered the overwhelming choice of the people if in addition he has the vote of the U.S. Senate Whip. And when the Peruvian military disagreed, there was a short month of pique on the part of the White House during which diplomatic relations were suspended and dollar assistance was withheld in an effort to discipline the junta, after which Washington wrote off the experience as just another in a continuing series of humiliations, another humiliating diplomatic rebuff, and relieved from duty the Ambassador under whom participation in the election of a president of Peru had failed.

In Brazil the more delicate the economic policy decision facing the Brazilian government, the more vigorously did the Embassy speak out as to what Brazil must do. There was no longer a place for diplomatic niceties in the relationship between these friends whose cooperation had been so great and effective in war and peace. The Embassy now went directly to the Brazilian people, as if it were a political party of Brazilian origin justified in challenging the views of "other" political parties. The scope of communist infiltration in the Brazilian government might be a burning political issue in Brazil but this did not stop the new political party (the U.S. Embassy) from entering the dispute directly. The Ambassador testified openly regarding the degree of infiltration, produced a very sensational statement which was published in a congressional document. There followed a week of confusion and perhaps prevarication, in which the State Department first claimed that the testimony had been wrongly identified, then stated that it shared the statement with the Ambassador, then finally issued an

---

[34] Letter to *Washington Post* from Miguel Ydigoras-Fuentes, commenting on an article (August 27, 1964) titled "Dictatorships of Right and Left Thrive in Latin America."

apology in the form of a statement dictated by the Brazilian government from Brasilia.

Senator Gruening might see a vital qualitative distinction between the dollar diplomacy of the earlier years which he had helped to discredit, and the new intervention of the Kennedy period, but the sight of the U.S. Embassy in Brazil, mobilizing its full financial power to force extravagant payments for properties owned by American companies who wanted to relieve themselves of the consequences of bad investment decisions, the sight of the Embassy willing to sacrifice the long-range interests of the United States in a stable prosperous Brazil to the immediate greed of several utility companies and using the sharp instrument of foreign aid as a political weapon to intimidate the Brazilian government, these were not calculated to impress anyone with the position that the so-called liberals were now assuming in their defense of and pressure for maximum intervention in the internal affairs of the once independent countries of Latin America.

And when finally the Brazilian President balked at endorsing an investment-guarantee treaty of which the Brazilian public and Congress obviously disapproved, and seemed to be putting obstacles in the way of a deal for a mining investment and also for the utility properties, and discouraged profit remittances, this was more than the Embassy could tolerate. Representative government might be alright but not when it carries with it such uncooperative tactics. This man had to go!

In Argentina, once a proud rival of the United States for hemisphere leadership, there was surprising willingness to try to have the United States accepted as the best judge of what is best for Argentina. The spectacle reported by major U.S. newspapers of the new political formula for governing Argentina from Washington would have shamed even the old-time "banana republics." No one denied that the U.S. Embassy had made of itself a major political force in Argentina, sufficient to dare challenge local political leaders whenever it saw fit.

The *Christian Science Monitor* reported the activity of the Ambassador "busy in accordance with his own working formula" for the political solution to Argentina's troubles. The *New York Times* found him equally busy seeking to preserve the succeeding administration. The *New York News* recounted the story of

Frondizi's desperate appeal to the Ambassador to save his administration and of the Ambassador's round-the-clock consultations with other Argentine leaders in the effort to hold Frondizi in office at least long enough for the petroleum concessions to pay off. (Frondizi had earned the eternal appreciation of the State Department by letting in certain companies under secretly-arrived-at deals on unprecedently generous terms apparently in exchange for a promise of political support and vast Alliance financing). The *New York Herald* noted that the Ambassador was "under orders from the State Department to do everything possible short of outright threats" to hold Frondizi in office and quoted the Ambassador as saying that he had tried never "to overstep the bounds of diplomatic decorum." The *Chicago Tribune* pointed out that the U.S. Ambassador had first "tried to stuff the unpalatable Peronistas down the throat of the anti-Peronistas," and noted the attacks by Argentine leaders in all walks of life against an Ambassador who was "indiscreet, imprudent, meddling." A leader of a major party noted that when Spruille Braden had indiscreetly battled Perón, at least "eminent Argentines had counselled Braden to imprudence in trying to block the rise of Perón to power. The new Ambassador has received no counsel for imprudence for acts on his own."

This did not end the story of course. Within a few years, the American Embassy was trying to hold an elected president in power in the Argentine. As the State Department described it: "We had the problem of dealing with the factual situation as opposed to the ideal. Ambassador Martin made it quite clear that we favored the constitutional government. That is our policy. When I was in Argentina this spring I spoke to some of those people who were talking military takeover. . . . They had grand ideas of some Gaullist-style government. . . . But I told them the country would make more progress sticking with the Illia government and that a military takeover would set them back." [35] The factual situation turned out to be a coup. Recognition came quickly. The U.S. position had been clear since the great takeover from a constitutional government in Brazil. Whatever the rhetoric, we were underwriting "stability" in Brazil whatever the cost politically, and the Argentine military had learned the lesson well.

"If there has been one pre-eminent disappointment about the

---

[35] *The National Observer*, July 11, 1966, p. 12 .

Alliance," the Vice-President of the United States wrote after the deterioration set in, "it is the failure of many Latin American countries to come forth with able responsible political leaders who are capable of mobilizing support for Alliance programs, of building political institutions and administrative structures which are able to sustain and implement the basic modifications of society that are needed." And when there seemed to be no end to the deterioration he warned that "until ways are found to strengthen the political fabric of Latin societies, we cannot be sure that military coups represent only a temporary aberration and not a permanent trend." [36]

Senator Javits cautioned that "the real danger lies in the continued erosion of the hope and faith of the people in the viability of democratic government; in the comparative ease with which successive coups can follow the path broken by prior ones; and in the frequent or prolonged absence of the democratic process." And he demanded a "realistic sanction" against military takeovers.[37] Was there such a thing? *The Observer* (London) had noted on an earlier occasion that "it is noteworthy that the threat to withdraw U.S. aid to Argentina if democratic processes were not adhered to has not worried the Peronistas, and has only modified if that the attitude of the military." [38] And Secretary Rusk persisted in his explanation that you simply cannot walk away from these situations. When Congressman Hays asked him: "What about the reports I read about Assistant Secretary of State Mann's decision to draft a few dictators for the ball game down there?" Rusk replied: "I think that that was speculation based on a fragmentary report of an off-the-record discussion which was inaccurate in the first place. We continue to throw our weight behind the constitutional governments. When we do have an incident or a coup in a particular country I don't believe we can simply walk away from the situation. We try in a country like Peru or in other situations to assist them to get back to constitutional procedures as quickly as possible. It isn't easy for us to pretend a particular country does not exist any more when it is faced with a particular violent situation." [39]

---

[36] *New York Times,* November 11, 1966.
[37] *Congressional Record,* June 28, 1966, p. 13788.
[38] April 1, 1962.
[39] *Hearings on Foreign Assistance Act of 1964,* House Foreign Affairs Committee, Part I, p. 22.

General Wood explained to the House Appropriations Committee that "the military takeover in many countries in Latin America is not particularly because of military capability but because of a vacuum in the civilian political structure so far as running the country is concerned, and the only force for stability and orderliness is the military." [40]

"The whole story," the *London Times* noted pessimistically, "is a melancholy repetition of a common theme in Latin America—the refusal of the army and the bourgeoisie to work with a populist movement towards real reform."

The crisis affecting the representative form of government and democratic institutions was of course a chronic affiliction of the region. Indeed, every year the State Department and the Pentagon delighted in alerting the Congress to the score: "The record shows that in the last thirty-six years there have been 106 unconstitutional changes of regime in Latin America, an average of three per year. The record in the last couple of years has been better. I am optimistic about the future." [41]

Optimism was in fact the operating device without which it could not be hoped to maintain the bureaucratic establishment — national and international — as a growing body. "The greatest progress has been political," [42] cried the chief phrase-maker of the Alliance, after the east coast of South America embracing almost half of the population of the Alliance beneficiaries had largely surrendered constitutional government. "The present situation with respect to the political structures of Latin America is an exceedingly favorable one," the State Department testified on the eve of a series of upheavals that took down eight governments in short order.[43] "The outlook for political stability in Latin America, with few exceptions, is more favorable today than it has been for many years," purred the Department of State on May 15, 1963,[44]

---

[40] *Hearings on Foreign Operations Appropriations for 1965,* House Appropriations Committee, Part I, p. 530.

[41] *Hearings on Foreign Assistance and Related Agencies Appropriations for 1967,* House Appropriations Committee, p. 662.

[42] *Congressional Record,* April 13, 1966, p. 7709.

[43] *Hearings on Foreign Assistance Act,* Senate Appropriations Committee, August 31, 1962, p. 306. Testimony of Assistant Secretary Martin.

[44] *Hearings on Foreign Assistance Act of 1963,* House Foreign Affairs Committee, p. 859.

only to have a great historian, Frank Tannenbaum, reply that "as long as the army is the only effective national institution the prospect for stable and democratic government will remain precarious." [45]   Not so, replied Senator McGee after a junket to the area: "while we carefully looked for evidence that military force was serving as a deterrent to democratic processes, our conclusions are to the contrary."   Latin dissatisfaction with the U.S. role?   Not so, explained Secretary Rusk: "We tend to put words into the mouths of Latin Americans generally on the assumption that they are very skittish and skeptical and resentful of a lot of things we do, when in fact it just isn't their opinion." [46]   This in defense particularly of the Dominican Republic intervention.

There was no shortage of bombast, of course.   Only a week before the Brazilian coup, the chairman of the Senate Foreign Relations Committee on Inter-American Affairs was still bellowing that "all of Latin America should know that there is a strong feeling in the United States that we will be no party after the fact or before the fact in aiding and abetting the overthrow of a constitutionally existing government . . . that if there is any potential military junta who believe they can proceed to overthrow constitutionally existing governments and be embraced by the United States they could not be more wrong." [47]   Shortly thereafter the coup occurred with full State Department support and blessing and for the moment it did not seriously disturb the Senator.

A very intelligent Latin American leader has explained the dilemma of progressive governments in this fashion, as he tried to explain the difficulties confronting a democratic party determined to carry forward the objectives of the Alliance when it attains power:

> (a) The electoral campaign arouses in the people great expectations of rapid economic and social improvement.   As it is impossible to achieve this quickly, a certain degree of disillusionment results.

> (b) The most important news media, almost always in the hands of the privileged classes that are opposed to change, encourage popular disenchantment by giving wide dissemination to unfounded criticisms.

---

[45] Letter to Editor, *New York Times,* October 4, 1963.

[46] *Hearings on Foreign Assistance and Related Agencies Appropriations for 1967,* House Appropriations Committee, p. 1065.

[47] *Congressional Record,* March 21, 1964, p. 5657.

(c) The leftist agitators, with the aid of international communism, also exploit the frustration of the people. The extremists of the left and the right thus conspire to undermine the effort of the reformist government.

(d) The wealthy classes then provoke subversion, in the hope that a military dictatorship will re-establish their privileges or keep them intact.

(e) The extremists of the left also encourage subversion, in the hope of taking over leadership of the anti-dictatorial movement that in all certainty will have to be forged.

(f) The impoverished masses end up aiding subversion, dreaming that the destruction of the established order will open the road to a better life.

He continued: "Even when subversion is not consumated, the stability of a democratic revolutionary party in power is always difficult to maintain. The short-term sacrifices that are imposed on the nation by structural reforms arouse an angry propaganda attack by the same businessmen who will benefit from the increase in the purchasing power of the majority of the people. And what is worse, the impoverished masses, for whose direct benefit the reforms are being made, translate their impatience into votes for the demagogic politicians of the opposition, ingenuously believing that their condition can be improved more rapidly than the growth of the national income will allow." He saw the challenge thus for democratic governments as one of gaining the confidence of the masses while carrying forward the slow and tedious process of development and at the same time avoiding the irreconcilable op-position of the wealthy. And for this there was required a true political mystique, "a crusade of political and social redemption that will capture the intellectual and emotional adherence of those who must give form to the new society." [48]

But after five years, the mystique undeveloped in Latin America, the United States had come to the conclusion that the key was "political stability" regardless of how it was achieved or by whom. In the presidential campaign of 1960, Kennedy had gone down the litany: "The people of Latin America have begun to feel that we are more interested in stable regimes than in free governments;

---

[48] This is taken from a very important paper by the Ambassador of Costa Rica, dated September 8, 1965, presented to the Council of the OAS. It is reprinted in part in *Inter-American Economic Affairs,* Volume 20, No. 2, pp. 91-96.

more interested in fighting against communism than in fighting for freedom; more interested in the possible loss of our investments than in the actual loss of the lives of the thousands of young Latins who have died fighting dictators and thus when the dictatorships fell, our actions of support were remembered and we have been distrusted because of them."[49]

After five years, his words seemed best to describe *precisely the situation that had now emerged.* Now, political stability was the goal, and the State Department felt that it had proved that the United States could not much care who would provide that stability, and that it was not prepared to balk at the character of the stability provided, however repugnant to the principles of democratic institutions. Now, policy was written definitely in terms of a fight against communism rather than as a fight for freedom of choice on the part of the Latin Americans. Now, the task of building support for the Alliance within the United States seemed to have dictated that "the possible loss of investments" must be an important key to U.S. policy.

It remained for Americans for Democratic Action, which served as an intellectual guide for the liberal senators in the Democratic Party, to throw in the sponge irretrievably. It resolved that "the United States should of course foster democracy *where feasible* but any government regardless of its form should be judged on the basis of its performance in economic, social and educational reform which provides the basis for advanced political democracy." [50]

There was provided no guide to determination of where democracy is *feasible.* But "the framework of democratic institutions" had apparently been abandoned.

---

[49] *The Speeches of John F. Kennedy, Presidential Campaign of 1960* (Government Printing Office, Washington 1961), p. 1161.

[50] *Congressional Record,* May 27, 1964, pp. 11713-74

Chapter VI

The Starving Jet Set

In five years Latin American defense expenditures absorbed $8 billion.[1] To this the United States added $0.4 billion in military assistance. Throughout this period the focus of public discussion was the U.S. military-aid component of this great outlay, its potential or alleged contribution — good or bad — to the objectives of the Alliance for Progress.

This confused the issue completely. The noisy opponents of the military-assistance program blasted away as if the decision on military aid by the United States were the decisive issue, with that frightful conceit of assuming on behalf of the United States the ultimate responsibility for what transpires in Latin America. But clearly the core decision, in a program theoretically geared to the planning of optimum priorities for social and economic development, was one wholly within the authority of each Latin American government. Did the Latin Americans feel that this $8 billion involved the optimum utilization of their resources? Did the Latin Americans feel that the diversion of $0.4 billion of U.S. aid from economic to military purposes involved the maximum use of external resources? It was their decision alone to make. And characteristically, at no time did the Latin Americans show any significant interest in the structural alteration which would have been necessary for a more satisfactory use of their resources.

President Kennedy had pinpointed the key decision during his election campaign when he pleaded with Latin America for "an arms control agreement in South (sic) America . . . which would end the wasteful arms race, which now absorbs sixty percent of the budget of some Latin American nations, dissipates resources which might be used for economic development, and increases

---

[1] This does not include Cuban military expenditures.

tension throughout the hemisphere." [2]   And the U.S. Coordinator for the Alliance, Teodoro Moscoso, had put the issue even more effectively: "A million dollars will buy a lot of things . . . maybe 40 tanks or a hundred howitzers . . . maybe a new jet fighter. . . . But this same million dollars can do many other things: It can build 500 rural schools, make graduate engineers out of 130 secondary school graduates, buy a daily glass of milk for 50,000 children for one year." He continued this most fruitful of all explorations: "With this million dollars in hand, you will probably be able to obtain an additional million from an external lending agency, and with the two million dollars you may be able to build 100 kilometers of fair weather road, or build an electric power plant with an output capacity of 10,000 kilowatts, or provide supervised agricultural credit to permit 4,000 small farmers to improve their farms." He was mild but firm in his exposition of the problem at the Conference of the American Armies at Fort Amador in July 1963: "While much of the military spending is for such high priority missions as internal security and civic action, I feel that money may be being spent for lower priority purposes, and expenditures for such purposes may result in the non-availability of resources needed for high priority economic and social development tasks." [3]

But as had been true in the other phases of the Alliance, the Latin Americans showed no serious interest in such ideas. The Alliance was a gimmick by which funds might be extracted from Washington. To expect them to initiate serious efforts at maximum use of their own resources was to exhibit naïveté which at best must be rejected politely. And the U.S. response was even more discreditable: The State Department and the Pentagon worked to construct a package justification for the continued waste, namely, that the military budgets were actually not large, that the nature of the expenditures was changing for the better, that the character of the military had changed.

Had President Kennedy thought there was large waste of resources, that military budgets in some cases ran to 60% of the budgets? Not at all, said the Pentagon. The conspicuous and

---

    [2] *The Speeches of Senator John F. Kennedy, Presidential Campaign of 1960.* (Government Printing Office, Washington), p. 1166.
    [3] Speech, July 19, 1963.

for policy purposes the central feature of the Latin American military picture, argued Defense Secretary McNamara, was the relatively *small* size of the military establishments. "Their military services are small relative to population. In only one case does a Latin American country have over 6.3 men in military service per thousand people. None of them, with one exception (Paraguay), has as many men in uniform per unit of population as does any nation in Europe other than Switzerland. Ten of nineteen countries to which we give aid spend less than ten percent of their government budgets on defense." Then the clincher: "The total number of tanks in the area is only 974, which is only 60% as many as Bulgaria has. And the inventory of combat aircraft is only 487 for the whole area." [4] In the United States defense expenditures were 55.4% of central government expenditures, in France 23.5%, in the United Kingdom 23.5%, but in Latin America defense expenditures were only 13% of central government expenditures, the House Foreign Affairs Committee was told.[5] Unfortunately, comparisons with Bulgaria or France or even the United States were quite meaningless. The important gauge of the military establishment was the function that the military needed to execute in each country. And here the Pentagon itself insisted that the role was narrowing. (See Table XIII).

The military assistance program originally had contemplated a hemisphere defense role of some magnitude for the Latin Americans. But the great alteration of policy incident to the underwriting of the Alliance for Progress had come when "the primary emphasis was changed from hemispheric defense to internal security." General O'Meara, U.S.A., Commander-in-Chief, Caribbean, put it this way: "The military assistance program which was designed at the time of the Korean crisis to prepare military units for hemisphere defense missions had been recast to concentrate on developing light mobile forces for internal security. And the hemisphere defense mission had been retained only in the antisubmarine warfare forces of the naval powers of South America." [6]

---

[4] *Hearings before the Senate Foreign Relations Committee on S. 2859,* pp. 177-8, 659. April 20, 1966.

[5] *Hearings on H.R. 10502,* House Foreign Affairs Committee, Part IV, p. 519.

[6] *Hearings on H.R. 5490,* House Foreign Affairs Committee, May 15, 1963, p. 914.

Table XIII

Latin American Military Expenses, 1964

	Host government expenditures			U.S. military assistance (millions of dollars)	
	Defense expenditures		Capital budget in-vestment as percent of total expenses	Grant assistance deliveries	Credit assistance sales
	As percent of total expenses	As a per-cent of GNP			
Argentina	15.0	2.3	17.1	1.5	....
Bolivia	6.8	1.1	20.2	3.2	....
Brazil	16.1	3.4	26.7	9.1	....
Chile	8.8	1.8	32.9	7.8	0.1
Colombia	12.2	1.3	38.9	6.2	....
Costa Rica	2.0	.4	38.8	.5	....
Dominican Republic	17.8	n.a.	15.7	1.5	....
Ecuador	10.0	2.0	17.6	2.6	....
El Salvador	8.8	1.2	32.4	.9	....
Guatemala	10.5	.9	16.6	1.4	....
Honduras	10.1	1.3	21.3	.4	....
Mexico	8.2	.7	25.5	.3	....
Nicaragua	16.5	1.8	23.2	1.2	....
Panama	.5	.1	16.1	.1	....
Paraguay	30.4	3.1	26.7	1.2	....
Peru	13.1	3.4	26.8	10.0	....
Uruguay	6.2	1.2	4.4	1.8	....
Venezuela	9.9	2.2	·39.6	1.5	4.6

Source: *Hearings before Senate Foreign Relations Committee on S. 2859,* p. 538.

As was the case throughout the Alliance effort, the influence of Castro was decisive here. "Events in Cuba and elsewhere have so sharpened the need for protection against threats to internal stability that it assumes an equal place with hemisphere defense among our common concerns," said the Secretary of Defense. He even went so far as to suggest that Batista might have been saved by the United States had we bolstered the military adequately. "Certain small expenditures might well have been all that were necessary. . . . That might have been all that would have been necessary to prevent Cuba from being taken over." [7]

Meanwhile, not only was the hemisphere defense role reduced to minor proportions, but also the Pentagon reached the conclusion that wars within Latin America had become very unlikely, and thus that another justification for the military expenditures was disappearing. "The Paraguayan-Bolivian war," testified the Pentagon, "is the last war we shall see in Latin America. First, because their economies cannot stand a war. And second, the

---

[7] *Hearings on S. 1983,* Senate Foreign Relations Committee, p. 658.

Inter-American peacekeeping machinery is getting stronger each day." [8]   It could be argued of course that the ability to afford a war did not always determine the entry into war, and the peace-keeping machinery still required vast improvement.   But what was important was that there was no serious re-definition of the role of the military and thus of the needs of the military establishments by the Latin Americans themselves.   Indeed, the appetite for sophisticated military equipment far beyond what was needed to maintain internal security *grew* throughout the period.   While President Johnson argued eloquently that their resources "might be better spent on feeding the hungry, healing the sick, teaching the uneducated," and warned the Latins against buying costly equipment for "illusory prestige," the plea fell on deaf ears. Secretary McNamara told the Senate Foreign Relations Committee of the efforts he had made to restrain the Latins in their purchases of highly sophisticated hardware and of their disdain for such advice. Indeed on September 19,1966 he was criticized by the respected trade journal *Aviation Week and Space Technology* because British and European manufacturers were about to sweep the South American jet fighter market for 150 fighters (roughly $150 million) all because "U.S. State and Defense Department officials have blocked permission for sale of supersonic jet aircraft to Latin America and have urged instead that they use the funds proposed for this purpose for programs that would directly benefit their poverty-stricken population. . . . They (the Latin Americans) have no intention of doing so."   There is no reason to challenge the Pentagon's statement that "we are seizing every opportunity to urge upon Latin American nations the need for a realistic correlation between both force levels and defense budgets and the actual requirements which must be met to insure their countries' security." [9] McNamara read the Committee a memorandum of conversation in which a Latin American ambassador warned him that if the United States did not furnish the ships and aircraft the country did not need, it would buy them from Europe.   He had protested vigorously the waste of money involved. But he wound up weakly arguing that there is nothing the United States can do when its

---

[8] *Hearings on Foreign Assistance and Related Agencies Appropriations 1967,* House Appropriations Committee, p. 801.

[9] *Hearings on the Foreign Assistance Act of 1966,* House Foreign Affairs Committee, Part II, p. 236.   Statement by Admiral Heinz, Director of Military Assistance, Office of the Assistant Secretary of Defense.

partners in the Alliance insist on wasting money for military purposes. Since they intend to buy elsewhere if the United States does not furnish the equipment, we *help* them when *we* provide the unneeded arms by saving foreign exchange for them." [10] This utterly defeatist or defeated attitude did not sit well with many members of the Congress, one of whom protested that "this is nothing but an argument for international blackmail on the part of these Latin American countries. . . . When they say: 'You either do it or we will go to Russia or France, or someone else, our answer ought to be Godspeed.' " [11]

The larger point however is the clear indication that the Latin Americans had no intention of adjusting their military expenditures to their requirements for defense. Achievement of the goals of the Alliance for Progress meant nothing to them, except as it referred to an enlargement of the flow of funds from the United States. There had been a total failure of communication as far as the Alliance was concerned.

And with the increasing tendency to make the winning of appropriations from the Congress an end in itself, there was the curious spectacle of the State Department defending the Latin American military. In the same week of 1966 in which the President of the United States insisted that "we must find a way to avoid the cost of procuring and maintaining unnecessary military equipment," the Assistant Secretary of State testified that he considered as "reasonable" the Latin American military's demand for modern advanced aircraft and the like. And he argued for even expanded military aid to the dictatorship that was digging in for a long hold on Brazil.

Despite the immense funds being wasted in the military establishment, each petty local disturbance prompted an urgent plea for major expansion of U.S. aid, lest "all be lost." Never in these situations did the military attend to the possibility that with better utilization of their existing funds, the plea for external aid might be avoided. Thus, instead of a force for self-help, the U.S. aid program had become an element in perpetuating the improper use of limited resources locally. And "stabilizing situation?" Let us examine a typical case:

---

[10] *Hearings on S. 2859*, Senate Foreign Relations Committee, p. 659.
[11] *Ibid.* Senator Morse.

In 1964 the Pentagon reported itself cheered by the information that "Argentina's plan is to increase greatly their defense budget." Argentina was spending $342 million per year, the national budget was running a fearful deficit since revenue collections were only one-third of expenditures, and most of the military establishment on which $342 million was being devoted was geared to a mythical non-existent external enemy whom it could not have fought anyway with the low efficiency of the establishment. Now, to justify the proposed expansion and to justify the demands on the U.S. taxpayer, the military found itself forced to find several hundred guerillas in the north who "threatened" a $342 million per year military establishment. As the *New York Times* drily put it, "current efforts of military leaders in Argentina to obtain modern equipment from the United States may have contributed to the government's decision to publicize guerilla activity." [12] In the Frondizi era, the military had been strong enough to force approval of a quarter-billion dollar expansion consisting largely of major naval and air units which had no relationship with the function of the Argentine military. And it had seen Frondizi fall and the financial situation continue to deteriorate too badly to permit the orders to be placed abroad, even though the United States had been willing to underwrite Frondizi's commitment as a reward for his assistance in allowing the oil companies to enter Argentina on their own terms and in some instances contrary to Argentine law. But the military never gives up, and now in 1964, with U.S. support, it was back fighting for a vast expansion in its outlays. And seeking valiantly to produce enough guerillas in evidence of the need for such expansion. The Pentagon was so enthused that when Congressman Passman suggested that any equipment Argentina had "bought" was probably "paid for with dollars we have given them," Deputy Assistant Secretary of Defense Sloan answered sharply that the Argentines are increasing their military budget so greatly that they would not only be given more aid but also they would be "purchasing more rather than less." "I said Argentina was one of our best customers in Latin America. They also do some purchasing in western Europe. We would like them to do that purchasing (of military equipment) in this country also." [13] And the excuse for the mendicant's use of additional

---

[12] July 4, 1964.

[13] *Hearings on Foreign Operations Appropriation for 1965,* House Appropriations Committee, Part I, p. 514.

funds for the military was that it could on demand locate some guerillas!

The Congress understood the problem:

Congressman Berry: "How have these governments we aid changed? Do they still want the same kind of equipment used before? Are they setting up to train properly? Are we giving them such training? Are they receptive or hard to sell?"

General Wood: "It varies. The countries where we emphasized internal security and civic action and de-emphasized hemisphere defense have generally accepted this. I would say truthfully there have been one or two cases where the military forces have felt it was all right to emphasize internal security and civic action AS LONG AS THEY DID NOT DECREASE THEIR CONVENTIONAL FORCES. That has not been true across the board. Even in (security deletion), which has been a principal country with that view, since the new government there, our rapport with the armed forces has increased tremendously." [14]

Not only were the Pentagon and the State Department trying to "sell" the notion of the "smallness' of the military expenditures of Latin America but also they found the character of the expenditures improved by the increasing adoption of civic action programs. Once the decision had been reached to surrender democracy to military tutelage, the Pentagon enthused at the device — civic action — that might improve the acceptability of the military to the population. "Civic action," General Taylor explained, "is bringing the Army closer to the people and is particularly applicable to underdeveloped countries." In insurgency-threatened countries, Secretary McNamara agreed, "civic action is designed to encourage and support the use of local forces and activities which contribute to social and economic development and to assist in the prevention or elimination of insurgencies inimical to U.S. interests by improving the relationship between the local military forces and the local populace. In countries not facing immediate insurgency problems, civic action is primarily designed to obtain low-cost economic and social by-product from the existing military and paramilitary capabilities." [15]   For even the liberals whose contempt for the military was an article of faith, there was something appealing in the idea of the "civic action programs in which soldiers help build dams

---

[14] *Ibid.*, p. 514-515.

[15] *Hearings on Foreign Operations Appropriations for 1964,* House Appropriations Committee, p. 119.

and roads." "Like the U.S. Army Engineering Corps in the United States," said the *New Republic,* much gratified.[16]

But General W. B. Palmer, Director of Military Assistance, preferred that the comparison with the work of the Army Engineering Corps in this country be avoided. "I don't like to say it is along that line because the civil functions of the U.S. Corps of Engineers haven't got much of the U.S. Army in them. There are a few officers at the top and a very large civilian structure spending a great deal of money. This 'civic action' is small stuff to which the military assistance contributes equipment and training by military people. In some cases the economic people put in some resources but all they are talking about is small jobs." His refinement of the definition continued: "The thought behind it is that in most of these countries historically the military has not had a very friendly relation with the civilian population or done anything in common with them. The idea was that the understanding of a more democratic type of living, a real community spirit, would be greatly improved if the military did get to assisting and working with the civilians around the country where they live. From the *military point of view* (italics added), the major point of emphasis on the thing is to build up a feeling of comradeship or community spirit between the military and the civilians." [17]

General O'Meara had examples to cite. "In Bolivia the school building, road building and medical programs of the armed forces convinced large groups of the Indian population that these armed forces which they had historically considered their enemies were in fact their friends. I believe this factor, together with the greatly increased effectiveness of the armed forces was decisive in convincing the government of Bolivia that it could win in a showdown with the miners. Proof of the pudding was the manner in which the mining area was surrounded and seized by a combination of army troops and peasant militia." [18] Presumably, too, the overthrow of the constitutional regime was an extra dividend! When the military took the government away from the official who had the support of the State Department, it even cost the United States

---

[16] October 19, 1963, p. 4.

[17] *Hearings on H.R. 13175,* Senate Appropriations Committee, p. 164.

[18] *Hearings on Foreign Assistance Act of 1964,* House Foreign Affairs Committee, Part III, p. 402.

the favor of the deposed President who wrote: "I knew my supporters including the police and the present militia were loyal but *we* were armed with outmoded weapons and the military was equipped with powerful arms supplied by the United States."[19] It would then have been too late for the Pentagon to remind the deposed official that it was he himself who had sought the heavily increased military aid in order to avert the consequences of his earlier inexcusable action in distributing arms to civilians.

In five years the United States budgeted $48 million in military assistance funds for civic action programs, to which properly should be added some of the funds charged against the economic side of the Alliance for civic action programs.[20] (See Table XIV). (In addition to the military aid program, the Agency for International Development was carrying out a variety of programs which directly or indirectly served "to combat subversion and the despair and frustration on which such subversion grows. After five years its "public safety program" had risen to a budgeted $33.1 million per year). After five years, the budget proposal for military aid (roughly $72 million per year) contemplated that 13.8% would go to civic action, 53.5% for internal security, 8.0% for maritime defense, 15.5% for general training, and 9.2% for supply operations. And credit assistance was contemplated which would enable the Latin Americans to finance $250 million of military equipment purchases from the United States in addition to the hardware they were buying elsewhere. The civic action programs were small by any standard at a time when Latin American mis sions were arriving in London and Paris and other shopping centers with lists totaling $50 million and $275 million and $25 million for sophisticated equipment to add to what could be extracted from Washington. And particularly so for an area spending perhaps $1.6 billion per year on its military establishment.

Not all Latin Americans were happy with the effort of the United States to buy the loyalty of the Latin American populations on behalf of the Latin American military. One newspaper put the problem well in a leading editorial:

---

[19] *Washington Post,* November 12, 1964.

[20] U.S. financing of the civic action programs was drawn roughly ⅔ from the military aid programs and one-third from Agency for International Development. AID provided the "clearly and purely civilian materials" such as pipe, well drilling materials, pumps, etc. in a water supply program.

Table XIV

U.S. MILITARY AID FUNDS FOR CIVIC ACTION
FISCAL 1962 — FISCAL 1966

(thousands of dollars)

	Fiscal 1962	Fiscal 1963	Fiscal 1964	Fiscal 1965	Fiscal 1966
Latin America:					
Argentina	——	——	298	1,253	539
Bolivia	——	1,817	397	239	114
Brazil	2,200	2,156	2,097	2,386	1,961
Chile	860	2,019	1,279	391	634
Colombia	——	1,488	1,655	550	696
Costa Rica	——	——	222	13	——
Dominican Republic	——	596	59	64	122
Ecuador	1,500	323	709	476	104
El Salvador	——	534	145	99	65
Guatemala	——	863	567	133	343
Honduras	——	84	20	240	71
Mexico	——	——	——	8	20
Nicaragua	——	59	——	3	——
Panama	——	——	2	44	22
Paraguay	——	840	1,111	596	576
Peru	1,135	2,794	1,271	2,411	2,871
Uruguay	——	546	431	286	103
Venezuela	——	——	23	47	59
Region					72
Area Total	5,695	14,119	10,286	9,239	8,372

Source: *Hearings on Foreign Assistance and Related Agencies Appropriations for 1967,* House Appropriations Subcommittee, p. 618.

"The maximum contribution of the Latin American armed forces to the progress of their respective nations should be their respect for the constitution and the laws and their indispensable subordination to the civil power of the republic. . . . If, with the pretext of civic action programs, the armed forces' chiefs devote themselves to promise to do, or to promise and not do, welfare works, it means that their budget is excessive and includes allocations which should be available to other departments of the government where the execution of programs for bridges, sanitation, road building, schools and the like is the normal function. . . . It is extremely dangerous for the democratic institutions and for the indispensable supremacy of the civil power that military chiefs with political ambitions, invoking a supposed preoccupation and mission of a civic social nature, devote themselves to activities that have nothing to do with their military functions, performing works that if they are really needed are the responsibility of other departments. The schools should be built by the Ministry of Education or the municipalities. The bridges and roads should be built by the Ministry of Public Works. The officers and soldiers should be in their barracks faithfully fulfilling their noble duty of maintaining the security of the nation, without invading the field of the civic power, without threatening the democratic institutions, and without being at the personal or political service of ambitious military chiefs." [21]

But forced to reject the notion that existing military budgets were excessive lest the Congress curtail military assistance programs, the Pentagon insisted that civic action represented a diversion of funds from the U.S. Treasury rather than from Latin American resources and should thus be found unobjectionable. This argument bogged down in the fact that there is at best a limit to the resources that can be made available from Washington, so that *any* diversion from expenditures contributing to the objectives of the Alliance was costly. This brought the State Department to the final "justification": That at least civic action is better than the *total* waste on sophisticated equipment. This was a pretty sickly basis for action. And unfortunately since simultaneously credit assistance was being offered for heavy purchases abroad, and since the manner of making economic assistance available was freeing funds for the purchase of sophisticated equipment in Europe, this left merely a bad smelling mess.

Yet, the defense of the Latin American military for their refusal to cut military expenditures and the praise for the tactics of improving their image at home was inevitable, given the political judgment made by Washington. In the thinking of the State Department, the military had become the "hope" of Latin America, not the bane of its existence. "In recent years," the Chairman of the Joint Chiefs of Staff found, "it has been the military establishment which in many instances has provided the greatest stabilizing factor for orderly change and continuity of constitutional government." [22] Again, "military assistance provides first of all a lever to put our ideas across. It provides a way to instill some initiative,"

---

[21] *Diario las Americas,* September 11, 1963.

[22] *Hearings on Foreign Assistance and Related Agencies 1967,* Senate Appropriations Committee, page 38.

Admiral Heinz told the House Appropriations Committee.[23] "The military are strong believers in the democratic system," General O'Meara noted.[24] Again, "we have trained thousands . . . and we have a feeling that the very type of responsibility to try to get away more and more from this constant interference in the elective process there, these are really products of the fact that they get training here," the Defense Department testified.[25] "Sometimes the military step in themselves without being called on (but) this is rare . . . the military has proved to be a major stabilizing force in Latin America." [26] More, "If more democratic institutions are to be built in these countries, the military forces will have to assist them in building them. The military is a powerful force which will continue to have great influence over what occurs in the future in many of these countries. It is to our interest to assist and influence the course of military development. That is a major reason for a U.S. military presence in Latin America, "General O'Meara concluded.

While the State Department statisticians were busy preparing the day-to-day tabulations which would show in orderly fashion eleven overthrows of constitutional government, the Deputy Assistant Secretary of State asked the House Appropriations Committee to remember that "the military in Latin America have acted in general in a very responsible way in recent years." The Assistant Secretary stepped in to top that: "The military are not universal supporters of those who oppose change as represented by the programs of the Alliance. The two worst dictators in Latin America today are not military men." [27] And his successor invoked the larger strategic picture to warn that "there are significant advantages from the general security point of view of the United States to have these relationships between the armed forces within Latin America with outside governments concentrated with the United States if that is

---

[23] *Hearings on Foreign Assistance and Related Agencies 1967*, House Appropriations Committee, p. 801.

[24] *Hearings on Foreign Assistance Act of 1964*, House Foreign Affairs Committee, Part III, p. 417.

[25] *Hearings on Foreign Assistance Appropriations for 1964*, Senate Appropriations Committee, p. 741.

[26] *Hearings on Foreign Assistance Act of 1964*, House Foreign Affairs Committee, Part III, p. 413.

[27] *New York Herald Tribune*, October 6, 1963.

possible." [28]   Indeed, "the support our political representatives abroad and our Secretary of State derive from this military assistance program is not well recognized by our public but it is very great indeed. I think the support it has given our military representatives is very great indeed. Whether that aid is invariably used in our interest is perhaps open to question. I think it is," said Secretary McNamara.[29]

A public affairs adviser of the Alliance for Progress urged Americans to remember than "with very few exceptions the traditional corrupt strongman type is being replaced by younger army men who are beginning to develop a civic consciousness." Sometimes of course it was hard to establish that this was a change for the better. For, when Assistant Secretary of State Martin boasted that "in most cases the top people in the Latin American military have now had some form of training in U.S. schools of one sort or another," [30] the press insisted on playing up the fact that the leadership at the palace revolt in Lima had graduated from the Ranger School at Fort Benning; that the senior membership of the Ecuadorean junta had graduated from the Navy's school at Monterrey; that the Dominican leaders' training had been at the Army School in the Panama Canal Zone and the Armor School at Fort Knox; that the Honduran junta leadership had been trained at U.S. Air Force bases; that the chief-of-staff to the Guatemalan junta leader had been trained by the Air Force; and so on. This suggested that training might be helping orient an influential group toward the United States but that the indoctrination with respect to support of legally constituted governments was falling far short of target, despite the "civic consciousness" of the new non-traditional military men.

The notion of a change in the character of the military was not limited to official circles. For instance, an extremely able journalist wrote in *The Spectator* early in 1963:

> "Latin American generals and colonels are usually portrayed in the likeness of Mexican bandits, with curling mustachios, unshaven chins and ill-fitting uniforms hung about with bandoliers or else in gold-

---

[28] *Hearings on S. 2859,* Senate Foreign Relations Committee, p. 539.

[29] *Hearings on Foreign Assistance and Related Agencies Appropriations 1967,* House Appropriations Committee, p. 579.

[30] *Hearings on Department of State Appropriation for 1964,* House Appropriations Committee, p. 417.

braided creations bedecked with medals. . . . In fact, they are staid professionals in khaki. . . . Nor do Latin American armies intervene in politics just for amusement or because they have been bribed by one faction to oust another The men who freed Latin America from Spain were soldiers and not politicians, and their successors regard themselves as the guardians of the spirit of their constitutions against the legalistic wiles of the civilian politicians, many of whom are in fact law graduates. . . . Today this ad hoc balance of forces has become anachronistic; in the highly complicated circumstances of the twentieth century it is impossible for an exasperated general to march on a capital and take over the government as though it were a parish council. The soldiers in general have realized this. . . . Nowadays a budding revolutionary is less likely to be found in the barracks or the hacienda than in the high school or the university." [31]

Again, an astute observer of Latin American affairs for the distinguished liberal journal *The New Leader* wrote that "behind the traditional rhetoric binding us to the conception that all military coups are *necessarily* undemocratic lies the possibility, still to be seriously examined in the United States, that the armed forces in Latin America (which differ widely in composition and function from ours) may be as reformist as the best democrats. They may be as anxious to preserve legality as the most juridical patriots and yet be determined to prevent the interests of their countries from deteriorating into petty partisanship, jockeying for position, corruption and hunger for power." [32] There was a growing inclination to broaden the responsibility beyond the military for what was happening. As he was going down to defeat, President Bosch noted: "The military do not conspire, unless civilian politicians urge them to do so. A conspiracy has been under way, but the military personnel are not responsible for it. Those who want power at any cost in this country wanted to use military officers as a stepping stone to seize it." And an organization which could claim to be less biased, the International Commission of Jurists, has concluded that the role in the coup of the "liberal elements of society, the technicians, the businessmen, and the large landowners" was perhaps greater than that of the military.[33] Bosch, seemingly providing an answer to the Pentagon's thesis that the military rarely step in "without being called on" to do so, wrote:

---

[31] J. Halcro Ferguson, "The Image of Latin America," *The Spectator*, January 11, 1963.

[32] August 6, 1962.

[33] *Bulletin*, December 1963, p. 17.

"In the majority of Latin American countries the military chiefs represent the proverbial gun in the hands of a child. . . . The existence of these oligarchies would not represent a mortal danger for democracy in Latin America if they did not have at their disposal armed forces supplied by irresponsible military chieftains who have no political education and who for that very reason are incapable of realizing where they are leading their own people's destiny." [34]

A fellow-deposed President, Ydigoras Fuentes of Guatemala, was unwilling to pay tribute to the "new" attitude of the Latin military: "The military in many Latin American countries are basically revolutionary, narrow-minded and authoritarian in character." And a fellow-countryman on whom the Central Intelligence Agency had relied for training areas in Guatemala for the Bay of Pigs disaster protested that there will never be any order "if every little man in uniform can disrupt a legal government by force of arms." [35]

Unfortunately "the fundamental objective of the Alliance for Progress security programs," as defined to the Congress, namely, "a Latin American leadership dedicated to the tasks of preserving democratic constitutional government and maintaining internal security" was defeated too many times in the five years to create any credence for the argument that the military are "strong believers in the democratic system." On the pretext of saving the country they had all too often overthrown constitutional governments by unconstitutional means. And the *Times* (London) was excusably pessimistic as we noted when it commented that "the whole story is a melancholy repetition of a common theme in Latin America—the refusal of the army and the bourgeoisie to work with a populist movement towards real reform." Secretary of State Rusk had early conceded that "the line between internal security of democratic and constitutional government on the one side and the abuse of military power on the other is a very difficult line to draw." [36] And clearly "the better trained and better equipped the military force is to deal with internal security, the better trained it is to seize domestic power." [37] The experience of five years offered up dismal proof of that thesis.

---

[34] *The New Leader,* October 14, 1963.

[35] *The Evening Star* (Washington), October 15, 1964.

[36] *Hearings on H.R. 5490,* Senate Appropriations Committee, p. 20.

[37] *Hearings on H.R. 13175,* Senate Appropriations Committee, p. 310.

If there was a "new" military in Latin America, it had to be demonstrated in two ways: (1) Respect for constitutional government. (2) A willingness to adjust military expenditures to the country's needs. In five years there was no demonstration of this kind. Nowhere were the Latin American military men willing to surrender to the fact that "in the context of the Latin American situation today, true military professionalism means among other things the recognition by the military of the real needs and demands of the people."[38] Since they rejected his thesis that "no amount of arms can assure Latin America of freedom and security while the resources are being dissipated in the fashion of the military budgets," they reinforced the fear expressed by Senator Humphrey for consequent failure of the Alliance for Progress.

This still left the U.S. Executive branch with the task of convincing the Congress that military aid is both politically and economically sound. Secretary McNamara refused to concede any inconsistency in continuing a high level of military assistance to a country that will not undertake sufficient self-help measures to qualify for economic development because "by this military assistance we are able to substitute *our* expenditures for *theirs* for military purposes." In other words, given the Latin Americans' refusal to make the basic decisions to reduce waste incident to their military establishments, the Pentagon felt that the alternative to U.S. military aid was for the Latins to spend even more of their *own* funds on military waste. To Congressman Cohelan's intelligent question: How do you justify any support (military) for a country where this becomes a pressure against their economic allocation of resources?" The Pentagon answered: *"They* have the last word on it and it is a fact of life we have to live with." Congressman Long rejected this: "No, *we* have the last word on whether we give them the money. If we think they have a military program which does not make any sense, we do not have to give them any money."[39] Here again was the supreme dilemma of the Alliance for Progress. Were we participants in a program with clearly defined goals? Or were we a prisoner of it? Did we further those goals by continuing to participate without parallel efforts on the other end or did we doom the goals by such participation? The

---

[38] Teodoro Moscoso's speech at Fort Amador, previously cited.

[39] *Hearings on Foreign Assistance and Related Agencies Appropriations 1967,* House Appropriations Committee, p. 804.

bureaucracy clearly was not inclined to yield the power that was daily building from the billion a year out of Washington and from the potential boost in the pace which its bureaucratic propagandists could hope to achieve. Yet in terms of public policy, in terms of alternative uses of U.S. resources, the question was very pertinent and the answer by no means as simple as the vested interests in the Alliance made it out to be.

On the political side, the Pentagon joined with the State Department to challenge the belief that the military assistance programs were detrimental to constitutional government. "We live," the Pentagon testified, "in an era of unscheduled or illegal changes of government. But we are also aware that within new and struggling nations the military leadership of these countries are frequently forced to act to prevent complete chaos, particularly when civil institutions collapse, the public loses confidence in the lawful regime, and the political process breaks down into violence and extremism. . . . Frequently their military establishments are the only cohesive elements with the power to preserve their nations as political entities and to provide temporary stability and security to permit the growth of responsible civil institutions. . . . The evidence hardly substantiates the view that U.S. military assistance is a cause or correlates with military coups." [40] Surveying the world picture of political violence over eight years, it found the true cause of instability to be relative economic status and the newness of nations. "Only seven percent of the rich nations had experienced internal conflicts on their own territory while 87% of the very poor nations had suffered such conflicts."

"It is obvious," the Department of Defense explained, "that a source that contributes only about six percent of military equipment and training in this area does not enable a military force to mount a revolution that it cannot mount with the men and equipment supplied by the other 94% of the budget." Conceding the force of this argument, and the likelihood that the disrespect for constitutional government would have been present even without military aid, it needed also to be pinpointed out however that the relative narrowness of U.S. military aid had to be analyzed in terms of the opposition, that is to say, there were cases in which $900 of U.S. arms and training per member of the armed forces confronted

---

[40] *Ibid.*, p. 529.

a population whose per-capita gross national product might be $200 or less. In these terms, even the limited aid became impressive.

Then, as "final evidence that resort to military rule may only be a phase characteristic of this era through which nations of lesser developed regions under stress may pass," the Pentagon offered up the "facts" on military government in Latin America, namely, that only 27% of the Latin American governments were headed by military men in 1957-66 compared with 28.7% in 1917-27 and 49.0% in 1937-47. (See Table XV). "It is too bad," Deputy

Table XV

PERCENT OF LATIN AMERICAN GOVERNMENTS WITH MILITARY MEN AS PRESIDENT OR HEAD OF STATE

1917 - 1927	28.7%
1927 - 1937	38.5
1937 - 1947	49.0
1947 - 1957	45.5
1957 - 1966	27.0

Source: *Hearings on Foreign Assistance and Related Agencies Appropriations for 1967,* House Appropriations Subcommittee, p. 529.

Assistant Secretary of Defense Frank Sloan deplored, "that the public is not aware of a pretty well known statistic and that is that the revolutions occurred at the same rate before there was ever a U.S. military assistance program down there as they do now." [41] For, "there have been fewer coups in the fifteen years since military assistance has been there than in the fifteen years before. From that we can draw at least the deduction that military assistance is not causing them." [42] (This was admittedly a rather negative appraisal of benefits from a program costing around three-quarters of a billion in grants). See Table XVI.

At a time when roughly half of the area's population was suffering under military rule, it would have been hard to find a less

[41] *Hearings on Foreign Assistance for 1964,* Senate Appropriations Committee, p. 741.

[42] *Hearings on Foreign Operations Appropriations for 1965,* House Appropriations Committee, Part I, p. 505.

Table XVI

MILITARY ASSISTANCE GRANT AID PROGRAMS,
CUMULATIVE, 1950 - 1966

In millions of dollars

Latin America	658.4	Guatemala	11.3
Argentina	38.2	Haiti	3.2
Bolivia	15.8	Honduras	5.5
Brazil	205.8	Jamaica	.8
Chile	88.8	Mexico	1.5
Colombia	75.5	Nicaragua	9.0
Costa Rica	2.2	Panama	2.1
Cuba	10.6	Paraguay	5.3
Dominican Republic	15.4	Peru	83.4
Ecuador	35.0	Uruguay	37.7
El Salvador	5.2	Venezuela	6.1

Source: *Hearings on Foreign Assistance and Related Agencies Appropriations,* House Appropriations Committee, p. 676. There are no satisfactory data on military aid to Latin America. Data issued by Department of Commerce and the Department of Defense differ widely. The National Advisory Council on International Monetary and Financial Problems shows calendar year 1961, 2, 3, 4, 5 military equipment and supplies furnished Latin America as follows: $133 million, $74 million, $63 million, $54 million, $59 million. And 1945-58 as $430 million.

meaningful answer to the charges that Senator Morse among others was making, namely, that "the military coups . . . fed by our military aid . . . are destroying the objectives of the Alliance for Progress in country after country. . . . The whole rationale that our military aid tends to teach civilians control of the military and to interest them in civic action has been totally refuted by events. It was bad enough when these coups occurred in the small nations of Central America. Now they have engulfed Brazil and Argentina. They are fed by our military aid and they are destroying the objectives of the Alliance for Progress." [43]

This is not to say that the almost exclusive emphasis on the U.S. military aid program as the cause of political instability was justified on the part of the many Congressmen who stressed this single fact. In fact, such an attitude only served to divert attention

[43] *Report of the Senate Foreign Relations Committee on S. 3583,* "Military Assistance and Sales Act," pp. 18-19.

from the real focus of policy decision as it affected the Alliance for Progress:

(1) The area was unwilling to make any serious effort to reduce the waste incident to military establishments that absorbed excessive portions of the national resources.

(2) There was no point in challenging the degree to which this waste was "excessive." If the billion dollars per year U.S. commitment to the Alliance had validity as the key to the goals of the Alliance, as the Latin Americans insisted it had, then it did not make sense to scoff at the "petty scope" of military expenditures. For, savings on a $1.6 billion annual outlay must be meaningful too if a billion dollars is so vastly important. In fact, even if, as the State Department claimed, the equipment outlay ran only $0.2 billion out of the $1.6 billion military budgets, this figured importantly for an area where foreign exchange is so limited and a billion in external commitments is termed so vital.

(3) Even with the maximum mobilization of its resources, the task of achieving the social and economic objectives of the Alliance promised to be strenuous in the extreme. Thus, any waste of the magnitude envisaged as present in the $1.6 billion outlay *did* have meaning.

(4) Given the concept that external assistance is at best limited, and all proponents of the Alliance agree on this, it made no sense to argue that at least part of the waste is being carried by the U.S. Treasury, for this meant merely a diversion of limited external resources from the central task. For instance, it was silly to argue when Chile launched its purchasing program for sophisticated aircraft in 1966 that since so much money was being donated to Chile through loose devices permitting diversion of funds to uneconomic expenditure in Europe, the deal for the planes still would represent *only* two months of donations and thus could be ignored. This confused the goals of the Alliance completely.

(5) The experience with Latin America's unwillingness to adopt a mystique which would comprehend the need for policies geared to the objectives of the Alliance set up a guideline for U.S. choices of policy alternatives.[44] It was imperative that the U.S. Executive,

---

[44] There were definitely alternatives. For instance, Vice-President Humphrey was at the time proclaiming that once the Viet Nam war is over, he

instead of concealing this fact lest an informed Congress act against further exfoliation of the bureaucratic establishment, face up frankly and boldly to the situation.

After five years the issue was clearly joined. The Latin American nations were independent countries. They quite correctly cherished their capacity to make their own political and economic decisions. If they were determined to make decisions inimical to the goals of the Alliance, this was their privilege. For the United States, however, there was equal capacity to make *our* decision, and in a democratic country an obligation on the part of the Executive not to conceal the facts nor to function in panic and seek to maintain a state of emergency for generations for policy options that had simply soured.

There was of course another school of thought which believed in U.S. leverage, that the United States could force Latin America to act as the U.S. saw fit in its infinite wisdom to designate as the optimum course of policy for Latin America. Senator Kennedy was of this school: When he belatedly (as usual) "discovered" the interest in sophisticated military equipment from Europe, he demanded that the U.S. issue a warning that any such purchases would be followed by parallel cuts in U.S. aid to the offending countries.[45] The State Department long ago had learned that the leverage which the U.S. has for such interference in Latin American decisions was very limited. As Assistant Secretary of State Martin once put it, even "in defense of legally constituted regimes U.S. leverage is "sometimes great but sometimes small." [46] And the early years of the Kennedy Administration had proven the point well. It was dangerous, after five years, still to be arguing that the goals of the Alliance could be reached by exercise of such leverage as long as Latin America itself was not prepared to make the policy decisions necessary for success of such a program.

---

would ask Americans to spend "the same amount to build a better America." Obviously, if efforts to build a better Latin America were failing for want of suitable response from the beneficiaries, sound public policy might warrant a diversion of the effort to the U.S.

[45] Senator Kennedy said: "I believe we must act now to discontinue sales of these unnecessary arms to Latin America, and if they persist in seeking arms elsewhere, wasting their own resources and depriving their own people, then we should take account of this waste in determining the amount of our own economic aid to them."

[46] *New York Herald Tribune,* October 6, 1963.

The problem of the starving jet set was not in process of solution. A study of the House Banking and Currency Committee put it well when it went into Colombia after five years of the Alliance to examine the situation: "In Cali the delegation observed a splendid air force academy on one side of the highway, with a vast slum on the other side of the highway. One wonders at the allocation of resources." [47]

---

[47] "Food for Progress in Latin America," Report of Subcommittee on International Finance, House Banking and Currency Committee, February 8, 1967.

Chapter VII
Private Investment at Public Risk

Without at least lip service to the role of U.S. private investment in Latin American development, it would have been impossible to clear the Alliance for Progress appropriations through the Congress. No one, however, could have anticipated that in five years the Alliance would have become for a large segment of the business community a substantial device for profiteering at public risk.

Without comprehension that at best the available resources—public and private together—must be badly strained to meet the goals of the Alliance, and that accordingly the maximum utilization and effectiveness of private foreign investment would be needed to complement the pledged governmental assistance, the Latin Americans could not possibly have been warranted in conceiving the goals to be realistic. No one, however, could have anticipated that the Latin Americans would simultaneously (1) establish an incompatible goal, largely political, that doomed this phase of the Alliance, and (2) in implementation thereof, permit the diversion of the public resources of the Alliance to provide an immense windfall for private investors already functioning in the area.

The piety of the initial presentation of the role of U.S. business could not be challenged:

First, private foreign capital must play a decisive role in realization of the goals. Treasury Secretary Dillon left no doubt of this: "The goal of two and one-half percent yearly increase in per-capita economic growth cannot be achieved without more private investment." [1] President Kennedy warned that "it is impossible for us to supply all the funds which are necessary for the development of Latin America. They must come through private sources. If local capital and American capital dry up, then all our hopes of a decade

---

[1] Speech in Buenos Aires, April 25, 1962.

of development in Latin America will be gone." [2]   Fowler Hamilton, head of the Agency for International Development, told the House Foreign Affairs Committee that "there will *have* to be a climate in the area that will attract foreign capital and keep domestic capital at home." [3]

It should perhaps be noted immediately that no one faced up to the policy decisions that would follow if the flow of private capital *failed* to materialize and if domestic capital continued to flee the area for reasons attributable to public policy in Latin America. What then? Would the Executive still be justified in demanding the billion dollars per year for what by its own definition had become goals that could not be achieved? The pledge established with the Charter of Punta del Este was after all contingent on certain performance on the part of the Latin Americans. What if that performance was not forthcoming? Would non-performance be ignored? Would there be intervention to compel performance? Reality in decision making had no place in Washington as long as rhetoric was the sole stock in trade.

Second, any attempt to use the donations or concealed donations of the Alliance for Progress to replace existing private investments or prospective private investments would seriously and perhaps fatally damage the capacity to meet the goals of the Alliance for which resources were already so limited. The State Department put it plainly: "When a government expropriates existing resources or uses its own funds to buy out existing operations rather than using these funds to create new wealth, new jobs and new taxpayers and to increase productivity, this action appears to be a step backward in the mobilization of all available resources for the success of the Alliance for Progress." [4]   Asst. Secretary of State Martin in this laudable economic analysis chose to take the argument forward: "We would also have the view," he said, "that there are some circumstances in which, while any government has the legal right to take property with just conpensation, it may or may not be a wise thing for the government to do and we would hold ourselves free

---

[2] Statement of May 9, 1962. See *Congressional Record,* May 25, 1962.

[3] *Hearings on Foreign Assistance Act of 1962,* House Foreign Affairs Committee, Part I, p. 30.

[4] Issued by Press Officer, carried by wire services February 17.

to discuss the question with them as to the wisdom from a policy standpoint." [5]

Again it is well to ask immediately: If "we" discussed it with the Latins and "they" rejected the U.S. view on optimum use of resources, what then? Would the Department of State still insist that the U.S. commitment of a billion per year was binding? Would it indeed demand from the Congress even larger commitments because the Latin American policy decisions were making it impossible to do the job with the prior level? Again, this was too realistic a question to tempt the "novice administration."

Third, the Department of State rejected the suggestion that assistance be cut off by legislative mandate to countries expropriating property of U.S. citizens without fair compensation. In a sense this answered the previous question, for if the Department was unwilling to discourage outright theft of property, it was unlikely to protest the simple misuse of U.S. government resources. The Department explained its position: Such action, the cutoff, would make it appear that "our assistance programs are substantially motivated by a desire to protect U.S. private investment and that they are in effect tools of U.S. capital." [6] More, "a vital and often crucial element of U.S. foreign policy would be placed at the mercy of one unreasonable action by a foreign official, perhaps not even a member of the national government of that country. There are often elements within a country not representative of the sentiments of the country as a whole and hostile to the United States that may appear to bring about an inadequately compensated expropriation in any individual case. Generally these are the very elements whose influence and power will be undermined if our aid program succeeds in promoting economic and social progress, and therefore they seek every opportunity to obstruct the effective implementation of that program. Providing for automatic termination or reduction of aid might well encourage them to attempt such expropriations."

Again, it suggested that such a cutoff might actually retard re-

---

[5] *Hearings on Nomination,* Senate Foreign Relations Committee. (Taken from transcript).

[6] The State Department's position, from which the quotations are taken, was outlined in a statement submitted to the Senate Foreign Relations Committee and reprinted in *Hearings on S. 2996,* pp. 557-558.

forms as for instance in connection with land reform requiring expropriation of estates owned by U.S. nationals. "The danger is that Latin American governments might avoid this type of reform, even though they intend to provide fair compensation, through fear that the United States would unilaterally determine the compensation inadequate or the procedures unfair and hence cut off all aid." Moreover, the cutoff policy "may well commit the whole policy into the hands of one intransigent American citizen whose actions could provoke expropriation and whose obstinacy could prevent a reasonable settlement. It may be hard for the United States to make a proper appraisal of his claims." And the reasonableness of compensation always being a difficult matter, "our public review of another country's court decision in a private case would be viewed as unwarranted interference in its internal affairs and would violate our own principle of the rule of law." Finally, and this as an extremely important statement, "in the administration of the program, AID will judge the entire use of a country's resources. If a particular country is dissipating its major resources in unproductive action such as the use of its foreign exchange to compensate for expropriated property, the aid given to such a country by the United States will reflect this fact."

Fourth, the Department was already on record with its distaste for the making of a "quick killing" by any company in Latin America. The concept of making a quick killing as a result of the incompetence or corruptness of a Latin regime in the granting of concessions was out of date, in the official Department position. During the previous administration Senator Morse had asked whether American oil companies are allowed "to go ahead without any control by the State Department? Can investors do anything they want to in South American countries by way of investment, even though that investment may result in subsequent exploitation and trouble to the State Department, trouble to our government conceivably, and great loss to the taxpayers of our country?" And the State Department had replied: "If ever it became clear that they (the corporations) were engaged in a policy which was contrary to their interest *and therefore to the interests of the United States Government,* I think we would undertake to so advise them." [7] As an added assurance it noted that the State

---

[7] *Hearings on Nomination of Roy R. Rubottom, Jr.,* Senate Foreign Relations Committee, pp. 60-64. (June 10, 1957).

Department is usually "familiar with the broad contract under which they do business," so that it is equipped to make a judgment on the acceptability of a business deal in terms of public policy. The implication that a policy contrary to the interest of Standard Oil would automatically be contrary to the interest of the United States (what's good for Standard Oil is good for the United States, to paraphrase an old refrain of the same administration) was startling but less revealing than the failure to say that a contract contrary to the interest of the United States must prompt a protest by the State Department regardless of the benefits that the company might think it offered to itself through quick exploitation of the foreign dictatorship or the incompetent regime that permitted such a concession to be written. In fairness, it is perhaps best to concede the mental lapse prompting the Assistant Secretary's statement, for it was by then generally understood that the Department of State had come to realize the menace of the quick "killings" that had featured the days of dollar diplomacy.

Veteran analysts of the Latin American scene might have been pardoned if they viewed with skepticism the policy on private investment offered up in support of the Alliance for Progress. After, all, the official philosopher of the Kennedy regime had already pontificated that "our mistake in the 1950s was to rely on private investment by the United States." [8] And Hubert Humphrey, before he became Vice-President, had already concluded that the standards of the American copper companies in Chile were faulty,[9] and again that jail rather than a rule of law is what ought to confront the corporations whether local or foreign which performed in such a fashion that standards of living continued to be low in Bolivia. When Bolivia had been put on the U.S. dole as a result of expropriation and total disaster to mining activity under the management of the expropriators, Senator Humphrey insisted that "this country ought to look into situations whereby the people of a country are exploited and the U.S. is forced to pour in millions of

---

[8] Arthur Schlesinger Jr., quoted in AP dispatch August 15, 1964, from Kent, Ohio. (Speech on campus of Kent University).

[9] Statement of August 18, 1961. Humphrey had apparently received two (repeat) two letters from constituents not identified in his speech. In the absence of any serious information of his own on the subject, this sufficed for such a statesman to say for wide dissemination in Chile: "I am not too happy about the American activities in the copper mines in Chile. . . . I think they should have better standards."

dollars. Expropriation is not enough. . . . In every case there is always a slick operator who has exploited everybody until the country is in an uproar and the taxpayers here have to bail them out. . . . It is the same trick all the time. . . . Name any country you want where you find trouble and somebody has made money out of the people. I am for American capital and other capital going into these countries. However, I am not for having people go in under our sponsorship and take out everything they can. After they have created revolution and hardship we are forced to bail out the country and they get away with it." Now he moved into high gear: "I think these people ought to be in jail. It is the same old trick all the time. They exploit everybody. . . . I hope they (the expropriated companies) haven't gotten a nickel back. We have the wrong people in jail. Everytime we hear of something that has gone wrong, the people behind it are at the French Riviera living off the fat of the land. If it is a Delaware corporation that means we are in it too. I want to know why our government has not looked into this." [10]

One demonstration of why our government has not looked into this was that in five years the integrity of the pious position so nicely put forth by the State Department to buy support for the Alliance for Progress had totally eroded. Within five years, the climate of investment had been so clouded by acts of Latin America that Washington began to offer more and more inducements to corporations as if to assume all the risks of foreign investments and leave only the profit for the corporation, all lest the public and the Congress take at face value the original thesis, as they understood it, that unless a suitable climate of investment is provided by Latin America, all bets are off, the goals cannot be reached, and the pledge of a billion dollars per year might become inoperative. In five years the appropriations for the Alliance for Progress had become a source of funds to compensate for evacuation of bad investments by American corporations which had milked the scene of all they could contemplate and now preferred to be given back their chips to play in some other form or other area. In five years the State Department had decided that cutting off assistance by legislature mandate was a proper threat because there were devices by which the threat could be reconciled with a

---

[10] *Hearings on the Mutual Security Act of 1956*, Senate Foreign Relations Committee, pp. 300-301.

private understanding with the Latin Americans so that in effect the Alliance would be used to pay for the expropriated properties and the criticism of the Congress thus blocked and the legislative mandate nullified. In five years the State Department decided that whatever was good for American companies in the short-run exploitative sense was good for the United States and it put U.S. government money behind the worst concessionary activity that had been seen in many a generation in U.S. policy.

Secretary of State Rusk had brought into the language of the Alliance the term "dollar diplomacy — modern style" in a revival of an odious term that had been thought permanently banned from the lexicon of inter-American relations. What was the "modern style"?

Direct investment in Latin America had always represented a free choice on the part of the investor. He might go into automobile production or operation of tramways or marketing of toothpaste or assembly of farm equipment or any other field. It was a free choice. When his choice proved wise, the profits could be very large and the gratification of the investor great. When his choice proved unwise, he did what any investor at home did — he suffered. Now dollar diplomacy — modern style offered an alternative. When a corporation had milked the scene to what seemed to be the maximum degree and there was no longer a prospect of satisfactory earnings, the State Department offered up a new course of action, courtesy of the unsuspecting U.S. taxpayer, namely, let the company's properties be nationalized by the Latin American government on a pledge by the U.S. government that sufficient donations would be forthcoming to make the properties in a sense the gift of the United States to the country, while the company bailed out with unexpected glee at the recovery of what seemed to be a hopelessly lost investment. In fact, to sweeten the pot, the United States encouraged especially generous treatment of the companies seeking to be bailed out, so that characteristically the corporations bailed out during the five years received better terms than would have been forthcoming if the Latin American country had been faced with use of its own funds for the purpose. And always, in this modern style dollar diplomacy there was the gimmick — unless the corporations were well and even overgenerously treated, there might be a diminution of the flow of resources from the Alliance pot.

It should be noted that this was totally unwarranted treatment of the private investor who moved to the foreign country of his own volition eager for the profits which he found to be potentially greater than alternative domestic outlets for his funds. The U.S. taxpayer had no obligation to sweeten the pot for such an investor. The U.S. taxpayer had no obligation to bail out such an investor once the investment soured. But the State Department implemented policy to this end because it seemed to fit with a political objective of the Latin Americans which was totally contrary to the goals of the Alliance. The disaffection with direct investments in Latin America was of long standing. Whether it was the mineral and petroleum industries whose huge profits often concealed the immense risks that had to be assumed, risks that the domestic investor or his government had been unwilling or unable to assume, or the public utility industries which had become a political issue over the matter of suitable rates and profits, Latin America in general was more keenly attuned to the desirability of ousting the foreign investor than it was to the thesis of the Alliance, namely, that in a capital-short area every dollar possible must be mobilized — public and private as well — and that any drainage to acquire existing physical facilities helps to doom achievement of the Alliance goals.

The Latin Americans saw profit remittances to the United States running three times as large as the target of new direct investment (which had never been reached) and running in fact eight or nine times as large as the actual direct investment flow during the five years of the Alliance, and concluded that this was an intolerable situation. This was "decapitalization," they argued ignorantly, failing to understand the contribution of direct investment to modernization of the productive mechanism of the countries, to expansion of exports and employment and public revenues and to the raising of the standards of living.

It must in fairness be remembered that seven percent of the economic activity of the area was already in the hands of foreigners, according to the Commerce Committee for the Alliance for Progress, which had seized on the coolness of the area to private investment to demand of the United States Government a series of measures and special assistance consistent with the newly adopted

principle of *private investment at public risk*.[11]   After all, even
in Canada, a wise Finance Minister was warning his country:

> "If we mean business, Canada must gradually take whatever steps are
> necessary, even if such steps are not popular in all circles, to regain
> a greater measure of control over her own economic affairs, including
> the policy decisions of Canadian corporations.   If we do not do this,
> Canadians may well wake up some day, and perhaps sooner than they
> think, and find that they have lost control not only of their economic
> destiny but of their political destiny as well."

If a sober intelligent Canadian official, analyzing his country's
situation without the emotion and political bias and concern for the
vote-catching potential such as the Latins were so often accused of,
could reach such a conclusion, was it at all surprising that the
Latins should be fearing the ultimate loss of control of their economic and political destiny?   In the dream world whence the Alliance had sprung, there was no place for such awkward facts or even
for technicians who might offer up such facts.   What if a Latin
American country deliberately chose a slower pace of development
as a result of a study of alternatives that indicated that the faster

---

[11] COMAP consisted of a group of businessmen set up to make recommendations to the U.S. Government on ways and means of stimulating
private investment.   It concluded in 1963 that "there is little hope for
creating the kind of climate that U.S. investors want in Latin America
without *increasing* substantially the amount of assistance which is being
extended, and *even then* it is unlikely that normal conditions attractive to
foreign capital can be created for a number of years."   It then seized the
opportunity to make another grab: it recommended special tax incentives,
special government loans to private investors, and other preferential treatment in keeping with the principle of private investment at public risk.
Report of the Commerce Committee for the Alliance for Progress
(COMAP), "Proposals to improve the flow of U.S. private investment to
Latin America" (Washington, Department of Commerce, March 1963),
p. 22.
   This report was quickly supplemented by an additional report by three
members of the Committee (Rockefeller, Collado, Wriston) which recommended that "the U.S. not provide aid in such a way as to finance the expropriation of privately owned companies in any field of endeavor," but
immediately nullified this by asking for "truly reasonable (sic) indemnification where nationalization has taken place" whether or not the capacity
to finance such purchases exists.   *A Reappraisal of the Alliance for Progress,* memorandum signed by Emilio G. Collado, (Standard Oil Company
of New Jersey), David Rockefeller (Chase Manhattan Bank), and Walter
B. Wriston (First National City Bank).

pace might involve loss of control over its economic and/or political destiny in a measure repugnant to the national sentiment?

On the part of the United States, the goals of the Alliance essentially having been rejected in favor of a more acceptable political objective in Latin America, the State Department had the choice of conceding that the billion dollar per year commitment no longer promised to mobilize the essential policy decisions which together had been held out to make likely the realization of the goals of the Alliance, or of converting by fraud the whole operation into a bailout affair for U.S. investors by a form of dollar diplomacy. The Alliance became a method of underwriting expropriations by an offer to finance the payoff for properties which the confiscating nation had no capacity to finance. This was a desperate effort to prevent the Congress of the United States from placing the Alliance for Progress in its proper proportions, a bureaucracy's effort to assure itself of the support of a powerful pressure group at the expense of other elements of the U.S. community.

It should not be thought that this was a minor incident in magnitude. In a period when $4 billion in booty was being disbursed to Latin America and $5.6 billion authorized, the State Department underwrote a bailout of around a half billion dollars in public utility properties and a Chilean adventure in mixed ownership of the copper industry which promised to divert a quarter billion or more to ends wholly inconsistent with realization of the goals of the Alliance. The magnitudes *were* great. And if there was any "magic" in the figure selected as the minimum capital inflow for the great objective, the new policy obviously doomed it.

There had of course been a buildup to the new policy. When at the outset of the Bolivian Revolution the mining properties were expropriated without capacity or serious intent to compensate adequately for them, a shift in U.S. policy, began, in the sense that for the first time a Latin American country was *rewarded* for confiscating private properties, by being allocated hundreds of millions of dollars in a futile effort to halt the damage to the economy and the standard of living that had occurred as a result of the confiscation. No serious effort to enforce just prompt and effective compensation was made by the State Department. And in a particularly stupid interpretation of U.S. interest, the State Department hammered on the new thesis that expropriation and confis-

cation were really out-dated concepts because the U.S. Government
was in many countries prepared to issue guarantees or insurance
against expropriation and thus prepared to burden the U.S. taxpayer any time that confiscation occurs.

There followed on the Bolivian example the expropriation of
in excess of one billion dollars worth of property of U.S. nationals
in Cuba, all without compensation. Then in February 1962, the
real test of policy occurred. On February 16, 1962 a decree was
issued by the governor of the State of Rio Grande do Sul (Brazil)
expropriating all the property of International Telephone and
Telegraph Corporation in that state. Bolivia after all had been
a small unimportant country with investments of relatively piddling proportions. Cuba, after all, represented a triumph of international communism and as such stood apart from the rule of
law governing the conduct of civilized nations. But Brazil was
big, big business, the cornerstone of the Alliance, the great friend
on whom the United States had in this century counted in war and
peace as its mainstay until the decision was made to shift emphasis
to Argentina in appreciation of the concessions Frondizi had
granted for entry of some $100 million of petroleum money,
partly in a manner and on terms inconsistent with Argentine law
and the Argentine constitution. Brazil's traditionally attractive
climate of investment had attracted perhaps the widest array of
American corporations ever to venture into a single Latin American
country and in an investment magnitude of truly important proportions. Now an expropriation had occurred. To an investing
community already made jittery by the uncertainties of the "Mexi-
canization" program of the Mexican Government, by the uneven-
ness of the Chilean Government's receptivity to major new investments, and by its tendency to squeeze profit margins by "creeping"
or "silent" expropriation, by the Cuban disaster, by the lessons of
the Bolivian experience, and by the great flight of Latin American
capital from Latin America, Governor Brizola's action in taking the
I.T.&T. property became decisive to the process of policy determination.[12] Now the issue was joined.

----

[12] The memorandum handed the Senate Foreign Relations Committee by
the State Department (*Hearings on S. 2996*, p. 417) noted:
  "The controversy is one of long standing. The company has been
  operating without a concession since 1953 and has been hard pressed
  to maintain or expand its operations because of the existing rate struc-

Brizola himself rather cutely said his expropriation was "a *favorable* movement for the Alliance for Progress. We have two problems holding back our programs, one the latifundistas and the other the foreign economic groups. Unless we get rid of these groups the Alliance will not work: they will eat all the dollars provided for aid and in less than ten years if these problem groups remain, all the dollars will be back in the United States." [13]

The State Department now had to respond to a Congress aroused by a vigorous and almost shameful public-relations campaign conducted by the company.[14]   It was ready with the ordinary replies:

---

ture. Public utility rates are set at a rate not exceeding a stipulated percentage of the company's capital investment and the state government has not permitted any significant change in rates since 1954. In 1959 the company approached the state government with an offer to invest $40 million in new facilities if it could obtain rate increases. This offer was not accepted and in 1960 the state government formed its own telephone company and requested I.T.&T. to participate. At that time, I.T.&T.'s representative in Brazil and officials of the state reached agreement on a valuation of the equivalent of $7.3 million for the property. However, this figure was not accepted by the governor of the state who considered it too high, and by I.T.&T. which considered it too low. The company also rejected participation in the proposed mixed company until terms of the proposed participation were made more clear. The long controversy culminated in the issuance on February 16, 1962, of a decree by the governor expropriating all the property of I.T.&T. in the state."

[13] AP dispatch out of Porto Alegre, February 20, 1962.

[14] The company launched a public-relations campaign in the U.S. and a campaign on Capitol Hill which badly besmirched Brazil and helped drain the reservoir of good will that the country had built up over the years in this country by fine cooperation in war and peace. It prevailed on the Congress to legislate that assistance would be cut off if any country seized property without just prompt and effective compensation. Pressure on Brazil from the U.S. Embassy was extreme and finally the Attorney General speaking for the White House intervened to prevail on Brazil to settle lest aid be cut off and with the understanding that aid would be so gratifying in amount that it would more than compensate for the drain by the company. After this damaging incident, the company had the nerve to declare breezily: "The expropriation in Brazil was exaggerated out of all proportion to what was seized — a $7.3 million company that was running in the red!"

The conduct of the company merited attention later when it proposed merger with American Broadcasting Company. Certain members of the Federal Communications Commission reminded their colleagues that the company is entangled in foreign policy and may some day find it profitable

"Fair compensation to American citizens is the absolute minimum.[15]
... We do not recognize the right of another government to con-
fiscate the property of American citizens without compensation."[16]
Then it reminded the Congress that this was in part a case of "dirty
hands." That is, that the complaints of Brizola against the service
provided by I.T.&T. were not unjustified. In fact, said Secretary
of State Rusk, "the State Department had pressed the utility for a
long time to expand its services because the actual extent of telephone services being offered was much less than the growing requirements demanded." [17] At the same time he conceded that
the company was suffering the risk that is inherent in all utility
operations which require government assent to rate increases. But
again this was a risk that had been openly entered into by the
company. It had profited during its good years. Now it had
come on unsatisfactory times. There was no obligation to bail it
out. But faced with the alternative of a review of the Alliance for
Progress by the Congress and an identification of the real potential of that assistance and the likely consequent decrease in appropriations, the State Department urged the Brazilians to settle with
the company, with an understanding that aid would be forthcoming to more than make it worthwhile. There was the threat to
Brazil of an inability to continue assistance in the event a settlement were not quickly forthcoming and an explanation of the in-
direct manner in which the expropriation's cost would fall on the
U.S. taxpayer if aid did continue. The "explanation' came from

---

to influence news media for positions it took abroad. "5.8% of its net
assets consist of U.S. dollar-AID guaranteed financing for its Chilean
utilities. It has a great stake in maintaining this guarantee and in encouraging other such guarantees. Chile, Peru, Brazil might someday wish to
nationalize properties which ITT owns in whole or in part. ABC news
personnel would have to comment on the nationalization and might wish
to editorialize. The potential for conflict with ITT's economic interest is
obvious."

[15] Asst. Secretary of State Martin. *Hearings on Nomination.*

[16] Secretary of State Rusk, *Hearings on Foreign Assistance Act of 1962,*
House Foreign Affairs Committee, Part IV, p. 812.

[17] *Hearings on Foreign Assistance Act of 1962,* House Foreign Affairs
Committee, Part IV, p. 819. Senator Morse noted that "we have been told
that incompetency is one of the troubles. The American company gave
such poor service that the request for a telephone was held up for three or
four years." *Hearing on S. 2996,* p. 418.

the top of the U.S. policy structure — the Secretary of State and the *Attorney General of the United States.*

The practice of bailing out companies from risks, the assumption of which was the reason for the profits which they had previously drained from the countries, created serious doubts even among the conservative press of the United States. The conservative *Business Week,* flagship of the McGraw-Hill publishing empire, predicted "an outcry from U.S. taxpayers if Alliance for Progress funds are used to help finance the transaction" and suggested that critics "may also ask whether the takeover would stop at utilities." The conservative *New York Herald Tribune* noted that the deal conforms with a pattern of "payment above market price." The conservative *Barron's* editorialized that the deal would contribute to inflation which "imposes cruel privations on the Brasilenos and jeopardizes the country's future growth." The Latin American specialist of the Scripps-Howard papers believed that "the good old American public would really balk" at the advance by the U.S. indirectly "of a billion in capital badly needed for other purposes to underwrite their purchase of Canadian properties" as well as at the "loan of even several millions in U.S. taxpayers' money to underwrite the expropriation of U.S. properties."

The Department rushed to make it clear that it was not entering the bailout operation on its own initiative. It was yielding to pressure which must otherwise hamper the ability to continue the great fraud which the Alliance had become. The solution supported by the United States, said Mr. Rusk, arose "on the initiative of some of the foreign utility companies. A number of them would prefer to sell out their holdings and then reinvest in industries in the same country that have access to a free market situation." [18] And of course they would milk as much from the country as was politically possible.

Once the road was cleared for the bailout and the diversion of Alliance money, the process expanded. There had been the early evacuation of Argentina by American & Foreign Power Company. In Argentina there had been a cluster of power properties into which no investment had been introduced for some twenty years. The U.S. Government allowed it to become known that if "proper"

---

[18] *Hearings on Foreign Assistance Act of 1962,* House Foreign Affairs Committee, Part IV, p. 811.

consideration were given the desires of the utility investors, heavy financing from U.S. government entities for Argentina would be forthcoming. An independent arbiter found the properties to be worth less than $30 million. Immediately there were reports that the U.S. Government did not feel that this was a "proper" enough consideration. A new evaluation followed and happily for the companies put the value at $53.6 million. The triumph was completed with an agreement by President Frondizi to pay off in *dollars* in thirteen years, to pay 6.5% interest meanwhile, with interest to be tax-free in Argentina, and to pay six percent interest on the valuation for the period 1958-61. The deal was accompanied by a gimmick which consisted of a promise by the company to invest the amount of the award in Argentina. Since the anticipated rates of return on this reinvestment were in the nature of things to be very high, the yields from the first three years of investment would thereafter meet the obligation to reinvest the annual payoff. Thus, the public-relations values of assuring the public that the award money would not leave the country were lacking in any substance. From properties that had been allowed to deteriorate by an absence of investment for twenty years, from properties that the owners said "have been unproductive for many years," the company was now able to proclaim that the *"immediate* effect should be to produce additional income of at least $3 million per year" and presumable much larger remittances afterward.

In Brazil the U.S. Embassy combined with American & Foreign Power Company to force Brazil to buy some $0.15 billion of utility properties that had ceased to be profitable. There was no limit to the drain from the pork barrel of the Alliance. The Company continued the sweep through Colombia, Chile where it was joined in the same effort by I.T.&T. In Costa Rica, bankrupt and living on budgetary support from the United States, the practice of drawing on the Alliance booty made attractive the idea of buying a British owned railway line. And shortly the benefits began to accrue to other foreign investors as distinct from U.S. investors. For Brazilian Traction Light and Power Company in Brazil there was an Alliance underwriting of a $96 million deal to dispose of unprofitable properties.

The melon was being split among speculators in these properties. Had the Brazilian revolution been a success? asked the conservative *Barron's* a year after the military had destroyed democratic government in Brazil. It found an easy answer: Look at the stock market quotations of Brazilian Traction. Did not a four fold rise in price speak for itself? And all this under the flag of the Alliance for Progress?

Price Range: Common Stock
1960 - 1965

Amer. & Foreign Power	6 - 20
Brazilian Traction	1¾ - 10

Keynes had once reminded a president of the United States that businessmen are "easily persuaded to be patriots, only too anxious to take a cheerful view, very unsure of themselves, pathetically responsive to a kind word." But in diverting a very large proportion of the Alliance's "public money" to assist three companies, in intervening directly in the legislative processes of Latin American countries and in practicing dollar diplomacy with all the pressures that it encompassed, the State Department had made a grab-bag of the Alliance. This was too much more than a "kind word."

On the eve of the Brazilian revolution, American & Foreign Power had informed its stockholders that it had had no income from Brazil since 1960. Within a year after Castelo Branco assumed office and took Brazil down the long road to dictatorship, the company was able to report that it had unloaded its properties for a fabulous sum and that it would be getting annually — this one company alone — more receipts from Brazil than were remitted by the whole $700 million of U.S. manufacturing investments in Brazil annually from 1963 to 1965. Nor does the story end there. Under President Goulart the company had reported that the deal would require when it went through "reinvestment of a substantial portion of the proceeds in other economic fields in Brazil." Two years later the company reported the successful evacuation of Latin America in these terms:

AMERICAN & FOREIGN POWER COMPANY
FUTURE PRINCIPAL PAYMENTS
(millions of dollars)

	Total	Unrestricted	To be reinvested in industry
Brazil	$139.4	$139.4	——
Argentina	27.9	——	$27.9
Colombia	26.9	26.9	——
Mexico	37.6	——	37.6
Chile	86.5	57.1	29.4

And in addition there were the assured lush interest payments to replace the dismal unrewarding record of recent years of the milked and worn out properties.

Brazilian Traction which was heavily owned by non-American investors had an even more exciting story to tell about the fruits in the grab bag of the Alliance. It had had a net income of zero for the two years 1962-63. Once Castelo Branco took over, it was able to unload some unprofitable properties (a very small percent of its total assets) for $96 million. It boosted net profits to $19.5 million in 1965. It boosted profits again to $14.7 million for a half year of 1966, and to $36.4 million for the full year. Its remittances from Brazil far exceeded what $700 million in U.S. manufacturing investments were able to net for their investors. The company's stock which had at market prices put a value on the whole company of only $30 million in March 1964, quickly rose four and even five fold. The company had in fact immediately told its stockholders that $7.2 million in arrears would be liquidated, *thanks to the volume of U.S. aid being poured into Brazil.* And when to all this the State Department put a cherry on the dessert in the form of a $40 million "loan", of the special "Alliance for Progress" type loans, it seemed almost too much to many congressmen. Senator Gore went to the floor of the Senate on July 22, 1966 to blast the deal. He protested that a Canadian company with heavy European ownership was being given $40 million in dollars to be repaid in *cruzeiros* at 5.5% at a time when the United States is paying 4.5% for its own borrowings and when money is worth a great deal more than 5.5% in Brazil. He pointed out that the Senate should investigate the dividends being made by the Brazilian Traction subsidiaries. And when asked to take pity on under-developed countries in a blanket avoidance of the practical issues, he told one of the representatives of the state of New York: "Some of your constituents in New York state have reaped a rich reward from their investments in that country. I do not criticize them at all. But I doubt that the American taxpayer should be called on to subsidize further investments from which they are enriched."

Even three leaders of the business community — David Rockefeller of the Chase Manhattan Bank, Emilio Collado of Standard Oil Company of New Jersey, and Walter B. Wriston of the First National City Bank — recognized the stickiness of the new modern style dollar diplomacy and recommended in their supplement to the report of the Commerce Committee for the Alliance for Progress that "the U.S. not provide aid in such a way as to finance the expropriation of privately-owned companies in any field of endeavor."

Curiously enough, for we are all inclined to downgrade all too often the public-policy sense of the Latin Americans, the concept of the grab-bag had been the initial reaction of many sober and serious-minded Latin Americans when Washington first put up the Alliance program. Especially in Chile there was the view: Give us the money so that we can buy out the copper companies and that will be it. To this the embarrassed novices on the White House smiled as if in appreciation of a big joke. But within five years, this is precisely what the Chileans did. They entered the copper industry courtesy of the Alliance for Progress donations. They negotiated partial ownership with the major companies. Note well: this was not a capital-surplus country. The per-capita volume of donations given Chile under the Alliance had been fabulous. Its further needs were by the Chileans' own testimony immense. Yet, as against the objectives of the Alliance, the Chileans decided that nationalization or partial nationalization of its major industry was more important than achievement of the goals of the Alliance. In fact, so eager was Chile to consummate the deals, that it gave the companies such favorable terms as to leave them wildly enthusiastic, and the stock market promptly evidenced the triumph of the companies. What in the world ever happened to the piously expressed thesis of the State Department that "when a government expropriates existing resources or uses its own funds to buy out existing operations rather than using these funds to create new wealth . . . this action appears to be a backward step . . . we would hold ourselves free to discuss the question as to the wisdom from a policy standpoint." The answer was simple: the goals of the Alliance had now been abandoned as not being practical. It was from the viewpoint of domestic U.S. politics much easier to provide a grab bag for private investors and thereby create a pressure group to support the appropriations sought from the Congress.

To the argument that the Chilean deal for partial participation in ownership would unleash a great expansion of facilities, it was pointed out that the companies had already offered to carry the whole burden of expansion themselves so that Chilean resources might have been put to other use for the vast requirements of social and economic development. As the companies exulted in the triumph over the Chileans, David Rockefeller crowed that the new investment by the companies "cannot fail to act as a major stimulant to economic growth — a stimulant which could not be matched by any program of government aid which Washington might find economically and politically feasible."[19] But he failed to mention that funds would be "borrowed" from Washington to accomplish this. And of course he missed completely the damage done by diversion of Chile's scarce resources to this purpose.

"As I look at the development program." protested Senator Gore, "it is primarily for the benefit of the (corporate) recipients of the loans. I see here a loan to Olinkraft Celulosa e Papel, a subsidiary of Olin Mathiesen. Olinkraft does not agree to repay the United States. It repays the government of Brazil and not in hard currency but in cruzeiros. The interest it pays the government of Brazil is 5.5%. The going rate of interest in Brazil on commercial loans is 2% per month so that even on these terms Olinkraft receives a favorable rate compared with commercial competitive enterprise. But it also gets the unusual benefit of repaying a hard loan with soft currency. It does not agree to repay the U.S. from whom it receives the dollars in any respect whatsoever. The Brazilian government receives a grace period of ten years at one percent; then the interest rate is 2.5% and amortization 40 years. The government of Brazil profits greatly too. It pays 1% for 10 years and 2.5% for 40 years. Meanwhile it has had the payment of the loan which it did not make in the first place and has the benefit and use of the money during all that time." [20]

The deterioration was a broad process. In the absence of a satisfactory climate of investment in Latin America, private investors were reluctant to invest. As we have seen, investment fell far short of the target detailed as the minimum needed to assure success of the Alliance. There were two possibilities of action: That Latin America make the climate of investment attractive; or that the United States Government shoulder increasingly the risks of investment so that the business community would be able to invest at public risk. There occurred thus during the five years a steady broadening of the investment-guarantee coverage so as to

[19] Press release of the Chase Manhattan Bank, October 27, 1966.
[20] *Congressional Record*, July 25, 1966, p. 16153.

enable businessmen to be assured of their profits with a minimum of risk, i.e., to make profits on Latin American operations disproportionate to the risk and to alternative investment operations elsewhere. Oddly enough, even this did not stimulate the flow in the magnitude sought. For businessmen understood that increasingly the position of the U.S. Government was being made to rest on the ability to offer more and more donations as inducements. In the event that a claim had to be entered against the guarantee and the investor was discharged with the obligation now one for the U.S. Government rather than the investor to negotiate, it became, as an Argentine enthusiast for the investment-guarantee treaty argued, a matter for the U.S. government itself "and an amicable solution may be arrived at when *political and diplomatic circumstances* make it advisable." It would always be possible for the United States Government to brandish the potential donations as an inducement to regularization of the situation. Many businessmen remembered however that the grab bag required annual refilling by the Congress of the United States and that at some point public consciousness of what was happening might balk a refill, causing the whole bargaining power to collapse. Thus, one finds in the period a great flow of investment to Mexico which *rejected* the challenge to its sovereignty implicit in the guarantee program, while investment lagged where guarantees were in effect. In Table XVII showing the guarantees that had been issued after five years, it should be remembered that these figures do not represent net outflow projected from the United States. In many cases, as little as one-sixth is the proper proportion to count on as net outflow projected.

Probably no phase of the Alliance for Progress saw such pressure exercised by the Department of State on Latin America as was the case with the investment-guarantee program. First, legislation was enacted which required a cutoff date for aid if the guarantees were not accepted by Latin America. And second, the record of private investment flow was so bad that the Department felt it was more than an affront, it was a real challenge to continuance of the fraud that the Alliance had become. In fact, the Department became a victim of panic to the point where it began to issue in some cases guarantees without the assent to the program of the Latin American countries, a completely unsound process. And in countries like Brazil, it put pressure on the military to assent to the program despite the open admission that the Congress and the people

Table XVII

INVESTMENT GUARANTIES ISSUED
THROUGH JUNE 30, 1966
(millions of dollars)

	Convertibility	Expropriation	War Risk	Combined	Total
Argentina	$373.2	$172.7	$82.9	$24.1	$652.9
Bolivia	12.2	32.4	5.6	——	50.2
Brazil	19.7	1.9	1.9	17.4	41.0
Chile	115.8	95.4	10.3	——	221.5
Colombia	66.9	71.4	44.9	0.4	183.6
Costa Rica	9.3	16.4	——	——	25.8
Dominican Rep.	3.6	7.5	30.8	——	42.0
Ecuador	17.7	17.8	8.9	——	44.5
El Salvador	5.3	5.5	——	——	10.8
Guatemala	0.4	2.8	——	——	3.2
Haiti	9.9	10.9	——	——	20.8
Honduras	5.9	30.5	——	——	36.3
Nicaragua	3.4	5.1	2.2	——	10.7
Panama	1.1	10.9	0.5	——	12.6
Paraguay	3.9	6.9	——	——	10.8
Peru	31.3	——	——	——	31.3
Venezuela	13.9	32.1	22.8	2.0	70.8
Latin America	694.0	520.3	211.0	43.9	1,469.0

of Brazil opposed any such action by Brazil. The ousted regime having resisted U.S. pressure, one of the first demands on the military when the revolution succeeded was that it sign the investment guarantee treaty. The Brazilian Congress balked and inserted a reservation interpreted by the American Embassy as limiting the right of diplomatic negotiation by the United States over claims against the Brazilian government. The U.S. Embassy promptly indicated its extreme distaste for this reservation which constituted in effect a final and pathetic show of independence unbecoming a client state. Finally the State Department arranged with the dictator a personal understanding that he would never invoke the legislative reservation and the State Department hastened to proceed with the issuance of guarantees. Oddly enough no American company raised its voice in support of the rule of law. Yet, dictators fall as well as rise, and this government might one day be thrown out, leaving only a personal arrangement with a dictator to govern important business relationships.

As the American Embassy lobbied for the whole package of concessions which had been the price of support for the military takeover — the profit remittance law, the investment guarantee treaty, the American Foreign Power deal implementation, the Hanna deal — even friendly editorial writers feared that "an error in judgment is involved which may boomerang against U.S. interests. . . . The effort to exert pressure on the Brazilian Congress revealed a lack of understanding of the revolution and/or a lack of faith in its leaders. Some Brazilians fear that because the first flagrant case of U.S. lobbying was in regard to profits, this would confirm the claims of anti-American forces that the American Embassy and American business are primarily concerned with profits and not with the development of Brazil." Others deplored the fact that at a time when real wages in Brazil were falling at a pace never before witnessed in Latin America, the attempt to gouge Brazil for the benefit of individual companies was frightfully timed.

Nor would the process stop at assumption of risks by guarantees. By the end of the five years, business was increasingly demanding tax preferences and other assistance if they were to enter the hostile climate of investment, and the State Department was becoming increasingly receptive.

Sometimes it seemed that there was no limit to the greed which had been unleashed by the attempt to keep the Alliance afloat. One is reminded of the story Sherman Adams told of President Eisenhower's discovery of the businessman's concept of the relationship with public policy:

> "Dulles had made a full-scale report on the critical role being played by Japan in the world balance. . . . George Humphrey had pointed to what he called critical unemployment in the Pittsburgh area because of Japanese competition in the electrical instrument industry, Eisenhower asked him if it were not possible for American businessmen to make sacrifices in such a situation in the interests of world peace. "No," Humphrey said candidly. "The American businessman believes in getting as much as he can while the getting is good." "Maybe that's the trouble with businessmen, George," Eisenhower said seriously."[21]

A Yale professor has written that "we have so far failed to reconcile the demands made on American policy by American firms in

---

[21] *Firsthand Report* (Harper & Brothers, New York, 1961), p. 449. A Greek historian outlining the decline of a nation has written: "At Carthage, nothing which results in profit is regarded as disgraceful."

Latin America with a variety of other American interests in that area, and here the pre-requisite adjustment must presumably be on terms less favorable to the American companies than now exist." [22] But the behavior of certain segments of American business in the five years of the Alliance did not represent an effort to reconcile the legitimate demands of the businessman with the objectives of public policy. The fact is that the great bulk of the business community would have benefited actually from devotion to principle by the State Department. For, the bulk of investors ultimately live or die by the degree to which there is respect for the rule of law. There is basically an identification of business and national interest, if only the State Department had had the integrity to function in the public interest and if business had had the intelligence to insist that a certain few corporations resist bribery and blackmail of the State Department.

Take for instance the case of the Argentine petroleum concessions. Petroleum had been a pivotal political issue in the Plate for a generation. During the 1956 campaign in the United States, Adlai Stevenson had reminded his audiences that "the U.S. Government's help in getting (from Perón) a concession for a U.S. oil company had angered the Argentine public not only against Perón but also against America and American businessmen." The conservative Aramburu had noted that "one of the prime motives of the revolutionary movement to overthrow Perón had been the threat of handing over the petroleum industry. And thanks to the revolution, the Argentine people had avoided the danger of giving away their oil." It was well known to the "business statesmen" of our generation and certainly to the State Department that any public policy or any business policy which failed to take account of the prevailing nationalistic sentiment regarding petroleum was unlikely to succeed.

But shortly before his inauguration, President Frondizi secretly negotiated agreements with certain oil interests to exploit oil that had already been discovered by the Argentine petroleum entity, so that the major risk of exploration had already been assumed by the government. Certain contracts were signed which were extremely

---

[22] Charles Lindbloom. See *Congressional Record*, January 21, 1963, pp. 609-611, or *Atlantic Monthly*, October 1962, "A New Look at Latin America."

unsound for Argentina economically, and were in fact quite out of line with mid-twentieth century practice in the oil industry the world over. The legislature had been short-cut in some cases in wholly improper fashion. We were back to the stage of the "quick-killings." The conservative *Fortune Magazine* remarked that these concessions had involved "political pressure tactics" of a type that had caused "eyebrow raising in both Buenos Aires and Washington." The conservative *Business Week* quoted American oilmen as considering some of the concessions "mighty juicy." The conservative *Financial Times* (London) editorialized that "the oil companies themselves privately admit that the contracts negotiated with them by President Frondizi are in some ways unfair to Y.P.F., the Argentine State oil entity." Knowing that the Argentine Congress would not permit such a giveaway, Frondizi had chosen to bypass the Congress despite the importance attaching to the petroleum question and despite his prior position opposing the entry of foreign companies on even economically sound terms.

Whether it feared to interfere with ex-U.S. officials who were busy negotiating questionable contracts in the Plate and other countries, or whether oil company influence was too much to challenge, the State Department made no effort to bring the oil concessions into line with mid-twentieth century practice. Instead, it proceeded to do everything that the U.S. Government could do to hold the Argentine President in office lest the situation blow up in everybody's face.

It is interesting to review the rapidity of the retreat of the State Department in the matter of the relationship of business to public policy as far as the Alliance for Progress is concerned. At the launching of the Alliance, John D. Moore, chairman of the U.S. Inter-American Council (an organization of 148 corporations representing perhaps 75 to 80 percent of U.S. investment in Latin America) had protested that the U.S. business community had been used merely as window-dressing advisers. "We were called 'consultants to the delegation' and we might just as well have been in Peoria as to have been in Punta del Este. We were not consulted, not in any meetings at all, and we were left strictly alone. We put our objectives to the delegation but nothing came of it. If a project like the Alliance for Progress is going to be formed that way and if our government friends are going to turn and say 'the principal responsibility falls on business' it is not fair. Businessmen cannot do a job on a blueprint that they had nothing to do with drawing, if it turns out to be as defective as some people think the Punta del Este blueprint was." He went on:

"You will recall that certain commitments or quasi-commitments were made, one of which was that there would be $300 million of net direct U.S. private investment as part of the $2 billion a year that was going to be brought to Latin America under the Alliance program. At the last minutes, about eight days before the meeting, the authorities in charge in the U.S. Government suggested that there be a business advisory group formed to go with the delegation. This had been characteristic of all OAS major economic conferences up to that time. Two or three businessmen had always been included. The business group (this time) was sought to be formed in such a way as to exclude the extractive industries from its membership, to exclude the utilities from its membership, and to exclude commercial banks. I might mention that those three categories include some of the most experienced and dedicated businessmen in the Latin American area. . . . We had the feeling we were there as window dressing. You will recall that there was no legislative delegation so that if somebody said something about business the answer would be that there was a business group there." [23]

But as the Alliance proceeded and the climate of investment deteriorated steadily while the State Department entered upon the orgy of beneficence and noisily proclaimed that violent revolution must follow if its activities failed as indeed they were visibly already failing, business succumbed to the temptation to insist on its "share" of the loot. It stressed increasingly that private investment must become "private investment at public risk" and it demanded even that this principle be applied retroactively so as to free it of its past mistakes. It had not been surprising to see a group of second-rate bureaucrats fighting for their positions by claiming that the public interest was involved in maintenance of the volume of government financing, but when businessmen abandoned principle and offered themselves to be bribed by the bureaucrats, they disgraced the community in the eyes of the public. If indeed other motives had caused the State Department orginally to keep business out of the councils in which the Alliance was being formed, there was now a demonstration of untrustworthiness as far as the enunciation of public policy is concerned which was extremely damaging to the image of the business community in our society.

---

[23] Hearings before the Subcommittee on International Organizations and Movements of the House Foreign Affairs Committee, *Winning the Cold War: The U.S. Ideological Offensive*, Part II, pp. 238-239.

Integrity and understanding were lost simultaneously. At the outset Secretary of State Rusk had been emphatic in outlining the relationship of business to public policy: "I don't believe that the United States can afford to stake its interests in other countries on a particular private investment in a particular situation because someone has to live with the results anyway. And we are affected by the results. We have to keep working at these things. We can't really quit and go home, quite frankly." [24] Again, "If we are going to tie American policy by law to the private investor overseas, to the extent you suggest, then I think we must of necessity reassure ourselves as to the operations, the conduct, the financial structure, and the other aspects of these private investors. It seems to me that we would have to intrude." [25] And 'unless we were ourselves to take control of American private investment abroad in terms of how they should conduct themselves, whether or not they should expand their facilities with this or that rate increase or not . . ." [26]

Yet in five years the "marked change in the attitude of those responsible for the Alliance," to use the words of David Rockefeller, head of the Chase Manhattan Bank, was such that business was convinced that the State Department now recognized that the "Alliance had been too much of an instrument of American foreign policy and had had too much emphasis on social reform." [27] Wayne Morse, accepting the allegations that U.S. businessmen had intervened in the overthrow of the President in the Dominican Republic, could bellow that "we cannot justify at any time any intermingling, intervention, muddling or meddling on the part of American businessmen abroad with American foreign policy." But when the government took the road on which bailouts were provided for dissatisfied investors out of the Alliance appropriations, financing was provided to identify the U.S. government as involved in private investments so that the hands of the foreign government were tied in its dealing lest sanctions be exercised, and guarantees were issued with more aids to come to reduce and eliminate risk while holding firm to expectations of profits geared to assumption of risk, it could no longer write itself or talk itself out of the requirements of such a situation. To use Rusk's words,

---

[24] *Hearings on S. 2996,* p. 31.
[25] *Hearings on S. 2996,* p. 32.
[26] *Hearings on Foreign Assistance Act of 1962,* House Foreign Affairs Committee, Part IV, p. 811.
[27] See press dispatches of February 19, 1964.

now we had actually tied "American policy by law to the private investor overseas," and it followed that *now* "we must of necessity reassure ourselves as to the operations, the conduct, the financial structure and the other aspects of these private investors." *Now* more than ever there was need for the careful scrutiny of private investment operations overseas which almost a decade previously Assistant Secretary Rubottom had told Senator Morse was within the policy capacity and operational concept of the State Department. But the Department failed to act.

It was not an entirely new situation. After all, for decades the Exim Bank had been used to bail out corporations which had extended credit too loosely in Latin America, to the damage of Latin America as well as of those innocent corporations who still felt that extension of credit was a risk of business rather than of government, and then came to Washington for the government to cover its errors in judgment. The same utilities which now claimed the ultimate privilege of being bailed out of investments that had soured had been aided for a generation in getting cheap credit as well as the desired identification of the U.S. government with their investments, and had left the U.S. government holding the bag. For instance, the Exim Bank had been persuaded to sink $40 million in Cuba for the American utilities in order to enable them to save interest charges on their financial requirements, to create an "umbrella" benefit by association with the U.S. Government which enabled them to justify rate increases as an imperative of the country's relationship with the United States — and when Batista fell, the U.S. taxpayer was left holding the bag for $35 million in defaulted loans. When I.T.&T. had made an unusually profitable sale of its properties to Perón at a price few dreamed could be gotten through legitimate negotiations there was no sharing of the windfall with the U.S. taxpayer and indeed not with the ultimate victim, the Argentine consumer of the services. But when its properties soured elsewhere, it permitted the U.S. taxpayer to assume the risks retroactively.

Surely the Alliance had not been intended as an instrument to reward overseas investors by distributing to them revenues raised from other U.S. taxpayers. But if the U.S. had erred fatally and had helped thereby further to handicap the Alliance, what had the Latin American done either to prevent the error or to meet the requirements of public policy on their own part?

After five years, an articulate spokesman for the Latin American community, Felipe Herrera, President of the Inter-American Development Bank, said that "the proportion of Latin American resources allocated to capital formation is dangerously low. Societies that are highly dynamic, that are striving to make up for lost decades and seeking new economic horizons allocate 25% or more of their resources to national development. But in Latin America this proportion is only 16%. . . . The current investment growth rate of 3.3% per year must be doubled if progress in per capita income level is to meet the minimum targets established in the Charter of Punta del Este." [28]   Yet, he had no protest to offer at the qualitative aspect of the problem, the determination of the area first to resist any serious enlargement of the flow of capital into private investment by creation of a suitable climate of investment, and second, to reduce the volume of capital that might make impact on the economies by using its own and external resources created by the Alliance to replace ownership rather than supplement existing physical facilities.

The rhetoric of the Alliance had not been at fault here. The Department of State in its initial presentations had shown that it understood the requirements of the situation. But when matters moved to the reality of action, the establishment by Latin America of goals, political in nature, that had nothing to do with the objectives of the Alliance had posed a fundamental problem for the United States: (1) We could accept the Latin disavowal of the objectives, but maintain the grab bag and proclaim it is every man for himself and the private U.S. investor must be given priority over the Latin Americans who had preferred to doom their countries to the failure. Or (2) We could present clearly the facts of the matter and concede the inability to meet objectives and thus then in fairness to the U.S. taxpayer adjust the appropriations to the realizable situation. This would have meant *no* grab bag for the private investors.

The choice that was made was obviously the wrong one.

It is true that to single out business may be on the surface unfair since virtually every organized element in the U.S. community was yielding to the temptation to drain funds from the grab bag. Labor,

---

[28] Address to the 33rd convention of the Association of Mexican Bankers, Monterrey Mexico, March 4, 1967. "Aspects in the International Financing of Latin American Development."

consumers, farm organizations, planning organizations, universities, bankers, building and loan executives, retired business executives, women's organizations, men's organizations, municipalities, states and counties, all recognized that they were pressure groups whose support the State Department needed and it was not hard to milk the situation for a few junkets and budgetary assistance and expansion of the private bureaucratic organization. These were essentially piddling operations. But business had ten billion dollars invested in Latin America, it was involved in commercial competition for a market of upwards of $10 billion annually, it had, properly conceived, an identification with what was *good for the United States* as its essential interest in public policy. Yet, once the deterioration set in and the Alliance was recognized as hopeless, it was unable to resist the temptation to grab for its share of the loot. And even when corporations saw how concentrated the distribution of the share appeared to be, how a few companies were grabbing an unfair share of the booty they hesitated to blow the whistle lest their turn in line be sacrificed.

Given the method employed in the Brazilian case it was particularly nauseating to hear the voice of International Telephone & Telegraph Company unctuously intoning: "Risk is always with us, the important thing is to weigh it calmly against the likely benefits — to us, our customers and our free enterprise system, for we must not forget that if we write off the under-developed parts of the world as risky, we yield them without a struggle to our enemies whose stated goal is to bury us along with our way of life." The position taken by all too many American business leaders during this period, whether expressed, or underlined by their silence, had no responsible relationship with sound public policy or the strategic requirements of national security.

For its part, Latin America had no intention of departing from the litany which had served so well to preserve its low standard of living. This consisted first in an increasingly well defined measurement of its capital requirements, and second, in policy decisions calculated not to maximize the resources available to meet these requirements but rather designed to discourage their realization. One of its spokesmen expressed the area's anguish: [29]

---

[29] Herrera, *op. cit.* Herrera cited the original target of $2 billion per year in external contributions from all sources. "If this figure is taken as a gross amount of financial contribution, that is, if it is to include amortizations, this target may be said to have been fulfilled. But if on the con-

"During the 1960-65 period investment rose by only 3.3% per year . . . population 2.7% per year. Thus we can understand why our society is still burdened with poverty and frustration. Little more than a half percent of capital is being added annually for each Latin American inhabitant to take care of the growingly urgent needs of 245 million Latin Americans. With this limited margin we are seeking to build more factories to provide needed jobs; to expand and improve farming to feed a growing population and still maintain an essential export trade; to supply the 12 million classrooms needed yearly for the   minimum education of our children; and to provide such basic services as electricity, water and transportation to accommodate the 7 million new inhabitants added annually to the Latin American population. . . . Each new industrial job requires a minimum additional investment of $5,000 which adds up to at least $5 billion in new overall investment in the manufacturing sector and today we still stand 25 to 30% short of this figure. This is one of the reasons why our streets and fields are confronted with the spectre of millions and millions of unemployed or underemployed young men and women who are barred from the sources of production, full employment and social well being."

"Any policy for economic growth in this region must give fundamental consideration to ways of securing more investment capital." Yet, it is significant and typical that even he did not find it possible to speak frankly on the means that were increasingly being used to discourage investment capital rather than attempting to secure more of it. Not for him an analysis of the cost of using scarce national savings to buy out existing foreign-owned facilities; not for him an attempt to measure the cost of the decades of discouragement of inflow of capital by the refusal to improve the climate of investment and to accept a rule of law. Instead, typically, the Latin American found a need for more "public" money at interest rates that would be less burdensome to the beneficiary. And he sounded the new theme: what is really needed is *net external* contributions more than double those of the first five years of the Alliance. Could the gimmickry of the Alliance provide them? From Washington?

---

trary it is viewed as a "net" contribution (exclusive of amortizations) then the goal has not been reached since the *net* cash contribution of foreign resources during the five year period may be estimated at $1.2 billion per year."

He then cited a certain new tentative and limited estimate that annually $2.8 billion in net external resources would be required by 1970 and $3.2 billion by 1975 to sustain an annual gross national product growth rate of from 5 to 6%. Such projections also assumed better mobilization of national savings by the Latin Americans themselves.

Chapter VIII
Gimmickry and
Pork-Barrel Diplomacy

Well into the sixth year of the Alliance, a new wave of "evaluation" touched off a renewed wave of prescriptioneering—this time by the heads of government themselves. The *Statist* (London) had wrapped up accurately the condition to which the charter of the Alliance for Progress had been reduced when it labelled it "so much transcendental hyperbole." But President Johnson felt that the rhetoric of the Alliance had enough life left in it for one more trip through the Congress and through the good-neighborhood generally.

"The peaceful and progressive revolution which is transforming Latin America," he informed the Congress with shocking disregard for the facts, "is one of the great inspirational movements of our time." [1]

Speaking for a major beneficiary of the Alliance (Chile), President Frei found reason to differ sharply: "The generous initial concepts, the commitments and the hopes which arose after the early success of some of its programs, have gone hand in hand with the renewed attacks against democracy, the loss of markets for Latin American primary commodities, the decline of foreign investment, the consolidation in power of unjust regimes and the acceptance of alternative evolutionary processes which only retard the revolutionary changes that so many of these countries need." [2]

---

[1] *Message to the Congress on the Latin American Summit Meeting,* March 13, 1967. (White House press release).

[2] Eduardo Frei Montalva, "The Alliance that Lost Its Way," *Foreign Affairs,* April 1967, pp. 437-448. Unless otherwise noted, quotations of Frei are taken from this article.

The reality of the Alliance was that it neither was transforming Latin America by a progressive revolution nor was it a great inspirational movement.

But it remained for the sober incoming president of Uruguay, which had fared badly in the distribution of the booty of the Alliance, to issue the really important finding: "If the Uruguayan people want to commit suicide, there is no government on earth that can prevent it. If they want to be saved, it lies in their power to do so."[3]

Individual circumstances dictated the differing prescriptions, of course. In President Johnson's case, it was vital that misrepresentation regarding the achievements of the Alliance be continued, lest the Congress withdraw support and the proliferation of the great bureaucracy of the Alliance — national and international — be brought to a crashing halt. Operational bungling or ineffectiveness could be concealed by reason of (1) the dimensions of the sheer physical task of scrutinizing the specific operations which were beyond the capacity of the press, (2) the lack of serious congressional interest in staffing its own inspector-general's office for so large a job,[4] and (3) the inter-relationship of the bureaucracy and the academic community (university and foundation alike) which assured immunity from serious critical examination as long as sympathetic consideration of the operations promised greater rewards in subsidies, travel, benefits and the like.

But policy analysis as against detailed operational examination was a different problem. Here the Executive sales effort domestically depended on gimmickry. Each time the appropriation proposals came to the hill, some gimmick had to be found to distract attention from the growing record of failure.[5] Thus in 1967 there

---

[3] Inaugural statement. UPI dispatch is cited.

[4] There is of course the Office of the Comptroller-General of the United States, but the task of detailed supervision and disclosure of the waste in Alliance financing would swamp such an organization. And disclosure would not be permitted by the State Department anyway. As has been noted many times on the floor of the Senate, the Department invariably demands that a secrecy label be attached to reports that reflect on the misuse of funds by AID.

[5] President Belaúnde of Peru did well to note "a common market, yes. but first we must integrate our national economices. There are vast new lands where farmers do not even have a road to get their produce to a

was economic integration as a gimmick which looked very good on paper as distinct from what experience indicated might be done with it when it went through the policy-decision making process of the various countries. Multilateralism in decision making, multinational projects, program loans designed to facilitate the flow of funds with less concern for the objectives of the Alliance, and similar gimmicks could be invoked on successive occasions to suggest new starts, as promising as the original ones had been, without looking too closely at the reasons for the existing failures and the likelihood of similar failures from new gimmicks under the prevailing conditions.

And for President Johnson there was the further circumstance that "the natives were restless," for which pork-barrel diplomacy had only one answer — "throw another piece of pork to the 'natives.' " This came in the form of a proposal to raise the U.S. commitment by 30%, which Congressman Gross chose to call a "greenback-wrapped carrot".

The "justification" handed the Congress was so faulty that it merely bolstered Congressman Curtis' earlier protest: "The year-end review of the Alliance for Progress . . . as far as giving information, is not worth the powder to blow it up. It is rhetoric. It does not have meaningful figures. When you try to zero in on some of the statistics that are set out, you end up with just words. They talk about modernization, expansion, a few disappointments, in one instance about reform, but you cannot find any meaning in the material. It is powder in the eyes. . . . It is propaganda, not reality. Talk about truth in lending and truth in packaging — we need a truth in labelling some of these programs in order to find out what they really are." [6]

Information was not totally lacking. But the misrepresentation was as great as Mr. Johnson's nonsense concerning a progressive revolution which is transforming Latin America, "one of the great inspirational movements of our time."

---

highway and there are provincial capitals which can be reached only by mule path." But policy-wise the point was that having failed in getting the necessary policy attention to such problems, the program could not be "sold" to the U.S. Congress again without new gimmicks.

[6] *Congressional Record,* February 16, 1967, pp. 1472-1478. Quotations from the Year end (1966) Report on the Alliance for Progress" subsequently used here are taken from *Congressional Record text.*

When the report distributed to the Congress stressed the "substantial overall economic growth," the Agency for International Development in a separate analysis conceded that even in the sixth year the per-capita growth in gross national product of 1.1% was less than half the target figure of the Alliance and of course much lower than the level which had prevailed before the Alliance was entered upon.

When the report to the Congress stressed that "all the American republics have adopted land reform legislation which is being implemented in a majority of the countries," the Inter-American Development Bank corrected it by noting that even "the year 1966 did not bring significant improvement in the pattern of land distribution and tenure in most Latin American countries . . . and the slowest progress was in land distribution . . . land taxation has not made a great impact on Latin America so far." [7]

When the report to the Congress stressed the "success" of the International Coffee Agreement and emphasized that the "success" must be defined in terms of raising prices to the consumer, an objective which President Kennedy had specifically denied in writing to be the objective of the Agreement and had indeed pledged to take the United States out of the Agreement if it were used for this purpose, other U.S. agencies emphasized that the cartel's price policy had actually destroyed the hopes of a growth in consumption and had accelerated the adverse consumption trend dangerously, had stimulated production, had worsened the statistical position of coffee in world markets, and that as the report was being issued, the capacity to continue to violate the originally outlined objectives of the Agreement might now be so impaired as to bring a breakdown. All this despite the immense burden imposed on the U.S. consumer (estimated at $2 billion for the period) in violation of the stated justification for U.S. legislative action to bring the United States into the arrangement.

When the report to the Congress alleged that "Latin America's deteriorating debt position has been halted and to some extent reversed", it was pointed out elsewhere that this merely represented the substitution of U.S. donations and concealed donations for

---

[7] Citations are from *Socio-Economic Progress in Latin America*, Sixth Annual Report 1966, Social Progress Trust Fund, Inter-American Development Bank (Washington 1967).

loans, and the Social Progress Trust Fund pointed out that the really significant element on balance of payments was that "Latin America has not benefited from the vigorous increase in world trade" even as compared with the performance of other under-developed areas, and even more significantly that "the unfavorable position is partly *due to unsuccessful policies and even a lack of policies" on the part of the Latin American countries.*

When the report to the Congress puffed the increase of over 15 to 20 percent per year in annual net tax revenues, the Inter-American Development Bank pointed out that at best the increase in tax receipts relative to gross national product had been 3.6% for the period of five years. And as far as Latin America meeting the investment goals through domestic savings to complement the U.S. donations, the Bank warned that "gross investment to which savings are destined actually declined as a percentage of gross domestic product in the period under review."

When the report to the Congress exulted in the fact that "free labor in Latin America *(which was in many instances operating under subsidy from the U.S. Treasury)* [8] has voiced its support of the Alliance and its goals," it was necessary to note also that typically in the new showcase of the Alliance (Brazil) the free labor movement had been crippled if not destroyed by the dicta-torship which had evolved under the aegis of the United States. And that situation was not unique.

When the report to the Congress laid stress on "the construction of new schools and related facilities," other U.S. agencies handed the Congress material emphasizing that the effectiveness of the educational effort was much less than that of the military effort of the Alliance and in the absence of a suitable mystique of social and economic development the data on relative expenditures for these purposes continued to point up the fault in the basic concept under which the Latin Americans were functioning. (See Tables XVIII and XIX).

Sometimes the data themselves seemed to be juggled for pur-poses of presentation of achievement, although it must be re-membered that in many areas the Latin American data are ex-tremely faulty in the first instance. Thus, when the preliminary data for 1966 were first given the press, Costa Rica was credited

---

[8] Italicized material added by author.

Table XVIII

PERCENTAGE OF FEDERAL GOVERNMENT EXPENDITURES
DEVOTED TO EDUCATION AND MILITARY*

	Education**	Military***
Argentina	12.8%	15.0%
Bolivia	25.2	6.8
Brazil	7.4	16.1
Chile	13.8	8.8
Colombia	16.1	12.2
Costa Rica	28.7	2.0
Dominican Rep.	11.5	17.8
Ecuador	11.6	10.0
El Salvador	22.1	8.8
Guatemala	14.0	10.5
Honduras	21.2	10.1
Haiti	10.8	?
Mexico	23.4	8.2
Nicaragua	15.6	16.5
Panama	22.4	0.5
Paraguay	16.3	30.4
Peru	24.0	13.1
Uruguay	16.4	6.2
Venezuela	10.5	9.9

* Data are extremely unsatisfactory and apart from central comparisons such as the relative importance of education and military expenditures in Mexico as compared with Brazil, etc., the crudeness of the data must be stressed. Shortly after these tables were prepared by official U.S. agencies, the Social Progress Trust Fund published its data on Education as a percentage of total expenditures. Among their figures are Argentina 17.2%, Chile 10.6%, Colombia 9.9%. The discrepancies have no official explanation. Data 1965 and 1966.

** *Hearings on Foreign Assistance and Related Agencies Appropriations for 1967*, House Appropriations Committee, p. 634.

*** *Hearings on Foreign Assistance*, 1966 Senate Foreign Relations Committee, p. 538.

with a per-capita increase in gross national product of 2.8% while the Embassy of the United States from which the data were presumably derived had sent in the figure of 0.7%. For a program in which worship of the gross national product — our Golden Calf — was predominant, "making" the data behave had become an objective in itself if the program were to survive.

George Humphrey, former Secretary of the Treasury, has remarked that "It is a terribly hard job to spend a billion dollars and get your money's worth." And although the explorations into performance were too scattered and limited to provide exact answers to how short we had come to getting our money's worth, the occasional safari of congressmen to the Latin American countries rarely failed to bring back evidence. A study prepared for the Senate Foreign Relations Committee put it well when it concluded that if a shot hits the target, it appears to be the result of accident rather than of careful aim. In 1966, for instance, Congressman Goodell, who professed to believe in foreign aid and particularly in community development and community action organizations, was shocked at the results of the showcase venture in Brazil — Vila Kennedy. "The entire project raises the question of whether or not the life of people has been in fact improved by their relocation." The low-cost housing project was found to be a "prime example of how visionary and totally unrealistic approaches can waste dollars. . . . Nobody thought about community development or about the need for a Brazilian agency to take over after it was built and nobody consulted the people themselves," with the result that "no jobs were available within normal commuting distance (transport costs were high, frequently involving 30% of monthly income and four hours a day in transportation), on-site training programs fizzled . . . there is no community development, self-help appears to be a totally unknown concept, the entire project is rapidly deteriorating." [9]   The U.S. program director was quoted as dismissing the operation with a sweeping "it's a stinker." [10] Perhaps more significantly, the *Wall Street Journal* reminded its readers that an AID man who had shown a congressman around the miserable operation "has since been shunted into what is described as a 'dead end job' that is unlikely to lead to future promotion." [11]

It may well be, indeed, that the increasing tendency to subvert the congressional process, to use Senator Fulbright's term, the tendency to circumvent the Congress in derogation of the separation of powers, the tendency to downgrade the legislative function, which is involved in the mass misrepresentation of the achieve-

---

[9] Quotations taken from report of the mission released to the press.
[10] *Wall Street Journal,* March 20, 1967.
[11] March 20, 1967.

Table XIX

ECONOMIC GROWTH, U.S. ASSISTANCE, EDUCATION AND
MILITARY EXPENDITURES PER CAPITA

Calendar Year 1966

	GNP Growth %	U.S. Donations and Concealed Donations Authorized	Expenditure for Education*	Expenditure for Military*
Argentina	−2.5%	$0.07	$7.56	$9.00
Bolivia	3.0	8.80	4.27	1.20
Brazil	0.4	3.90	2.24	4.90
Chile	3.3	11.00	8.85	7.30
Colombia	2.8	2.10	2.56	3.20
Costa Rica	2.8	2.70	11.51	1.00
Dom. Rep.	−0.4	17.00	5.03	6.70
Ecuador	0.9	3.10	4.40	2.80
El Salvador	2.2	2.70	7.17	2.70
Guatemala	3.0	0.90	4.46	3.20
Honduras	3.0	3.20	5.82	2.90
Mexico	3.3	——	8.19	2.90
Nicaragua	2.7	10.00	5.86	5.80
Panama	3.7	1.75	18.94	0.40
Paraguay	1.4	8.00	3.17	5.70
Peru	3.0	2.50	14.00	6.70
Uruguay	−0.7	2.50	23.17	5.50
Venezuela	1.5	0.70	20.43	17.00

* Data are extremely unreliable, although relations as between countries
and as between types of expenditures are of some value. Data prepared as
follows: Column 1 and 2 — Agency for International Development.
Column 3 — Social Progress Trust Fund (Inter-American Development
Bank) for 1965 in 1963 dollars. Column 4 — U.S. Department of Defense.

ments of the Alliance, is a cost for a democratic nation that it
should not be asked to pay.[12] One would, for instance, look in
vain through the published hearings on legislation to find details
of the experiences in Brazil which when exposed were admitted

---

[12] Fulbright asked: "If they cannot get the money from the Congress,
why do they not assume that perhaps it should not be done?" *Congressional
Record*, March 16, 1967, S3944.

by the officials involved, whether it be the housing experience or the educational ventures. In 1966, for instance, there was the freshly produced material on the school construction program in Brazil: "the many schools suffering from inadequate construction with some showing serious danger of roof or wall collapse; contracts awarded to unregistered firms on a non-competitive basis with some contract adjustments awarding a slow contractor double the contract price; schools built under the program being allowed to deteriorate with no provision in most cases for even minimal maintenance." [13]

Sometimes the President himself found his position contradicted by his own Executive agencies. When he justified preferential treatment of Colombia in 1967 in terms of the "encouraging economic trends" there, a spurious justification which had been used and disproved to the satisfaction of virtually every observer except the President in previous years also, the Agency for International Development hastened to point out that the per-capita gross national product growth rate in 1965-66 was only one-quarter that of the period 1957-58 to 1964-65, that there had been an unprecedented collapse in 1966, and that Colombia's performance had not only been far below the target of the Alliance but that it had been the *worst* performance of the seventeen countries for which data are available except Uruguay. And the House Banking and Currency Committee released a report emphasizing that not only was the growth rate unsatisfactory but also the distribution of incomes was becoming more inequitable: "Personal income appears to be falling among the poorer or lower income levels in agriculture. . . . Per capita foodsupplies have been decreasing. . . . Recent rates of growth in the agricultural sector have lagged behind the 3.1% rate of population growth." Even the Minister of Government of Colombia in December 1966 was moved to note that despite the years of disproportionate aid from the United States, "la economía colombiana es la más débil de todo el continente." Encouraging trend, indeed!

The total separation of rhetoric from reality, the presentation of fiction as fact, was not limited to the United States of course. When the Brazilian regime was well on the way to destroying democratic institutions in Brazil, the Minister of Planning lectured the Inter-

---

[13] Congressman Goodell's report, cited previously.

American Press Association that "one should not be afraid of the workings of the democratic process for recent history has proved that communist revolutions have only been successful when projected against authoritarian states." [14]   And the flow of announcements on economic achievements offered up as the reward for destruction of democratic institutions was breath-taking in its deviation from fact. While AID was informing the Congress that per-capita growth at the rate of 0.4% in 1966 left per-capita gross national product barely at the level achieved in Brazil in 1961 before the lush flow of funds from Washington had really become effective, and that the distribution was known to have become less equitable, if such a thing was possible, under the devastating decline in real wages, the Brazilians continued to send up data on improvement that simply embarrassed their friends.

The U.S. Executive found itself increasingly thrown back on a cataloguing of performance in terms of quantity of houses built or school rooms prepared or textbooks published, etc., as a substitute for both the qualitative aspect (getting the dollar's worth in top priority expenditures) and the larger matter of the real objectives of the program. Thus, in 1967 the President informed the Congress that: [15]

1. 350,000 housing units have been, or are now being built.

2. 2,000 rural wells and 1,170 portable water supply systems have been built to benefit some 20 million persons.

3. 1,200 health centers including hospitals and mobile medical units are in operation or soon will be.

4. 100 million people are being protected from malaria. In ten countries, deaths caused by malaria dropped from 10,810, to 2,280 in three years time.

5. More than 14 million textbooks have been distributed.

6. 13 million school children and 3 million pre-schoolers participate in school lunch programs.

7. 160,000 teachers have been trained or given additional training.

8. 28,000 classrooms have been built.

9. Primary school enrollments have increased by 23%; secondary school by 50%; university enrollments by 39%.

---

[14] Meeting at San Diego, California, October 12, 1965.

[15] *Message to the Congress on the Latin American Summit Meeting.*

10. Sixteen countries have legislation dealing directly with land reform; with U.S. aid, 1.1 million acres have been irrigated and 106,000 acres reclaimed.

11. More than 0.7 million agricultural loans benefited 3.5 million people.

12. 15,000 miles of road have been built or improved, many of them farm-to-market access roads.

But from left and right alike, such listings brought only disrespect for the shift in emphasis represented by such justifications for continuing appropriations. The conservative *Business Week*, duly noting the data that appeared yearly, insisted that the record continues to be one of failure because there had been a failure to achieve the *real* objectives of the Alliance: (1) The mobilization of the resources of the Latin Americans themselves with the help of U.S. public and private capital to make a concerted assult on poverty and under-development; and (2) The reform of outmoded social structures in order to demonstrate to the under-privileged masses that they need not resort to revolution to get a better deal. "Nowhere," it insisted, "has a country been denied aid because it has failed to make basic social reforms." [16] Washington had eased up on talk of reform and now emphasized stability — economic and political alike — even though stability might reinforce the very evils to whose correction the Alliance was directed. Rather than championing change, U.S. officials now talked of "not expecting the Latin Americans to change overnight." And when a U.S. labor leader dared urge that higher priority be given to *change* than to *non-violence* in the campaign for *non-violent change* in Latin America, the State Department edited out the remark in its translation of his statement to the Conference of Hemisphere Labor Ministers at Caracas. [17]

From the left President Frei was especially effective on this point. Conceding the advances in number of classrooms and miles of road and administration of anti-malaria measures and the like, he nevertheless noted that these could have been secured "simply with the financial assistance of the United States plus of course the demand that these additional resources be used rationally by the recipient countries." The heart of the problem, he said, was

---

[16] June 11, 1966, p. 128.
[17] Speech by AFL-CIO vice-president Joseph Beirne.

that "the ultimate objective of the Alliance — the formation of just, stable, democratic and dynamic societies — is as distant today as it was five years ago. The problem is that what was fundamental to the Alliance — a revolutionary approach to the need for reform — has not been achieved. Less than half of the Latin American countries have started serious programs of agrarian reform. Drastic changes in the tax system are even scarcer, while the number of genuinely democratic regimes far from increasing has actually declined."

Yet, his prescription too, built as it was on the peculiar circumstances of his own country, was faulty in the extreme. He insisted that "it is inadmissible that the mere (sic) fact of making available financial aid gives any nation the right to demand that another (nation) implement specific types of structural changes. This would constitute an intolerable infringement of national sovereignty." Essentially this meant that each country must be the sole judge of the degree to which it has met the U.S. stipulation of suitable self-help. It should have been clear to President Frei that the exploitation of the U.S. Treasury for a program destined to last generations could not continue without an accounting to the American people in terms of achievement or partial achievement of the real objectives which prompted the appropriation of their hard-earned funds. And this measurement must inevitably have to be in terms of self-help criteria that satisfied the United States rather than in terms of politically flexible criteria that a foreign government might set up. It should have been clear to President Frei that he was entirely correct in believing that Uruguay's national sovereignty requires that it be free to retire on nearly full pay government workers in their mid-40s, that government rosters there have half again more workers than are needed, that if the wisdom of the Uruguayan government so dictated, national sovereignty assured it the capacity to continue to allow men to milk the government budgets by drawing pay as wet nurses in the widespread cheating of the Uruguayan welfare system. Frei was obviously correct in believing that national sovereignty gave Colombia the full privilege of restricting world consumption of its coffee and piling up unsalable surpluses by an unwise price policy. Frei was obviously correct in relating national sovereignty to the capacity to commit national suicide. The rub comes in the notion that U.S. donations should be made without stipulation that these mistakes be eradicated.

As a matter of fact, Frei's concept broke down badly when the contradictions of his philosophical analysis and Chilean policies were studied. For instance, his pious support of the U.S. thesis that "the armaments race diverts important resources which should be utilized to satisfy the urgent need for economic and social development" contrasts sharply with his performance in touching off the west coast armament race in 1966 with orders for sophisticated military equipment unrelated to Chilean defense requirements. Admittedly, the decision was one that fell wholly within the privilege of national soverignty. But the U.S. taxpayer properly could protest that he did not wish to underwrite such waste and that the U.S. criteria would insist on Frei's philosophical utterance as the guide rather than on his practical bid for military gains against Peru and Argentina.

Again, his decision to use a major portion of the potential capital inflow from the Alliance for the political objectives of nationalization was well within the privilege of national sovereignty. But it was equally certain that U.S. criteria properly could not accept this diversion of scarce resources for objectives that would inevitably defeat the major objectives of the Alliance. And the fact that the deal had been sweetened for certain U.S. business interests properly could not determine U.S. public policy. At least not as long as lip service was being given to the concept of an inspirational movement, a progressive revolution.

Frei was clearly correct when he warned that for many of the countries that signed the Charter of Punta del Este "the reforms and structural changes were regarded only as marginal conditions . . . clearly less important than the increase in financial aid." Yet, all too often he had shown the same aversion to making policy decisions focussed directly on the objectives of the Alliance. Even as he protested that "foreign aid is a mirage . . . our country belongs to us," he had devised and sold the Latin American countries on the thesis that they have a *right* to take what they need from the U.S. Treasury, that it might well be the condition for supporting the U.S. in political objectives in the hemisphere on which the Latins themselves placed a low priority. If $5.6 billion was merely a mirage, the U.S. taxpayer too might ultimately feel that "our country belongs to us" rather than to the new claimants to a 'right' to access to the U.S. Treasury.

Nor did it substantially alter the situation to propose, as Frei did, that the allocation of funds provided by the United States henceforth be made by an inter-American body on which the U.S. would be easily outvoted, and where the "one donation for you, one donation for me, one donation for you, one donation for me" tactic assured a policy concensus on the part of the Lation Americans. A quarter century earlier in the United States itself the Supreme Court had suggested that "it is hardly lack of due process for the government to regulate that which it subsidizes." Now, the question was arising whether inter-American relationships for client states could be such as to permit subsidies without the attachment of specific conditions for the flow of the money.

Was not the basic error that in arguing against infringement of national sovereignty, Frei failed to understand that sovereign states are supposed to function as independent and equal states, and that once they abandon this role and appear, as Senator Dirksen's famous phrase had it, as bearers of the tin cup, they have in fact abandoned their status of equals? The fault would appear to lie with the initial decision to rely on mendicancy as a substitute for suitable internal action, and to promote the desired results of mendicancy by reinforcing it with blackmail. The Kennedy adviser who argued that in the absence of acceptance by the Latin Americans of the necessary mystique of the Alliance, the business of the Alliance would be transacted as "disguised blackmail operations on the Latin American side and disguised bribery or payoff on our own" [18] anticipated that the whole process could become one of asking for as much as possible, on the part of the Latins, and paying as little as possible on the part of the United States.

It is significant in this respect that when in 1967 President Johnson was persuaded to offer the Latins a 30% boost as a *reward* for *failing* in the first five years to perform in the manner necessary for the achievement of the objectives of the Alliance, he was confronted with indignation on the part of the Latin Americans. *"Solamente un mil quinientos millones de dolares quiere dar Johnson,"* the headlines ran. "Una broma," "una propina," "a pittance" the Latin diplomats sneered. The chairman of the Senate Foreign Ielations Committee protested that "one and a half billion dollars is significant to us even though a pittance to Latin America." [19]

---

[18] "Our Good-Neighbors Should Come First," *New York Times Magazine,* June 6, 1965.

[19] *Congressional Record,* March 16, 1967, S 3944.

Even the *New York Times,* always in favor of foreign aid expansion whatever the record which it so often avoided examining, was moved to insist that "the Latin countries have no legitimate cause to grumble . . . the offer of $300 million (additions) a year for five years is a generous one," even as it agreed that "a gesture of interest is needed" in furtherance of the prevailing concept of pork-barrel diplomacy.[20] More to the point was the Scripps-Howard label: "Dollar Diplomacy — Latin Style." [21] For, each concession made to enable the Latin Americans to avoid the critical internal decisions, made without any serious indication that the suitable decisions would be forthcoming, reinforced the rising impression that a "right" to the U.S. Treasury had been created. Senator Church had a good suggestion when confronted with the proposal to raise Alliance expenditures by 30%. "Let us first know what the Latin Americans are doing — not what they are promising or proposing but what they are doing. It is interesting that no Latin American president has asked *his* Congress for a resolution before the Punta del Este Conference making a prior commitment to land reform, tax increases and reduction of trade barriers." [22] Protesting the President's demand for an advance commitment by the Congress, Senator Fulbright suggested mildly that "when the administration has found it necessary to cut back on our highway funds . . . if our circumstances are so stringent that our own people cannot have sewers . . . recent developments such as the Watts riots and similar disturbances . . . have made me feel much greater urgency to do something about preventing the deterioration of our society here at home." Instead of a "right" to draw on the U.S. Treasury, implemented by "dollar diplomacy Latin style (blackmail)" it might prove necessary to respect an order of priorities within the United States which provided alternatives to the waste of funds for objectives unrelated to social and economic development in Latin America.

The issue was clearly joined: The program director for the Agency for International Development in Rio put it well: "We want them to help themselves more. *The question is how hard do you pound on the table to get them to do it.*" [23] President Frei's

---

[20] March 18, 1967.

[21] *Washington Daily News,* March 18, 1967.

[22] Congressional Record, March 23, 1967, S 4389-90.

[23] *Wall Street Journal,* March 20, 1967.

answer was that you do not pound the table because that infringes national sovereignty. Such a concept was wholly unacceptable to the United States Congress. To this the U.S. Executive Branch had its own answer: If the Congress can be prevented from finding out that we had abandoned the necessary pounding on the table, it might be bamboozled indefinitely into support of larger and larger appropriations. Was this a proper procedure for public policy making in a democracy affecting objectives whose realization would be extending over a generation?

The deterioration of the Alliance from an imaginative bold dynamic commitment to a label to be applied to everything from donations to dictators to protests against consumer substitution of Coca Cola for coffee drinking had been apparent as early as the first year of the Alliance and reflected dismally the utter failure to understand the concept. Within months after the Charter of Punta del Este came into being, the Latin Americans were seeking to profit from application of the Alliance label to any complaint against the United States. When for instance, the Coast Guard enforced U.S. safety rules in order to protect passengers against potentially dangerous conditions on a Latin American cruise ship, there was the angry protest that "They had better not ever again use the phrase 'Alliance for Progress' in Mexico. . . . This is a blow to the pride of the Mexican people." After all, had not the Alliance for Progress assured U.S. travellers the opportunity to ride in ships considered unsafe by the U.S. Coast Guard? Had not the Alliance assured Latin America the right to risk the lives of American passengers in vessels deemed unsafe? The spirit was contagious. When a U.S. owner of some Spanish-language newspapers was denied press-gallery privileges by the group which checks the rules for Senate-House gallery privileges, it was only to be expected that he would blast out that this "might be a body-blow to the Alliance for Progress." How fragile the name in which all damage seemed to be done.

Conversely, the Alliance was a label to be attached by the U.S. Executive to any accomplishment, real or imaginary. Every piddling piece of legislation passed in Latin America, whatever its history or the unlikelihood of implementation, had to be attributed to the Alliance by the eager beavers in Washington, in their hungry search for something to cite as an accomplishment. Surely civilization in Latin America had not dated alone from the Alliance, and surely there had been at least a sprinkling of economic and social legislation of merit long before the Alliance came into being. Yet, now the expanding corps of bureaucrats was mobilizing to pounce on just anything that might be pulled under the label of the Alliance. For the new experts on the new frontier, development in Latin America started with the Punta del Este agreement. Yet, this area had had immense economic achievements to its credit long before this. If the Exim Bank made a loan of the type it had been making for twenty-five years, it now became an "Alliance for Progress" loan, even though it would have been forthcoming even without the Alliance program. The elegance of the rhetoric was matched only by the utter contempt that prompted this effort at puffery and only made a mockery of the Alliance.

After five years, Brazil's spokesman for the Alliance was insisting that "between those cynics who judge what has been done with excessive severity and the utopians who under-estimate the difficulty of the task, the truth remains with those who are realistic and patient enough to face up to the contradictions and have the firmness to continue." The danger now, however, was that the abandonment of all the basic objectives in favor of a day to day yielding to pressures for money in"flexible" (sic) conditions which permitted it to be used without relationship to objectives would only intensify problems and assure the alternative drastic solutions which the United States had sought to avoid.

It has been said that history sometimes indulges in jokes of dubious taste. In 1961 with all the hoopla surrounding the launching of the Alliance no one would have believed that a program intended to function within a framework of democratic institutions would be allowed to deteriorate into U.S. support for the very elimination of such institutions in Brazil and Argentina and a number of lesser countries. In 1961 no one would have believed that Latin American leadership would remain so out of touch with the popular masses as to be unable to rally to a mystique of political social and economic development that would balk or make unnecessary more turbulent solutions. In 1961 no one would have believed that the concentration camps and the abandonment of the rule of law of the Bolivian Revolution would have become the ideal pattern which President Kennedy suggested he would like to see generalized in Latin America. In 1961 no one would have anticipated that the role of private investment would have been converted into a bailout operation for greedy investors, into private investment at public risk under the label "dollar diplomacy — modern style." In 1961 no one would have believed that the Latin American military would be encouraged to expand their role by open and generous support of the United States. In 1961 no one would have believed that Latin American leadership was so bankrupt and lacking in self-respect that blackmail would become the key to the Latin American approach. In 1961 no one would have believed that the U.S. Executive would resort increasingly to misrepresentation within the United States to make sure that public policy did not suffer the scrutiny of an informed public. In 1961 no one would have believed that the quiet dignity of the Latin American people would be surrendered to the temptation of successful mendicancy. In 1961 no one would have believed that the program would be used to reward rather than to penalize resistance to change. In 1961 no one would have believed that the potential of U.S. assistance — technical and financial — as a catalytic agent would have been so dissipated that per-capita growth rate deteriorated and the distribution of income became even more unsatisfactory.

It was after all a century since Ponciano Arriaga had suggested that instead of waiting for foreign colonization to cure the poverty of his country it might be better to rely on local colonization in the sense of redistribution of land among the country's own citizens and revision of local policies to the end of creating a successful formula of social and economic advance. It was more than a generation since a former President of Panama had urged that "we Latin Americans must realize the truth that we are the only ones to cure our own evils." Now again the fundamental truth appeared in the rhetoric of the time, as General Gestido called on his fellow-citizens to heed his warning that "si el pueblo uruguayo quiere salvarse, está en sus manos y en las de nadie más el hacerlo."

Yet, five years of the Alliance for Progress found Latin America losing ground politically, economically and socially in its response to the challenge of the times. And five years found Latin America increasingly willing to avoid the basic decisions as long as the alternative of drawing on the U.S. Treasury remained open.